DEC 2017

Critical Concepts™ Series . . .

Crappie Location

Finding Crappies in Lakes, Rivers & Reservoirs

799.17
Cra

Tombigbee Regional Library
436 Commerce Street
West Point, MS 39773-2986

Critical Concepts™ Series . . .

Crappie Location

Finding Crappies in Lakes, Rivers & Reservoirs

Expert Advice from North America's
Foremost Authority on Freshwater Fishing

THE IN-FISHERMAN STAFF

Critical Concepts™ Series . . .
Crappie Location—Finding Crappies in Lakes, Rivers & Reservoirs

Publisher *Steve Hoffman*
Assistant Publisher *Chuck Nelson*
Editor In Chief *Doug Stange*
Managing Editor *Dr. Rob Neumann*
Project Editor *Matt Straw*
Editors *Steve Quinn, Jeff Simpson*
Copy Editor *Kathy Callaway*
Layout *Amy Jackson, Jan Schneider*
Editorial Assistant *Claudette Kitzman*
Cover *Jim Pfaff*

Acknowledgments
Roger Bullock, Location in new lakes, ch. 9; **Ronnie Capps, Steve Coleman**, "Winning Crappie Secrets," chs. 4, 5; **Ron Finger**, illustrations, chs. 1, 2, 3, 4, 5, 7; **Bill Fletcher**, Hill-land reservoir movements, p. 79; **Dave Genz**, "Micro Seasons," p. 62; **Dr. Chris Guy**, South Dakota St. Univ. & Assist. Unit Leader, radio-telemetry study, p. 47, KS Fish & Wildlife Coop. Research Unit, ch. 3; **Chris Guy, Robert M. Neumann, D.W. Willis**, "Movement Patterns of Adult Black Crappies," *J. Freshwater Ecol.*, 7(2): p. 137-147; ch. 7; **Bob Holmes**, Reelfoot, brushpile designs, p. 123-124; **Ned Kehde**, Flatland-reservoir location, p. 74; **John Kolbeck**, Wisconsin flowages, p. 106; **Gary Korsgaden**, Natural lake movements, ch. 3; **Bill Lindner**, photos, pp. 197 and 200; **Ralph Manns**, "The Weather Connection," ch. 6; **Joe Monteleone**, Tennessee creeks, p. 102; **National Weather Service**, chart, p. 177, ch. 8; **Ryan Oster**, "Behavioral Patterns of White and Black Crappie . . . Kentucky Lake," ch. 1; **Pete Pritchard**, brushpile designs, p. 146; **Paul Radomski**, biologist, Minnesota DNR, aquatic plants, p. 151; **R. Radomski, T.J. Goeman**, "Consequences of Human Lakeshore Development," *N. Amer. Journal Fish. Mgmt.* 21(1):46-61; ch. 7; **Rich Zaleski**, Tidal-river movements, p. 108.

Crappie Location—Finding Crappies in Lakes, Rivers & Reservoirs

Copyright © 2007 by In-Fisherman, an InterMedia Outdoors company. All rights reserved. Printed in the United States of America. No part of this book may be used or reproduced in any manner without written permission except in the case of brief quotations embodied in critical articles and reviews. For information write Editor In Chief, In-Fisherman, 7819 Highland Scenic Rd., Baxter, MN 56425-8011.

First Edition

Library of Congress Cataloging-in-Publication Data
ISBN: 1-892947-89-7

Dedication

To the *In-Fisherman* reader, whose passion for crappies and cutting-edge information keeps our ongoing quest for piscatorial knowledge alive.

Contents

Foreword ix
Introduction xi

1. **Overall Perspectives**
   Year of the Crappie 1
2. **Location**
   Classifying Crappie Waters 19
3. **Understanding Seasonal Movements—I**
   Crappies in Natural Lakes 35
4. **Understanding Seasonal Movements—II**
   Understanding Movements in Reservoirs 69
5. **Understanding Seasonal Movements—III**
   Crappie Location in Rivers 99
6. **Weather and Location**
   The Weather Connection 113
7. **Crappies and Cover**
   How Crappies Relate to Cover 135
8. **Modern Electronics Made Easy**
   Tools for Fine-Tuning Crappie Location 159
9. **Ultimate Locational Factors**
   Finding Crappies Fast 181
10. **Final Factors**
    Where the Slabs Are 195

Foreword

THE L PART

Taking kids crappie fishing is to climb out on a long limb. Your status as a provider is on the line. Far be it from us to suggest that your ability to catch crappies, or not, defines you as a parent or as a person. It wasn't our idea to make fishing a competitive sport, and we can't help what society does to your kids when we're not looking. But if you come back to the dock empty-handed while Jimmy's dad has a bucketful, your children may look up at you with bewildered, accusing eyes. This can't be helped. You will read things into that look that you probably shouldn't. We can't help you with that either.

But we can help you find crappies. Find crappies, and your kids will stop looking at you like that.

Our first *Critical Concepts* book on crappies provided a foundation for understanding the basic needs, distribution, and habitat requirements of the crappie—the **F** part. This book represents the **L** part of our formula: **Fish** (behavior) plus **Location** (seasonal needs) plus **Presentation** (angling tactics) equals **Success**. **F+L+P=S** has been helping us organize these writings about crappies for decades, and the primary results of those inquiries into the **L** part of the equation can be found in the pages of this book.

When crappies follow traditional paths and arrive in seasonal habitat at the usual time and conditions are just right, finding them seems like such an easy game to play. But the search for knowledge, the kind required to find crappies in every possible situation, is infinite. Lifetimes can be spent in this pursuit without knowing all there is to know. But, along the way, crappies can fall into your lap by the thousands, because they proliferate quite well in so many different kinds of waters. The crappie is an adaptable creature. But that can work against us, too. They adapt quickly to adversity and move to locations that suit them best in every possible situation. Locating them can be easy or hard, depending on the water, the season, and the conditions you face.

We would like to suggest taking your kids when it's easy, when crappies are concentrated in the right kind of water, at the right time of year. That's why the **L** is so important. Knowing a little about the environment of crappies, their forage, and their physical needs, goes a long way toward finding them at any point in the year. Ever taken kids out for a fishless day in search of crappies? Then you know what we're talking about.

Introduction

From the Project Editor—
A Word about This Book

This book is all about finding crappies, in every type of water they inhabit, in every season, in every type of cover, and in most conditions. *In-Fisherman* readers, we assume, are acutely aware of the word "most" in the first sentence. They expect us to deliver the word on every possible condition, not just "most" of them. But we can't discuss all possible conditions here because we don't know what they all are, and neither do you. The world is in a constant state of flux. Archeologists proclaim that certain changes (like the rate of increase of carbon dioxide in the atmosphere) are happening faster than at any point in the planet's history. The rate of flux is increasing, and all living things, crappies and humans included, must adapt relatively quickly. Consider this example:

Ice fishing is something many crappie fishermen never do, but winter habitats are very similar everywhere. Crappies tend to winter in depths of 20 to 50 feet, depending on the overall size, depth, and lake type they inhabit. In recent winters in Minnesota lakes, however, we often find the biggest crappies in any given system inhabiting depths of 10 feet or less under the ice in January. In some lakes, crappies are typically found in 5 feet of water or so, under the ice in March, but only in those bays, smaller connected lakes, and shoreline areas they tend to inhabit after ice-out and throughout early spring. For many years we've found crappies in 6-foot holes in canals and river backwaters throughout winter, too. But we believe it's new and different to find winter crappies shallow in natural lakes along shoreline areas they seldom inhabit in spring, and in lakes where shallow movements never seemed to occur during winter in the past.

For many years, big crappies were typically found in depths of 18 to 22 feet in many of the lakes in question. For the past few seasons, only small crappies appear in those depths, while the biggest specimens are caught in depths of 8 feet or so. This behavioral change can only be called "apparent," as no scientific studies we know of can be called upon to back it up. But behavioral changes do take place among fish, caused in most cases by environmental change or a dramatic increase in fishing pressure. If 100 or more anglers per day are dropping jigs into a 25-foot basin area on a medium-sized lake, will the biggest crappies remain there until all are removed? It appears that way, at times. Will some adapt and move shallow, or deeper? We can only suppose.

But the kind of change being discussed here, if valid, is often attributed to ongoing or permanent environmental alterations, such as depletions and substitutions within the forage base. One environmental change impossible to ignore in this instance is the overall warming of the environment. The National Weather Service concludes that 10 of the hottest years on record (with 125 years of data to refer to) have occurred since 1994, 13 years prior to the printing of this book. The warmest years on record tend to be accompanied by early springs, late falls, thinner ice, and less snow cover. Ice thickness and snow cover have a direct bearing on how much light penetrates and how deep it penetrates into the water. With less ice and snow to block sunlight, plankton and aquatic weeds will fare better. Oxygen counts remain more stable, perhaps, around those green weeds, and crappies may prefer green weeds over dead weeds for cover. Food, in the form of plankton, may increase. Invertebrates and minnows that inhabit shallow areas may survive the winter in greater numbers, increasing the food supply somewhat. And the depth of water reading 34°F or less (studies indicate crappies may lose motor function in water 34°F or colder) will be higher in the water column during winters with higher average temperatures.

All these factors would favor the movement of crappies into shallower habitats in winter. But that doesn't prove they will move shallow, nor that they did move shallow. All we know for certain is that we can now catch crappies shallower during winter, in some lakes, than in the past. And we can only guess why. Doesn't sound like much to go on, but how to argue with results? In coming years, many of the movements and activities of crappies may seem equally mysterious, with even more tenuous explanations.

Global warming might be an extreme example, but we dare say all of us will soon see changes within our local fisheries because of it. We do know that, at the northern end of their range, crappies are moving into habitats once considered too cold and harsh for their survival. Though discussed only briefly in this book, extremes happen. Rivers are rerouted, lakes are drained, "dead zones" persist in Lake Erie, and increases in raw sewage are causing severe algae blooms the likes of which have not been seen since the early 1970s. As this book goes to print, we have mining companies leveling mountains. Congress outlawed the practice 50 years ago, but powerful lobbyists pushed hard enough to have that law rescinded. Strip-mining companies may not bury any crappie lakes, but they have buried nearly 2,000 miles of trout habitat in the form of streams since 2000. Doubtless to say, the migration routes of trout have changed drastically in those areas.

The complete removal of a river from the surface of the planet is about as extreme as it gets, from a fisherman's perspective. But extremes can be perfect for pointing out that we sometimes need to think outside the box to locate fish (given they have water left to swim in). This book is a resource for developing that kind of mindset. All the tools and formulas and science we might apply to locate crappies can be found right here, but the best tool for the task isn't in the book. It's between your ears. The charts, formulas, electronics, maps, and studies are only guidelines on the path to becoming a complete angler, one who can think independently and find crappies no matter how difficult the world tries to make it.

This book is about finding crappies. When you can't find them, think about what they need, what they eat, and which factor is most critical under the conditions at hand. Think about seasonal habitat, the weather, and options for cover. This book discusses all that and more, but you have to make the next step and find them where they shouldn't be, when conventional wisdom fails. Nobody knows everything there is to know about crappies and, perhaps, nobody ever will. The complexity and adaptability of living things should always be able to amaze us. A certain sense of well-being follows when the understanding of crappies—what they need, what they eat and what limits they have—reaches the point where we can intuit the next move and find them when others can't. Not because it makes us better than anybody else, but because we took the time to understand something real, and to understand well enough to find it.

Matt Straw

Overall Perspectives

Chapter 1

Year of the Crappie

SECRETS TO SEASONAL MIGRATIONS, HABITS AND HABITATS

As the seasons change, so do the attitudes and environmental needs of fish. With the passing seasons, crappies alter many things, including type of diet, activity levels, location, even behavior. But the calendar year of a fish isn't divided into neat mathematical units like our Gregorian calendar of 12 months of relatively equal length. The crappie's calendar is determined by seasonal needs. Each season brings particular requirements for a certain type of habitat, which may be related to forage abundance, depth, substrate types—whatever the environment demands for survival, growth, or propagation at that point in time.

Year of the Crappie 1

Seasons of Change

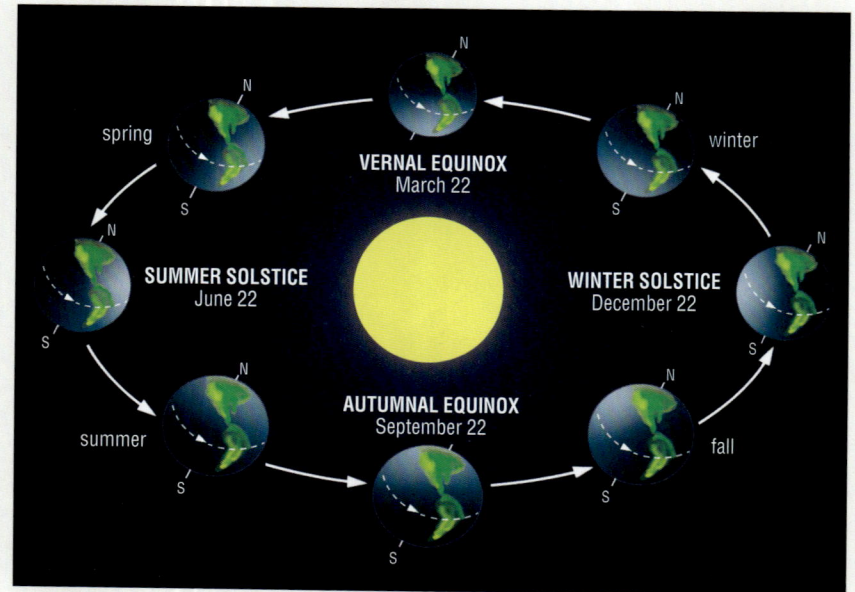

Spring, summer, fall, winter. The pendulum swings between seasons, bringing evident changes on land but more difficult-to-define changes underwater. Studies show that photoperiod (length of daylight) influences the tempo of the environment, from microorganisms to top-of-the-line predators. The intensity and duration of light in a yearly cycle influences migrations, spawning, and feeding.

    In-Fisherman founders Al and Ron Lindner developed the basic concept of the In-Fisherman Calendar of Fish Activity before publishing the first issue of *In-Fisherman* in 1975. They used the concept while working as guides early in their careers, and *In-Fisherman* editors fine-tuned the concept as the years passed. All fish go through activity periods based on seasonal needs. These and resulting activities are determined by genetics and modified by conditions. Each species is triggered by its own internal clock, its own unique reactions to day length, water temperature, and other environmental cues.

    The In-Fisherman Calendar breaks down the annual cycle of a fish species into 10 distinct periods, varying in length and timing according to the makeup and needs of the fish in question. Dividing the year into 10 periods is somewhat arbitrary, and periods often overlap as individual fish may vary in the timing of activities, and bodies of water differ from one end to the other. But each time frame on this calendar represents basic modes of an annual cycle followed by fish as they move through stages of: Preparing for and carrying out reproductive duties (Prespawn and Spawn Periods); finding forage in warm water (Summer Period); stocking up on stored energy (Postsummer and Turnover Periods); and seeking environmental stability during the harshest time of their year (Coldwater Period).

This chapter describes the fundamental principles for determining crappie location based on seasonal changes that crappies experience annually. How those seasons compare to the months of the Gregorian calendar depends largely upon latitude. In the North, crappies have an extended Coldwater Period and a compressed Summer Period. In the South, it's just the opposite. When crappies spawn in the South, their northern cousins might still be locked under the ice and entrenched in the Coldwater Period. Though the periods may start at different times in different regions, crappies within the same period exhibit similar behavior in similar environments. So, no matter where crappies live, the In-Fisherman Calendar can be used as a guideline to determine what mode of activity crappies might be engaged in (foraging, spawning, migrating) and what general locational patterns they might be following (shallow, deep, in-between, suspending, or on structure).

The In-Fisherman Calendar also notes the general mood of fish through the various periods. Active fish are moving, feeding fish and are generally easiest to catch on artificials. Neutral fish are ambivalent about biting but can generally be triggered with bait, finesse tactics, or specific triggers. Inactive fish are the most difficult to catch and require thoughtful, patient techniques. Certain Periods encourage high activity levels on a large, overall scale, while other Periods inspire the opposite. Though these are generalities, the In-Fisherman Calendar helps identify which bodies of water to seek and which to avoid throughout the year. The Fall Turnover Period, for instance, can result in masses of largely inactive fish.

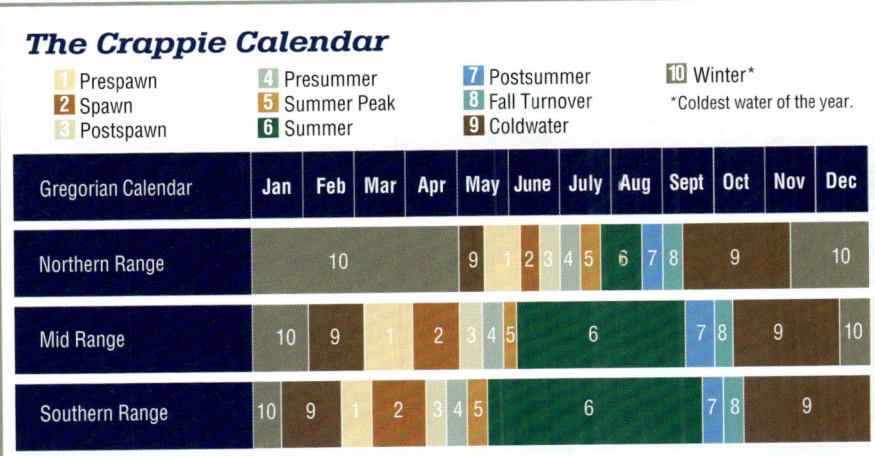

The 10 In-Fisherman Calendar Periods of fish response vary in length from year to year. Unusually warm or cool weather affects the length of the periods that can vary as much as four weeks from year to year. The Periods aren't based on the Gregorian calendar, so they don't occur on specific dates each year. Instead, calendar periods are based on nature's clock.

In addition, Calendar Periods vary by region. Rivers of the South experience an extended Summer Period and a brief Winter Period. In contrast, rivers along the U.S.-Canadian border have extended Coldwater and Winter Periods. Crappies in Florida could be in the Spawn Period while those in northern Minnesota are still in the Winter Period.

You can learn to identify events related to the passing seasons, to avoid the wrong lakes and gravitate to the right bodies of water to fish.

Though the Lindners first developed the Calendar to describe the passing of seasons for fish in lakes and reservoirs, the same general changes take place in rivers. River crappies tend to find all their needs met in fairly confined areas, but sometimes they migrate much farther between Calendar Periods than do crappies that dwell in lakes. To better understand what environments crappies seek and use during the various periods, the Lindners also classified lake, river, and reservoir types in fishing terms. Crappies in the same type of environment tend to behave in a similar fashion. The Calendar Periods and lake-classification system work together to provide you with a complete picture of how crappies relate to their world in every corner of ours.

COLDWATER PERIOD (Spring)
Water Temperature: Warming slightly from annual minimum to above 50°F
General Fish Mood: Neutral

Crappies move from coldwater wintering haunts to spring foraging areas during this period of transitions. In the North, this period begins at ice-out, as waters climb into the low 40°F range—usually sometime in April. In the South, crappies move from deep water to coves and the back ends of creek arms as the water

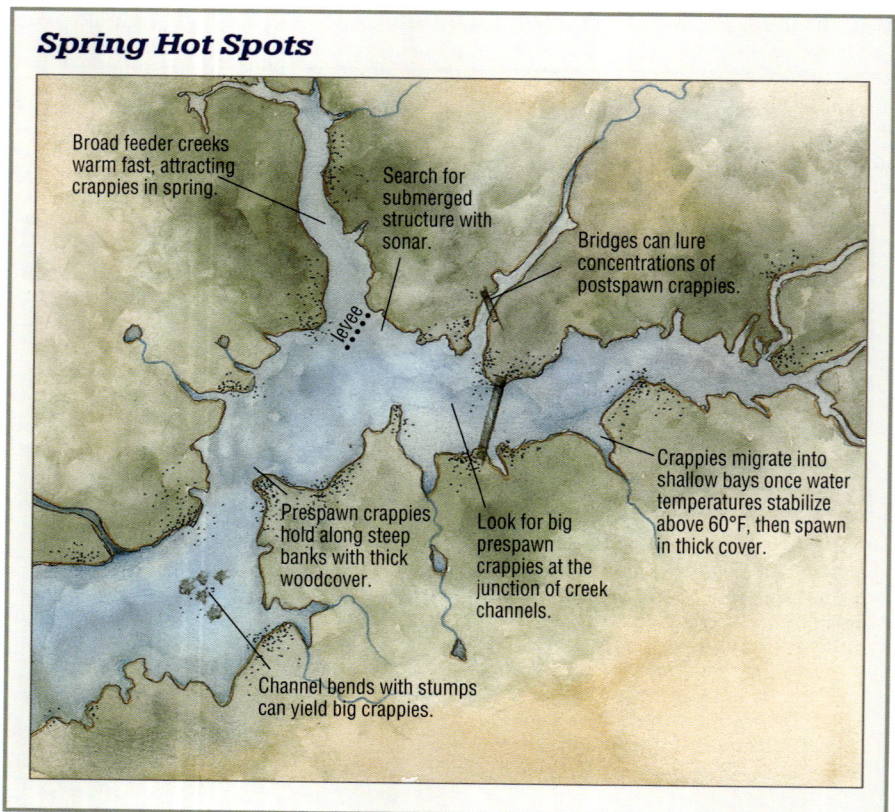

Spring Hot Spots

- Broad feeder creeks warm fast, attracting crappies in spring.
- Search for submerged structure with sonar.
- Bridges can lure concentrations of postspawn crappies.
- Prespawn crappies hold along steep banks with thick woodcover.
- Look for big prespawn crappies at the junction of creek channels.
- Crappies migrate into shallow bays once water temperatures stabilize above 60°F, then spawn in thick cover.
- Channel bends with stumps can yield big crappies.

warms into the mid-40°F range, usually sometime between late February and the end of March. In the most southerly latitudes, crappies may bypass this period and instead experience an extended Prespawn Period.

In large lakes and reservoirs across the country, it's typical for crappies to stage and suspend over depths of 20 to 40 feet, somewhere beyond the first drop-off leading into the shallow zones they later use to forage and spawn. In reservoirs, this typically takes place in creek arms. In lakes, it usually happens near the mouth of shallow bays or coves, or along shorelines studded with reeds or woodcover. In small lakes or ponds, it's not uncommon for such staging to take place over the center of the deepest hole in the lake.

During warm, stable weather and particularly on sunny days, crappies are drawn into the shallows to feed in dark, muck-bottomed bays, old reedbeds, around brushpiles and fallen trees, or in the best habitat they can find. Channels, boat canals, cuts, harbors, and backwaters draw crappies, too. The key is finding shallow, wind-protected spots that warm faster than the main lake. The best spots often extend from the north shore of lakes or impoundments, where sun exposure is longest throughout the day and the north wind is blocked. These spots draw baitfish early. Early moves to water less than 10 feet deep are for feeding and have little to do with spawning activities. Crappies are hungry in spring, and their first order of business is to compensate for the energy deficit brought on by simply surviving the extremes of winter. Sometimes crappies eventually spawn in the same general areas, but often not.

Stable weather draws crappies in, and cold fronts drive them back out.

Lakes and reservoirs with lots of shallow, protected habitat promote these shallow feeding binges. The best bays, coves, and cuts are shallow, usually no deeper than 10 feet. The best harbors, canals, and channels are closed, with only one way in or out. Open channels allow currents to develop, and strong winds blow the warm water back out into the lake. These areas concentrate fish, but crappies tend to concentrate in early spring, anyway. Lakes without shallow, protected areas may take several additional weeks to draw shallow movements by crappies. Crappies in these lakes bunch in fairly tight groups, too, but suspend just off the first drop-off into depths of 15 to 40 feet, just outside the bay, cut, cove, channel, or whatever feature draws them once the main-lake shallows warm enough to attract them.

Stable weather draws crappies in, and cold fronts drive them back out, where they suspend in the areas just described. Ideal conditions (unzip the jacket, take off the hood) bring crappies shallow, and the bite can be hot. It's a great time for flyrods, tiny twistertails, and bait under a bobber. Intermediate conditions (zip it back up), like cool weather several days after the passage of a front, find neutral crappies riding in pods along the edge of that first drop-off. They'll bite, but it may require some patience. Bobbers are key. On cold-front days (hood, gloves, long johns), crappies suspend and often refuse to bite all but the most motionless presentations. Crappies typically suspend 5 to 20 feet down over 15 to 40 feet of water in these conditions. The focus shifts to vertical jigging or slip-drifting (deploying a driftsock to negate the wind, with aid of the trolling motor) and using sonar and marker buoys to stay on the schools.

As the water continues to warm past 50°F, the environment grows more stable. Most activity is now confined between the first drop-off and the extreme shallows. Movements toward actual spawning habitat begin, which may or may not be the same areas used during the earliest foraging forays. It all depends on what habitat the lake has to offer.

THE PRESPAWN PERIOD
Surface temperatures: 50°F to 63°F
General fish mood: Neutral to positive

As the water warms, the focus of crappies shifts toward spawning activities. Crappies require (1) a sufficiently soft bottom like sand-marl—but usually not muck—where they can sweep out a nest; (2) some form of cover (stumps, fallen trees, brushpiles, reeds, or the stalks of old weeds) at (3) the appropriate depth. Depth is determined to a large degree by water clarity. The clearer the water, the deeper crappies spawn—down to about 20 feet in the clearest lakes and reservoirs. In average water clarity,

The Recruitment Puzzle

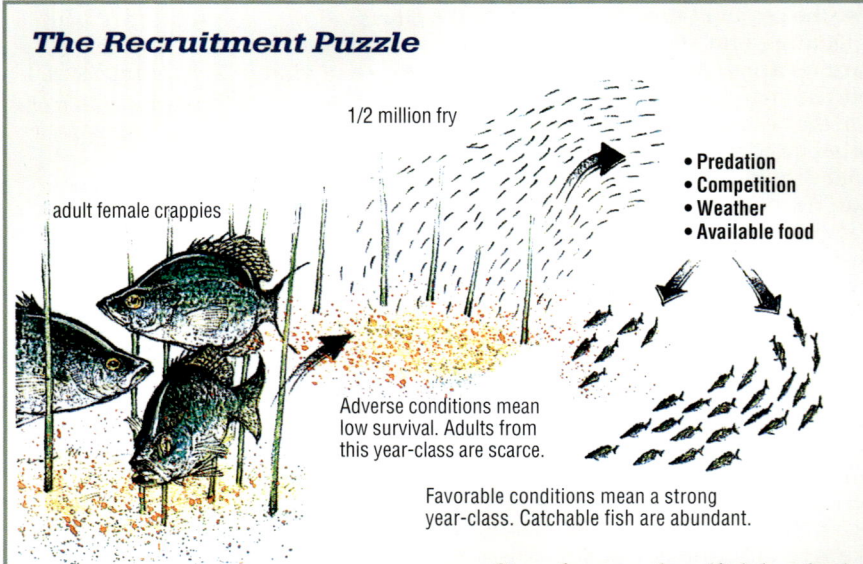

1/2 million fry

adult female crappies

- Predation
- Competition
- Weather
- Available food

Adverse conditions mean low survival. Adults from this year-class are scarce.

Favorable conditions mean a strong year-class. Catchable fish are abundant.

Recruitment is the process whereby fish are added to a catchable population. The number of eggs produced doesn't determine how many crappies will be available to fishermen in the next generation.

After leaving the nest, crappie fry live in open water. Abundant food (appropriate-sized zooplankton) is essential for survival.

Predation by larger fish and competition for food with other small fish are important. Temperature, wind, and water level also have direct and indirect effects on survival of small crappies.

Size of a year-class (fish hatched in a particular year) is determined during the first year. Naturally, crappies can die between their first birthday and the time they reach catchable size, but the relationship between the number of one-year-old fish and three-year-old fish is much more predictable. Future studies of crappie biology can define the crucial factors for survival of young crappies. Catch-and-release, either voluntary or by regulation, can increase the number and size of fish in the catchable population, but probably doesn't affect future generations unless the population is very low.

crappies spawn at about 3 to 6 feet. In muddy conditions, the bulk of the spawn may take place in 2 feet of water or less. The right depth is just below the point of maximum sunlight penetration. Light penetration is required down to the depth of the eggs, providing warmth for the optimum incubation period. If the hatch is delayed, survival is affected. But eggs placed too shallow are subjected to additional ultraviolet light, which also affects overall survival rates. Lakes with widely variable clarity in spring tend to have inconsistent year-classes of crappies.

Bays, coves, and backwaters with woodcover and the right substrates (gravel-sand, sand, sand-marl, sand-silt) draw the most crappies. Without the right substrate at the right depth, or in the face of competition for spawning areas with other species, crappies sometimes spawn on the limbs of submerged timber. Female crappies begin moving in and out of the primary cover, often holding on the deep fringe around these sites as the surface temperatures broach 50°F. Males tend to move right into the cover and stay put at this point. When males first arrive, they may mill around and spook easily. As the water warms, they become more aggressive and territorial.

Males turn dark as hormonal changes occur. As the water broaches the 60°F mark, the males often bite like tigers, becoming easy to catch with a variety of bobber systems and, in clearer lakes, vertical techniques. This is especially true after the males select a spawning site and begin clearing and defending it. The females remain edgy, slipping in and out of cover, but they often bite a carefully presented bait quite well until the water nears the mid-60°F range. Females finally join males on their selected nests, but not until they're ready to spawn. In most bodies of water, spawning takes place when surface temperatures read somewhere between 64°F and 72°F, but some conjecture exists as to the importance of temperature. The most important factor determining when crappies spawn could be day length. After a cold spring, crappies may spawn in water colder than 62°F if that day-length window is about to close. Conversely, if the water warms exceptionally fast in spring, crappies may be forced to spawn in water warmer than 72°F. Over tens of thousands of years, nature culls late spawners out of the gene pool because their progeny have insufficient time to grow large enough to survive the rigors of winter. Genetics over time fine-tunes an optimum "day-length window" that corresponds to the same specific week or two on our calendar—the human calendar—every year.

THE SPAWN PERIOD
Water Temperature: 64°F to 72°F
General Fish Mood: Negative

All the crappies in any given body of water do not spawn at the same time. Those that spawn in fast-warming bays and coves spawn first, followed by crappies using the north-facing bays, and finally by spawners on main-lake shorelines that warm slowest. In any given area, actual egg laying can be completed in as little as one day, or could be spread out over weeks or more if cold fronts continue to interrupt.

Typical Spawning Months

Area	Months
Florida	March-April
Alabama-Georgia	March-April
Texas-Oklahoma	March-May
Kentucky-Tennessee	April-May
Missouri-Illinois-Iowa	April-June
Ohio	April-July
Oregon	March-June
Minnesota-Wisconsin	May-July
Ontario	June-August

The actual act of spawning for individual fish takes only a couple of hours, but females rarely drop all their eggs at once. They may repeat the spawning ritual two or three times over a period of several days as eggs continue to mature and ripen within their body cavities, but under stable conditions most females complete the task within 24 hours.

The spawn is a relatively brief and variable period. In smaller bodies of water, the bulk of the spawning occurs within a two-week window. In huge reservoirs and vast, sprawling lakes—encompassing slightly different climates between the north and south ends of the lake, with crappies spawning everywhere from shallow interior bays within bays to deep main-lake timber—the Spawn Period could drag on for well over a month. In Lake of the Woods on the Minnesota-Ontario border, for example, crappies in the far south end of the lake often finish spawning while crappies in the north end remain in prespawn mode.

If spawning habitat is limited, crappies from different areas of the lake may occupy it in waves. The first to arrive (those that winter closest) spawn earliest in the low 60°F range and, as other areas of the lake warm at varying rates, more crappies continue to appear and spawn in the same area. This might leave the impression that the spawn is a long, drawn-out affair for individual fish. That isn't the case. Each individual female generally finishes her duties within a day, sometimes within hours.

Calendar Period Regional Timetable

The timing of the crappie Spawn Period illustrates the region-by-region progression of the calendar periods. Region (latitude), water temperature, weather trends, length of daylight, and competition for habitat are just a few of the factors influencing the exact timing of the spawn. Not all crappies spawn at the same time even in the same body of water. While the bulk of adult fish may spawn during a few days of ideal conditions, some fish spawn early and some late. Regionally, the onset of crappie spawning may begin in early March in the South and as late as July in southern Canada.

Crappie Spawning Conditions
Graphs show the best conditions for crappies spawning.

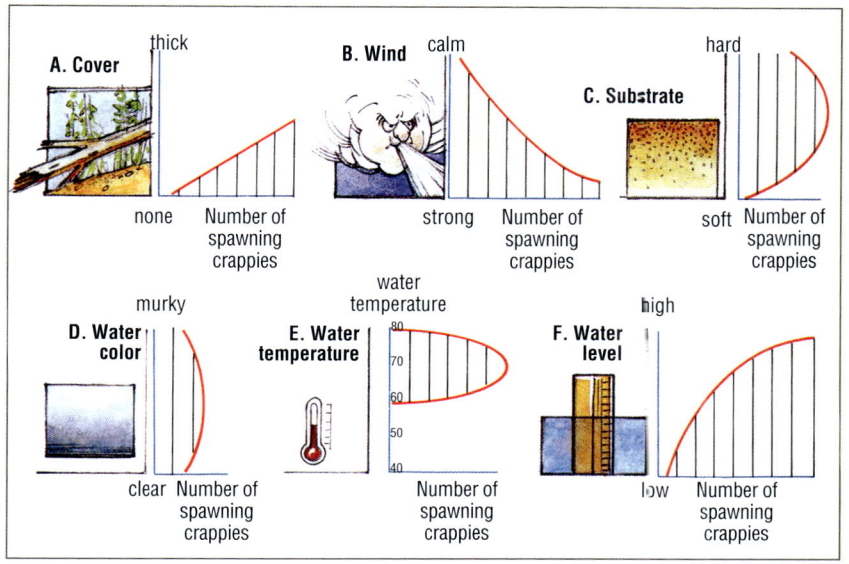

A. Crappies can spawn without cover, but thick cover draws large concentrations of fish. As a rule, cover is weeds in lakes and wood in reservoirs. Reservoirs with abundant vegetation function like lakes. Fallen trees are prime spawning sites for crappies.
B. Crappies spawn in calm areas, avoiding wind. They leave nests if strong winds arise.
C. Substrate of medium hardness is best. Crappies do spawn on rock and stumps, but rarely. A muck or silt bottom is unsatisfactory because the male can't fan the eggs without smothering them.
D. Crappies can spawn in all but the muddiest water. They generally choose water clarity with 2- to 4-foot visibility, however. As a general rule, the clearer the water, the deeper they spawn. Heavy cover like reeds or brush draws spawners shallow.
E. Crappies begin spawning when water temperature rises into the low 60°F range. Peak activity is around 70°F. Lakes and reservoirs don't warm uniformly, though, so spawning may continue for 6 weeks in a given body of water.
F. A quick rise in water level when crappies are almost ready to spawn often causes a flurry of spawning activity. They take advantage of high water to spawn around inundated brush and grass. Falling water levels disrupt spawning, and in extreme cases, beds are left high and dry.

After laying eggs, females abruptly leave, filtering out into deeper water. Males remain behind to guard the nests and fan them to keep sediment from settling, and to maintain a steady supply of oxygen to the eggs, which hatch in about a week in optimal conditions. Males remain for several days after the hatch to guard the fry. When the males are harassed by too many anglers at this critical juncture, the result can be a poor year-class of crappies for the lake, especially in waters with limited spawning habitat. Unguarded, the young fry become easy pickings for other panfish, small bass, and a host of other species.

Crappie Spawning Location in Reservoirs

[Illustration showing underwater reservoir habitat with labels: brush, sunken Christmas Trees, stumps]

Most experts say fishing pressure has no effect on year-classes or overall spawning success, which is probably true on those "fish factory" lakes with a prolific population of crappies that produce consistently strong year-classes. Some lakes, however, particularly at the northern edge of crappie distribution, have limited spawning habitat, inconsistent year-classes, and pendulous swings in forage abundance. No states or provinces enforce spawning closures, and interest in crappie fishing peaks around spawning time in most areas. No effects have been documented, but harvesting or harassing spawning crappies on such lakes can't be beneficial.

POSTSPAWN PERIOD

Water Temperature: Mid-70°F range
General Fish Mood: Neutral to negative

Depending on the body of water and local weather conditions, crappies may take a week or two to recuperate from the rigors of spawning. That doesn't mean they aren't hungry, but they aren't inclined to chase. The energy deficit produced by spawning has to be addressed, and crappies will feed. But the spawning ordeal is difficult enough that many crappies don't survive. Fungus-infested fish are common in some lakes during this period.

After leaving the nest, females filter across adjacent flats to the edge of deep water. Small groups of crappies may linger around shallow cover like brushpiles and weed clumps. In shallow lakes, those become key spots during this period of recuperation. In general, however, crappies move to the developing deep weedline or to the nearest drop-off into deeper water. It's common to find them suspending 5 to 15 feet below the surface off the edge of the break, waiting for pods of small minnows or casually cropping off larger forms of zooplankton. It's also common to find loose groups of crappies roaming the edges of channels, drop-offs, and developing weedlines, sometimes holding above deeper points.

Once the hatchlings leave the nest, males join the females in this roaming, casual feeding activity, as the Postspawn Period dovetails into the Presummer Period. At that point, the bite begins to heat up.

PRESUMMER PERIOD
Water Temperature: 70°F range
General Fish Mood: Neutral to positive

Resumption of regular feeding patterns marks the beginning of the Presummer Period. Water temperatures could be in the mid-70°F range or above. Presummer is the Calendar Period during which weedgrowth and food chains develop toward peak summer levels.

Feeding opportunities and patterns for crappies develop at different depths. Some fish are found in weedbeds, some on flats, some on breaks, and some are suspended—all at the same time. The Presummer Period is yet another time of transition for crappies. In deep southern reservoirs, crappies appear on primary and secondary points in the main lake, establishing ever-deeper patterns. Deep, timbered channel edges harbor steadily increasing numbers of crappies through this period, while the extreme shallows become nearly devoid of fish.

In northern natural lakes, crappies establish themselves in the habitat they use all summer long and show an increasing tendency to suspend farther from structure. In smaller lakes and ponds, points and turns along deep weededges draw increasing numbers of fish, and a classic summer pattern begins: Crappies suspend during the day, then hover near the deep weededge as the sun drops lower or the wind rises, moving to the weededges and over the weeds in low-light periods (evening, night, dawn).

The passing of the cool-water periods of spring into the warmest period of the year encourages crappies to switch to classic patterns that match the long, stable period of summer. A recent tracking study on Kentucky Lake revealed major differences between white and black crappies in habitat selected after spawning and in movement patterns. While white crappies quickly departed spawning areas and moved to deeper water near secondary river channel ledges and submerged structure, black crappies remained in the same type of shallow brushy habitat where they'd spawned. Interestingly, local anglers keyed on offshore patterns and had difficulty catching these increasingly abundant black crappies.

SUMMER PEAK PERIOD
Water Temperature: Mid- to upper 70°F range
General Fish Mood: Positive

During the Summer Peak, weeds have arrived at their zenith, the food chain is humming along at peak production levels, and the metabolism of crappies reaches its apex for the year. The transformation from a cool to a warm environment is complete. Hatching insects leave millions of husks scattered on the surface film. Rooted aquatic plants reach the surface and begin to bend there, along the roof of their world.

In natural lakes, deep weeds develop a distinct edge, and crappies roam that edge like caribou skirting a pipeline. In reservoirs, crappies follow the year's biggest schools of shad, gorging on and around the edges of creek and river channels. Crappies again group tightly, and fishing can be fast and furious.

The Summer Peak is one of the year's prime times to be on the water. Crappies are more likely to be in a positive feeding mood than at any other time until fall arrives. Hungry, aggressive, and fully recovered from the postspawn blues, they school tightly, which promotes competitive feeding. To top it all off, the water is alive and brimming with food. Crappies now tend to throw caution to the wind.

One key to recognizing this period is establishing that the last crappies to spawn finished a week or two previously. Typically, deep cabbage tops appear for the first time through the surface film. The water first reached 70°F two or three weeks prior. The Summer Peak generally coincides with the point at which the water broaches the mid-70°F mark, and crappies reveal a propensity to consistently chase lures like jig-twistertail combos and small suspending minnowbaits.

By human standards, some years seem to have no fall season, jumping right from an extended summer to an early winter. By the same token, those years when weather is unseasonably cold and cloudy for several weeks after panfish spawn seem to have no Summer Peak Period on the crappie calendar, either. But even in such adverse situations, this time frame offers the best post cold-front fishing for crappies of the entire year.

SUMMER PERIOD
Water Temperature: Annual maximum
General Fish Mood: Variable

As summer progresses, crappies become far less "suicidal" than during the Summer Peak Period. The sun is converting energy into life all around, and forage is plentiful in the form of plankton, insects, minnows, fry, and fingerlings. No longer driven by energy deficits, crappies can afford to be more selective and judicious in their feeding.

Scorching sun and high humidity mark the dog days of summer for humans, but life underwater is in high gear. Thermoclines develop in many natural lakes and reservoirs. Other controlling factors like increased sunlight, competing species, and an increased metabolism demand order. Nature responds by regulating feeding times.

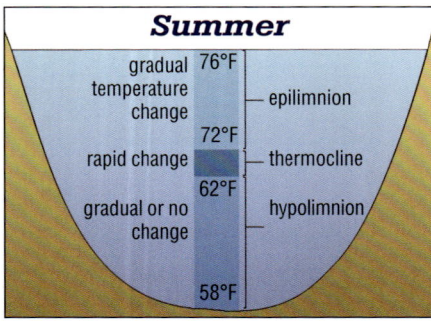

The upper (warmwater) layer may be from 12 to 40 feet thick, while the thermocline may be 2 to 15 feet thick. The lower (coldwater) level usually contains less dissolved oxygen than the upper layer.

In some systems, big crappies vacate the shallows. During the Summer Period, they suspend more, roaming the edges of cover at night or during low-light periods. Most activity in the daytime is confined to depths ranging from 12 to 24 feet in larger lakes and reservoirs. The clearer the water, the deeper crappies suspend. The cloudier the water, the more they tend to use cover during the day. Active fish may be on the edge of cover or slightly within it, while inactive fish bury deep.

In natural lakes and vegetated impoundments, the best summer areas tend to be deep weededges. Crappies hold along points and turns in those edges. On deeper flats, rockpiles that rise slightly above the level of deepest sunlight penetration often hold large schools of crappies. Tall trees that fall across or slide down steep-dropping shorelines and intersect depths of 15 feet or deeper are crappie magnets. Similar spots in strip pits, ponds, and impoundments attract crappies in summer, as well.

In most reservoirs, flooded timber, deep stumps, brushpiles, and other man-made fish attractors substitute for natural weedcover or woodcover, but patterns are similar. Crappies use the best wood along the edges of creek and river channels and select depths based on water clarity. The precise location of the "best wood" can alter from year to year, depending on pool level and changes in water clarity. Active crappies hold in or next to cover. Suspended fish near cover can be negative or actively feeding. When marking large schools of shad around cover, assume suspended fish are feeding, especially those fish highest in the water column.

Crappies often suspend during the Summer Period, particularly in the daytime. In clear water, they become most active at dusk and during the night. During the heart of summer, the best fishing tends to be around classically positioned cover in the evening, at night, and at dawn. But in lakes and ponds with dark, stained, or cloudy water, the best bite tends to occur sometime between 9 a.m. and 3 p.m.

As a general rule, summer activity tends to take place deeper than spring activity, although crappies remain above the thermocline once it develops (usually somewhere between 18 and 30 feet). Crappies show a decided preference for roaming confined open water during the day and invading cover at night, holding at depths determined by water clarity. During the Summer Period, crappies group less tightly and forage more sporadically than during the Summer Peak.

POSTSUMMER PERIOD

Water Temperature: Rapidly cooling from annual maximum
General Fish Mood: Neutral to positive

The Postsummer Period is a reversal of the Presummer process, occurring at the end of summer when waters begin to cool. Hot days with dead-calm periods followed by cool nights are typical. Days are growing noticeably shorter. With less sunlight, the ecosystem begins winding down. Food production grinds to a near halt.

Ongoing predation by all species continues to reduce the now-finite food supply. Weeds begin to thin out. Insect hatches dwindle in size and number. Water levels in rivers and feeder creeks may reach annual low points, forcing fish into the deepest holes.

Crappies generally respond to this changing environment by holding tighter to cover and showing less tendency to suspend. Fish a weedline or timberline and you may not spot a single suspended

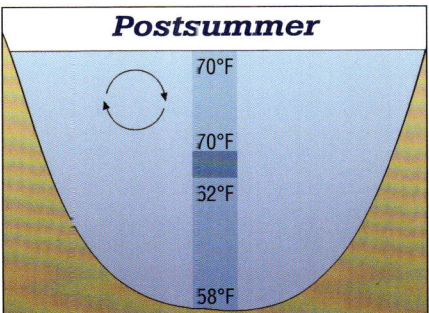

The surface of the water radiates heat to the atmosphere at right as water above the thermocline gradually cools. The thermocline remains intact but becomes closer in temperature to the layer above. Oxygen-poor water remains trapped below the thermocline.

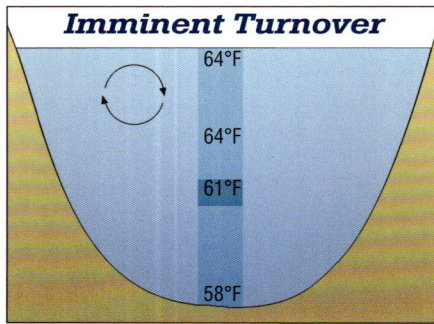

The thermocline shrinks when it approaches the same temperature as the uniform mass of water above.

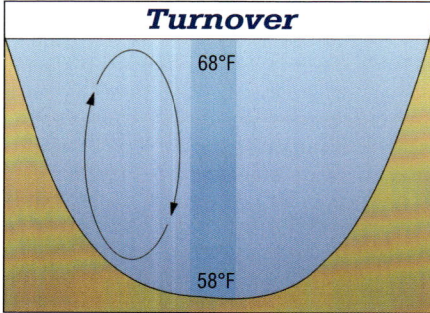

The thermocline disintegrates, and water mixes from surface to bottom. The water continues to cool as it circulates, aided by wind. The oxygen level of the water drops for a short time as the oxygen-depleted hypolimnion mixes with the water above.

fish on sonar. Pitch a jig to those edges, however, and you just might catch a boatload. Now it becomes necessary to fish them in order to find them, rather than depending on the depthfinder to locate schools.

Once again, crappies begin to concentrate more. Key spots become the edges of prime cover, making them easier to find and catch. Key locations tend to retain crappies for extended periods. A hot bite generally repeats itself for weeks on the same spot during Postsummer, but it all comes to an abrupt halt when the lake "turns over."

TURNOVER PERIOD

Water Temperature: *60°F to low 50°F range*
General Fish Mood: *Negative*

Many lakes stratify by temperature in summer, with heavier, denser, cold water deep and lighter, warmer, less-dense water on top. Turnover occurs when the temperature on top drops to a point where it equalizes with water temperature below the thermocline. It's a dramatic event for aquatic life and a visual event for us. When the temperature drops below 60°F, look for detritus, clumps of bottom algae, and old, dead weedstalks littering the surface on lakes that thermocline in summer. The flotsam is dragged topside by currents created as the water in the lake mixes top to bottom. Sometimes the stagnant bottom water of the lake releases a sulfurous odor as it reaches the surface and mixes with the air on windy days. You also may detect suspended debris on sonar.

Turnover is like one big off-switch. The crappie bite, consistent for so many weeks, now abruptly shuts down for several days to a week. Turnover is usually brought on by cool winds after a cold snap or a cold rain that chills the surface of the lake. Shallower bodies of water never develop thermoclines and don't turn over in fall. The Turnover Period can be a great time to seek crappies in rivers, backwaters, flowages, and other shallow impoundments. Or, if that isn't an option, look shallow. In many environments, predators like pike, walleyes, and crappies follow hordes of baitfish right up to the beaches and into shoreline cover during the turnover, where they find more environmental stability in terms of temperature and oxygen content. In-flowing creeks and other current areas become key spots. The bite's slow, but better shallow than in deeper areas. In fact, deeper spots, which crappies otherwise flock to, can be entirely devoid of fish in many lakes during this period.

As the days get shorter in fall, the first really hard cold snap followed by several days of windy, cold weather generally precipitates turnover and heralds the approach of the Coldwater Period. As the temperature on the surface of the lake drops to about 55°F and the water perceptibly clears, coldwater fishing patterns for crappies begin to emerge.

THE COLDWATER PERIOD (Fall)
Surface Water Temperature: 55°F down to the coldest temperatures of the year
General Fish Mood: Neutral
This period spans the entire time frame from turnover to freeze-up, or down to the lowest temperatures of the year on waters that never freeze. It represents a gradual slowing down and stabilization of the entire ecosystem. The metabolism of a crappie slows in direct proportion to the gradually dropping temperatures. A cooling environment, however, triggers the instinctive need to feed. Winter, and all the stress it represents, is drawing near. Crappies may be moving more slowly, but they rarely pass up an opportunistic meal during this period. Even cold fronts can trigger activity.

In larger, deeper lakes and reservoirs, the passing of the Turnover Period opens the door to deeper, formerly unusable tracts of water that were below the thermocline in summer. Turnover sends oxygenated water deep, providing crappies the chance to forage for invertebrates that were out of reach for months. Minnows soon seek the same areas in search of environmental stability. And, slowly but surely, deeper spots become the most stable areas of the lake. After ice-up, the warmest water is on bottom, the coldest water on top. Water, unlike other liquids, almost reverses the laws of physics as it continues to cool down to about 38°F. At that point, it begins to expand. The coldest water—ice—becomes the lightest. Water is most dense at 39°F and sinks to bottom, so that's about as cold as water ever gets in deeper portions of frozen lakes. It's a strange twist of nature that provides for life in northern lakes. If water were most dense at 32°F, lakes would freeze solid from the bottom up.

Within a few days to a week after turnover, crappies begin showing up in deeper haunts. They may linger on the deep edge of healthy weedbeds for some time. Some suspend in the open water of deeper bays or between points over main-lake basins where they spend the winter. Deep rocky points, sunken islands, humps, and other main-lake structural elements experience increasing use by crappies. Transitions from hard to soft bottom at the base of main-lake shorelines crappies use in summer become important, often in depths of 30 to 45 feet in larger lakes. In shallow, bowl-shaped lakes with little structure, crappies may suspend right in the middle of the lake, over basins in the 20- to 30-foot range where they winter.

In reservoirs, crappies begin schooling in deep (15- to 35-foot) creek channels. They collect where the channel bends, usually along the steepest break. Some suspend between primary and secondary points, depending on the

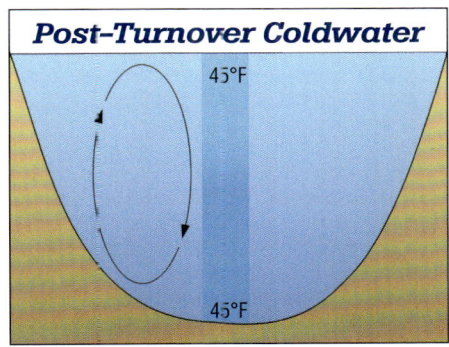

Post-Turnover Coldwater

Temperature becomes uniform. Wind action circulates and oxygenates water, which reaches a uniform temperature.

type of reservoir. On large rivers, crappies leave current areas for deeper 5- to 15-foot backwaters or connected natural lakes. Huge schools form by late fall. In small rivers without deep backwaters, they move into deeper pools as water levels drop.

In all environments, crappies rarely suspend near the surface after the water cools into the high 40°F range. They may suspend, but increasingly closer to bottom. Typically, the Coldwater Period of fall finds them within 5 or 10 feet of bottom. They begin to hold on bottom, a posture they may assume with increasing regularity as the water dips into the low 40°F range and as it becomes even colder. Inactive crappies are pinned to the bottom and difficult to see with sonar. Active fish rise 5 to 10 feet above bottom, becoming easier to mark.

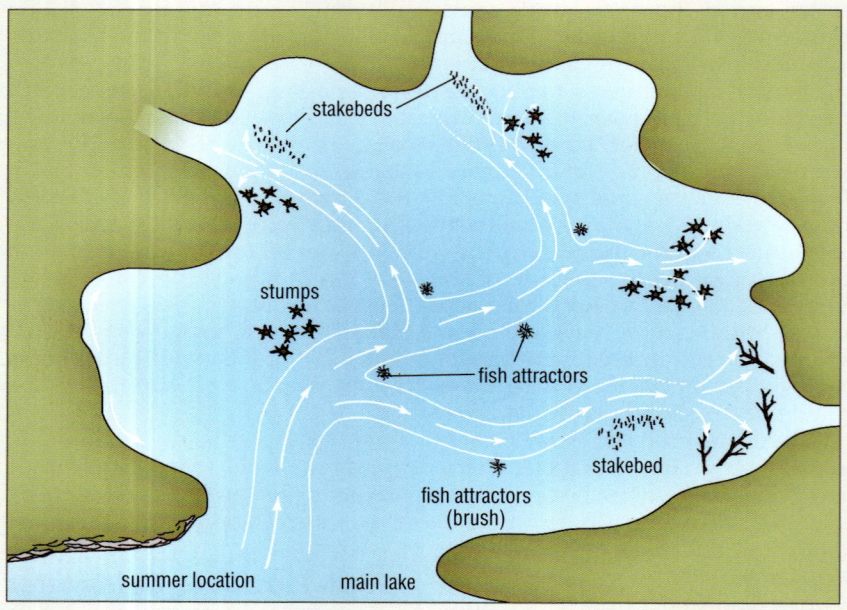

Crappie Movements during Fall

Fall migrations begin after the first cold front in September. After leaving the main channel, crappies follow the same routes they used in spring. Their first stop or staging area is a pocket of stumps; mid-depth fish attractors; an old roadbed; or the junction of a creek, slough, or ditch. They remain in these areas until cooler temperatures push them shallower into brushpiles.

Fish attractors placed along migration routes pay greater dividends during fall than during any other season. Stakebeds are particularly effective, although any kind of attractor can hold fish, because cover is at a premium during fall and winter drawdowns. Note the location of the fish attractors—sites for crappies, when they're properly built and anchored.

In fall, because of the water clarity, cast jigs on ultralight gear or work them under a slip cork for spooky crappies. Most reservoirs draw down their water level in winter, which leaves cover dry that was underwater in spring and summer.

The stable Coldwater Period is prime time for crappie fishing. Schooling behavior concentrates fish in distinct areas that they continue to use for months. Once they're located in fall, consistent action lasts for weeks. Successful anglers drift slowly and employ a combination of bottom-oriented techniques, presentations that maintain baited rigs a specific distance from bottom, and vertical jigging. If too many people don't harvest too many fish, the open-water bite lasts for six weeks to two months.

WINTER OR FROZEN-WATER PERIOD

Water Temperature: Coldest of the year
General Fish Mood: Neutral

In far northern waters, Winter or Frozen-Water is the longest calendar period of the year for crappies. In many northern waters, ice covers lakes for up to five months. In southern waters, the temperature may never drop below 40°F and rarely dips below 50°F in the far south. In lakes like Florida's famous Okeechobee, a temperature reading below 50°F is almost as rare as a polar-bear sighting.

Crappies feed on small invertebrates and minnows through the Winter Period, providing excellent ice-fishing in the North. In the South, open-water angling can be good, too, especially since few anglers pursue crappies at this time of year. Fishing small jigs 30 feet deep from a boat in the face of rain or sleet in a stiff wind is too much discomfort for most folks. Fishing from a toasty fish house on the ice, on the other hand, is easier and far more comfortable.

In general, crappies occupy the same areas they used during the Fall Coldwater Period. Basin areas are key in ponds, small lakes, and northern natural lakes, especially around hard-to-soft transitions. Deep edges of cover (weeds or timber), channel edges, and rocky humps continue to produce fish. The best areas lie in less than 30 feet of water but may be as deep as 45 feet. Active crappies often suspend within 5 feet of bottom during this period, sometimes higher. In clear weedy lakes, they also roam flats from 5 to 10 feet deep, apparently feeding on invertebrates, tiny bluegill, and minnows under ice cover.

During the middle stretches of the Winter Period, snow cover and thickening ice decrease light penetration. Along with shorter days, the dwindling light supply reduces plankton production to its lowest point of the year. In small or shallow northern lakes, crappies become lethargic, almost dormant, as oxygen counts drop. Best to concentrate on larger lakes at this point. Later in the period, as ice cover thins, they may suspend closer to the surface again. In some lakes, fish move to shallow areas less than 6 feet deep slightly before ice-out, especially in smaller lakes that may experience low oxygen levels. As the ice pulls from shore, life-giving oxygen again mixes into the water on windy days, and the bite improves dramatically.

Most crappie activity under the ice occurs at midday in normal to cloudy water clarity, but continues to occur during the low-light periods of dawn and dusk, or at night on clearer bodies of water. Night-fishing can be surprisingly productive during winter, north or south. Dropping a lantern below the surface (where legal) attracts baitfish and in turn attracts crappies. Lantern light flooding down the holes from ice houses often attracts the fish at night and activity levels increase, especially on lakes that receive heavy fishing pressure during the day.

During winter, crappies are concentrated and catchable on small lures or livebait presented slowly at or slightly above their depth level. Use sonar to determine the depths fish are using, then experiment with combinations of ice flies, spoons, and jigs tipped with minnows or insect larvae (maggots, waxworms).

In the South, most winter crappie activity is centered around brushpiles. As in the Fall Coldwater Period, active fish tend to stay within 5 or 10 feet of bottom, but may suspend in the tops of taller piles. Catching them means finding brushpiles situated at the right depth levels. In most cases, they use slightly different spots each year, depending on pool level and water clarity, but the right depth remains generally constant from year to year. As the days lengthen and the water begins to warm, they begin to suspend, often rising straight up and staging within 5 or 10 feet of the surface. When the water warms slightly again, they begin moving from main-lake areas back into the creek arms where they eventually spawn, which brings us full cycle once again to the beginning of the year of the crappie.

Location
Chapter 2

Classifying Crappie Waters

CATEGORIZING LAKE, RIVER AND RESERVOIR TYPES

Classifying lake, river, and reservoir types is important because crappies in hill-land reservoirs in the South behave much the same as crappies in hill-land reservoirs in the North, East, or West. Crappies react differently in small, cloudy ponds and natural lakes, feeding at different times and in different areas than they do in large impoundments. But crappies in small, cloudy lakes in the North behave much the same as crappies in similar environments in the South.

When combined with the Calendar Periods, In-Fisherman's lake classification system helps fine-tune and pinpoint crappie location throughout the year. It also serves as a basis for communication. When anglers from the same general region discuss crappie fishing over the phone, with one catching crappies from an oligotrophic lake in Minnesota while the other is fishing a deep impoundment in Wisconsin, they're really comparing apples and oranges. Without a classification system, the conversation produces more questions than answers.

<u>Understand a little bit about how a lake was formed, and it becomes easier to find a range of similar attributes within all such lakes.</u>

The ability to classify lakes, rivers, and reservoirs is another critical concept that helps anglers understand the structural makeup of different bodies of water. Similar patterns emerge for finding crappies, as well. Classifying different waters helps anglers note similarities and differences in fish behavior in differing environments and place them within a defined context. After catching crappies from a canyon reservoir for many years, an angler might be surprised how differently they behave in a middle-aged natural lake. The depths crappies use, the structure they seek out, the forage they prefer, and many other factors, will vary. And, if these two lakes are geographically close, anglers can confirm how differently the Calendar Periods play out within these two very different bodies of water. Some crappies in a canyon reservoir probably remain in Prespawn even as the lake fish are following Presummer patterns. Deep, clear lakes warm much more slowly in spring than shallower lakes, which have higher counts of plankton and more suspended particles that catch sunlight and give off energy in the form of heat.

Surprisingly, the thousands of lakes, rivers, and reservoirs across North America fall somewhat neatly into little more than a dozen categories, relatively easy to grasp and remember, with use. Plan your work and work your plan, yes. But first, the plan has to work. Learning lake categories is the second step in our process of pinpointing patterns, even before the boat gets wet.

NATURAL LAKES

Obviously, no two lakes are exactly alike. Broadly, though, all can be classified into one of three environmental age groups: Oligotrophic (young, in geologic terms), mesotrophic (middle-aged), and eutrophic (old). Factors like predator-prey relationships, the amounts and types of aquatic vegetation, and many other structural considerations, help to determine the basic lake classification. This helps you decide where crappies should be located during each Calendar Period.

No matter where your favorite lake is located, it's changing. In some waters, observable change may take centuries. In others, due to siltation caused by construction, logging, natural disasters, or any of a number of factors, change occur in only a few years. This aging process is often called eutrophication, and all lakes pass through it. A lake grows older not only in time, but in condition. The initial stages of eutrophication may take thousands of years. The final stages may happen quickly, especially with the intervention of man.

Throughout this process, the lake environment—structural makeup, food chains, vegetation levels, and dominant fish species—changes. Eutrophication brought on by human activity is primarily due to our rapidly increasing population. Waste disposal, fertilizer runoff from lawns and golf courses, removal of vegetation bordering the water—all these things and many more speed up the eutrophication

Middle-Stage Oligotrophic

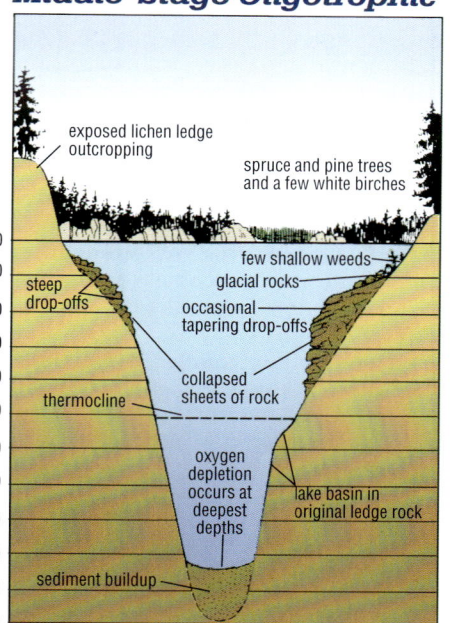

YOUNG

Middle-Stage Mesotrophic

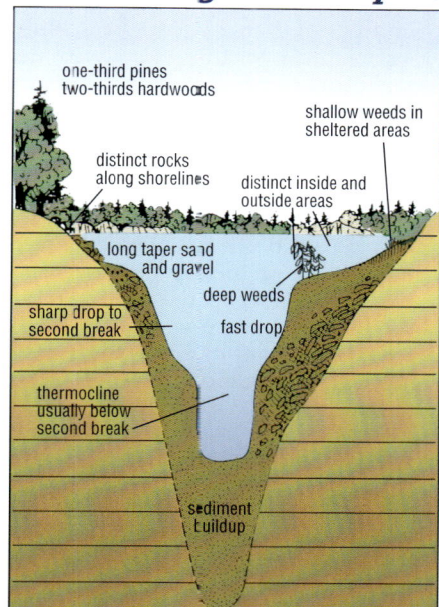

MIDDLE AGED

Middle-Stage Eutrophic

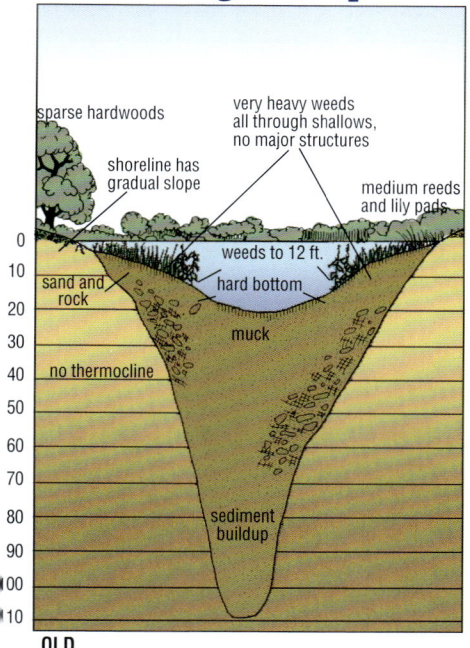

OLD

The Aging Processes

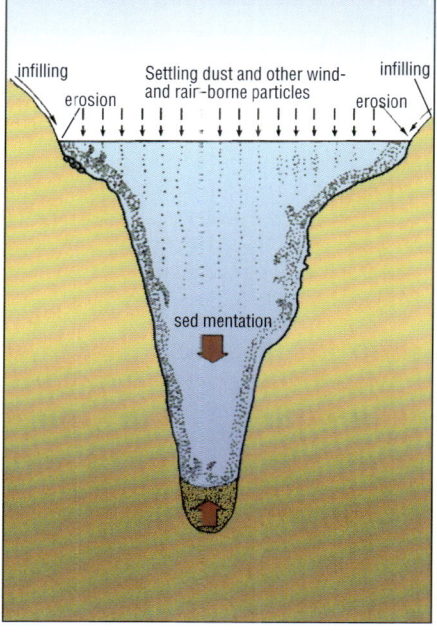

process. Within a generation, humans cause changes that would take nature hundreds of years to effect. Each individual living on the shoreline accepts some responsibility for this, along with neighboring municipalities, industries, and agriculture. Laws restricting human activity along waterways have increased for decades.

Because of the manmade changes on most North American lakes, we classify them according to environmental condition rather than chronological age. Each category is a point of reference, making it easier to recognize similarities between various bodies of water. This, in turn, makes it easier to transfer patterns of fishing from one body of water to the next. The logical process for fine-tuning those patterns to meet the demands of each specific environment becomes easier to follow, too. Soon it becomes second nature to pursue patterns for catching crappies based on experience on other waters in the same category.

As a lake ages, its character changes. Environmentally young lakes are deep and clear, while older lakes are shallow and murky. Young lakes tend to be deep, cool, and oxygen rich, ideal for species like lake trout and whitefish, while crappies tend to run small but can be fairly populous though confined to bays and "lake-within-lake" scenarios. Old lakes are weed-choked and oxygen poor, supporting species like carp and bullhead, while crappies tend to be sparse but sometimes grow large. Between those two extremes lie the optimum lake environments for crappies—usually mid-mesotrophic to early eutrophic natural lakes. While it's possible to have a weed-choked, late eutrophic lake produce crappies of good number and size, it's the exception and not the rule.

The three basic categories of natural lakes can be subdivided further into early-, mid-, and late-stage, creating nine specific categories. First, however, let's consider the three basic categories.

OLIGOTROPHIC LAKES

The youngest and least fertile lakes typically have rock basins and, since many were formed in the most recent Ice Age, are found almost exclusively within the northern latitudes of North America. Oligotrophic lakes have steep drop-offs, few weeds, and shorelines punctuated with conifers or surrounded by tundra. Big boulders and huge slabs of bedrock are common in the shallows. The nutrient level of the water is typically low, and oxygen is available at all depths. These lakes usually support only a few pounds of gamefish per acre and are most suitable to cold-water species like char, whitefish, and tulibee. Crappies most often appear in oligotrophic lakes during the later stages of this lake classification, and then only within bays or confined basins that more closely resemble mesotrophic or eutrophic environments.

MESOTROPHIC LAKES

Mesotrophic or middle-aged lakes typically have shorelines less gorgelike and drop-offs less steep than oligotrophic lakes, having less depth overall. Huge boulders and bedrock give way to smaller rocks with occasional boulders. Sand and gravel substrates are more apparent. Shallow flats appear, where direct sunlight contacts more bottom-area of the lake. Aquatic vegetation is usually abundant. Shoreline terrain is more varied and plant life more diverse. The water contains more nutrients. The lake is moderately fertile, the water characterized as "cool" overall, and many pounds of fish are present per acre. Mesotrophic lakes support a wider range of species than oligotrophic lakes. Crappies thrive in mesotrophic lakes.

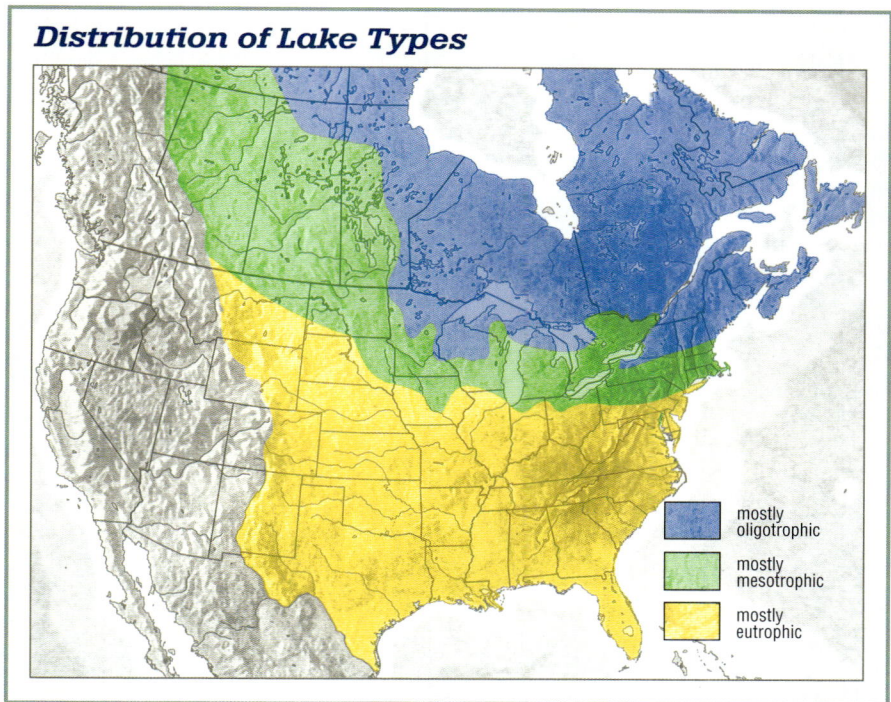

Distribution of Lake Types

- mostly oligotrophic
- mostly mesotrophic
- mostly eutrophic

EUTROPHIC LAKES

The oldest lakes, in geologic terms, tend to be warmwater environments. Shallow weedgrowth is thick where the water remains clear. In murky eutrophic lakes, weeds may be sparse, while clear ones often become weed-choked in summer. Lake bottoms consist of muck, marl, or clay—sediment that piled up in the lake's basin over the millenia, filling in a formerly mesotrophic environment. Typically shallow flats are expansive, with gradual drop-offs that taper to the main basin—the bottom of the lake. Secondary drop-offs are rare and maximum depths are less than 40 feet. Marshes normally surround part or all of these lakes. Hardwood trees and flat shorelines are the rule.

Sometimes eutrophic lakes are called "dishpan lakes" because of their more uniform shape and shallow depth. Typically, these old lakes are the most fertile and have large fish populations. Crappies do well in early- to mid-stage eutrophic lakes, but become sparse in older, marshier lakes. In the far South, however, crappies fare well in bayous and many other shallow, marshy environments. In most parts of the country, as these lakes age, they begin to favor species like carp, bullheads, bowfin, and other species better suited to low-oxygen environments.

RIVERS

Rivers come in many sizes and shapes, provide habitat for many fish species. Different stretches of the same river can have contrasting personalities, producing entirely different aquatic flora and fauna. For example, a young, clear, coldwater river plunges from mountainous terrain, flowing over and cutting through bedrock. Here, trout, grayling, and whitefish thrive, but not crappies.

Classifying Crappie Waters 23

River Type Continuum

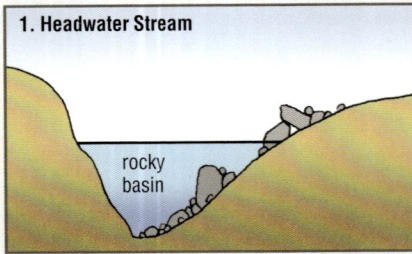

1. Headwater Stream

Bottom rocky; water cool and clear; depth shallow; width narrow; gradient steep; current fast; no aquatic vegetation. Poor crappie habitat.

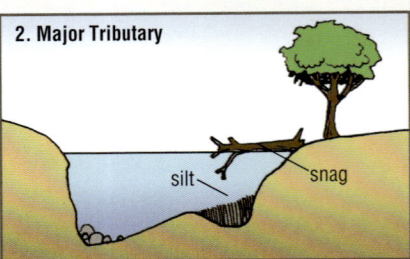

2. Major Tributary

Bottom variable; deeper pools common; water warmer and more turbid, especially after rain; gradient and flow rate reduced; typical riffle-pool-run sequence. Spotty and seasonal crappie habitat.

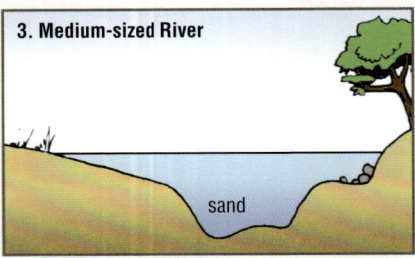

3. Medium-sized River

Bottom variable; riffle-pool-run sequence occurs, but not as well defined; vegetation may be present on shallow banks; tributaries common. Fair crappie habitat.

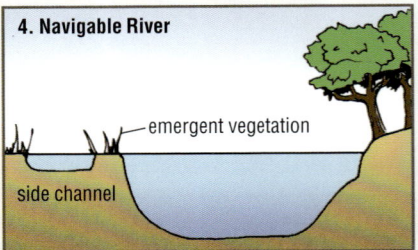

4. Navigable River

Current moderate; channel complex, possibly dredged; aquatic vegetation locally abundant; bottom soft; water murky and warm. Crappies may be abundant in backwaters and slow-moving stretches.

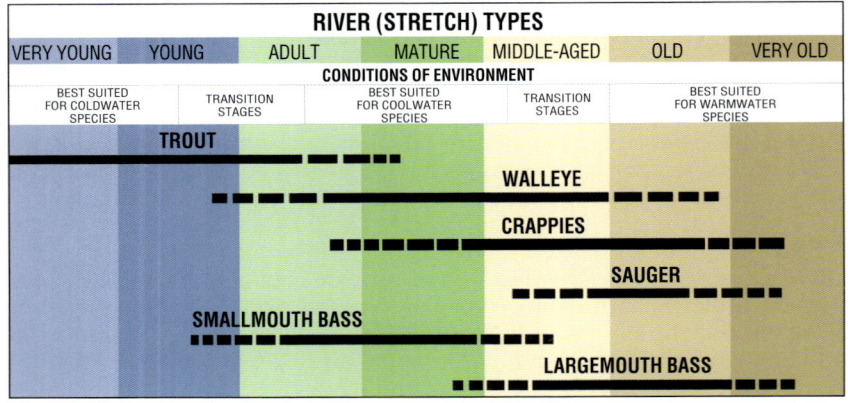

24 Critical Concepts . . . All About Finding Crappies

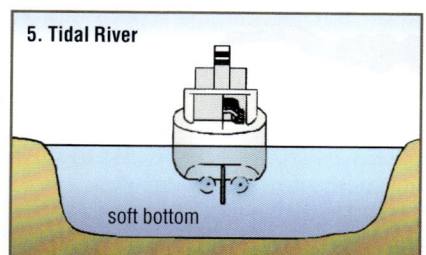

5. Tidal River

Water subject to tidal influence; salinity varies with location, tide, and rainfall. Crappies inhabit backwater ponds, feeder creeks, and river structure, but move seasonally in response to flow and salinity.

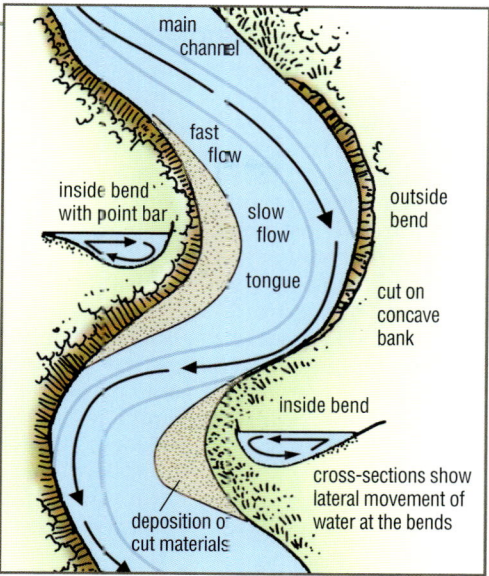

The force of water is constantly remodeling the riverscape. Over time, rivers change their courses. It is this change that constructs adjacent floodplains. If a river stretch does not have an extensive adjoining floodplain, it means that its bed is stable or the river is geologically very young. Water is a universal solvent; given time, it can chew away granite, dissolve iron, and move mountains.

In streams, the action of water along with the meandering effect cuts materials on the outside bend, where current flow is swift and deposits other materials on the inside bend where current speed and force are reduced. Notice how the current has created a tongue-like structure. The deepest part of any river stretch is always on the outside bend.

The same river plunges into an area of hilly terrain. It widens and slows, becoming home to large trout, a few bass, pike, and walleyes—perhaps a few crappies in impoundments and in backwaters. Finally, the river empties into truly flat terrain, meandering easily, leaving its banks and creating new channels where soft substrates in the floodplain give way to create oxbow lakes, backwaters, and marshes. This is where crappies and species like largemouth bass, gar, and catfish thrive.

Middle-aged and old rivers are slow-flowing, shallow, and accompanied by broad floodplains. These wide floodplains create complex backwater areas with abundant habitat for crappies. Everywhere along the Mississippi River, for example—from Minnesota to Louisiana—backwater areas harbor excellent populations of crappies. Many of these backwaters have maximum depths of only 5 or 6 feet, but enough current finds its way in to reestablish oxygen content on a regular basis, while vast areas lie out of the current—the kind of habitat crappies utilize most in rivers. Brushpiles, stumpfields, deadfalls, and other woodcover are common crappie magnets within these areas.

RIVER CLASSIFICATION

Streams must be examined segment by segment. A stream can be shallow with only gradual gradient changes for miles, replete with backwaters, oxbows, and primarily soft-bottom habitat where crappies find an adequate home. Downstream, the river may cascade down a steep grade in the landscape, creating multiple sets of rapids, riffles, chutes, and falls—and harbor only trout. Eventually, the same stream could revert back to crappie-catfish water.

Rarely is a river the same from beginning to end, because few regions are topographically consistent. Because of these flow variations from fast to slow within the same river, we use the following method to classify rivers. "Very young" or "very old" are, perhaps, misnomers in most cases, as some old rivers run quite fast out of the Blue Ridge and Smokey mountains. The key is understanding gradient. The steeper the drop, the harder the bottom will be, as softer substrates are washed away by powerful currents. In flatter terrain, the sediments settle, covering the rock with sand and silt. Most river stretches in North America fall within one of seven categories. River stretches, though, often exhibit transitional tendencies, just as a natural lake may have eutrophic bays while its main body is mesotrophic.

Because crappies are on the cusp between coolwater and warmwater designations as a species, they thrive in all kinds of impoundments throughout the continent.

RESERVOIRS

A reservoir is a body of water impounded behind a dam on a river. When the dam is completed, water floods the terrestrial landscape, covering marshes, plains, forests, road beds—even houses and barns, in some cases. We classify reservoirs based on the topography of the terrain where the river is dammed, from deep canyon reservoirs to shallow lowland-wetland impoundments. Reservoirs in the North, West, and East produce cooler environments than those in the South, Southwest, and Southeast. Because crappies are on the cusp between coolwater and warmwater designations as a species, they thrive in all kinds of impoundments throughout the continent.

In general, impoundments make fantastic homes for crappies from Arizona to Maine. From low, swampy, flat regions to hill-land, and even in highland and canyon reservoirs, crappies seem well adapted to carving out a niche.

Reservoirs in these various landforms have the same basic configuration. Each is deepest by the dam and shallowest at the upstream end, so we divide the reservoir into thirds. The deepest water in each segment is always in the old river channel, unless it silts in. Wherever creeks flow into an area that's impounded, a "creek arm" is created that wanders back between the hills. The confluence of an old creek channel with the old river channel within the impoundment is always a key spot for one species or another. The other end, or back end, of these creek arms and connecting coves becomes a critical spot for spawning crappies in spring.

Shape and depth of the pool and the surrounding topography determine how we categorize a reservoir. By studying a topographical map, you can usually determine what classification an impoundment falls into. Other facets of a reservoir's personality include (1) annual fluctuation of water level, (2) overall water clarity, (3) fertility, and (4) temperature.

Reading Reservoir Features

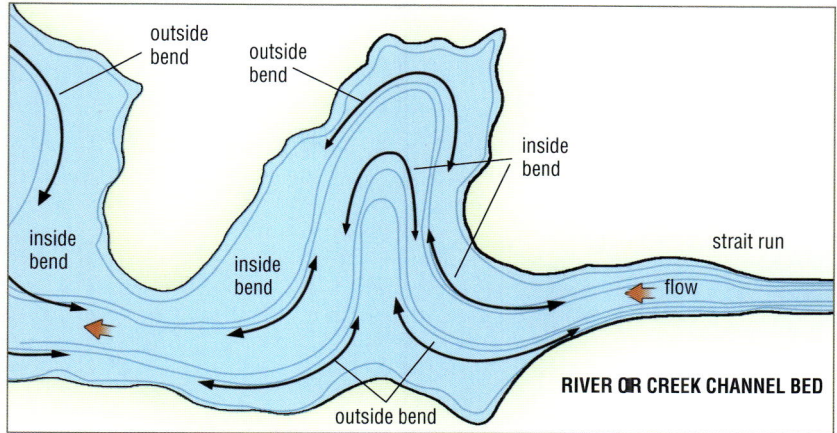

This illustration shows the difference between an inside and outside bend. The outside bend of a river or creek is "washed" the hardest by the water flow. Tongue areas are especially attractive. Obstructions such as a fallen tree can slow the flow and provide cover.

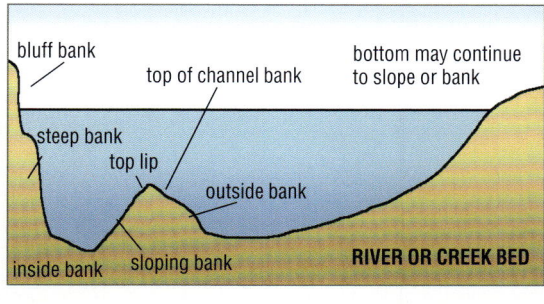

River and creek channels with the proper depth are the "main highways" in a reservoir. Bends, the degree of bank slope, the make-up of the bank top, the amount of timber or bush at the top of the banks, and obstructions in the channel itself affect the exact location of fish.

IMPOUNDMENT CLASSIFICATION

We use six broad categories to classify reservoirs: canyon, plateau, highland, hill-land, flatland, and lowland (or wetland). These classes are based on regional and geological aspects of North America's wildly various landforms. Both natural and manmade characteristics determine what class an impoundment fits into. There are, of course, many exceptions. Some small reservoirs and "flowages" are hard to classify. Also, some reservoirs have portions characteristic of different classes, just as rivers and lakes do.

LOWLAND IMPOUNDMENTS

Lowland impoundments are the shallowest category of reservoir, sometimes with a maximum depth of fewer than 15 feet, usually found in the old creek channel. A small dam blocks a small river, causing a wetland to fill and spread

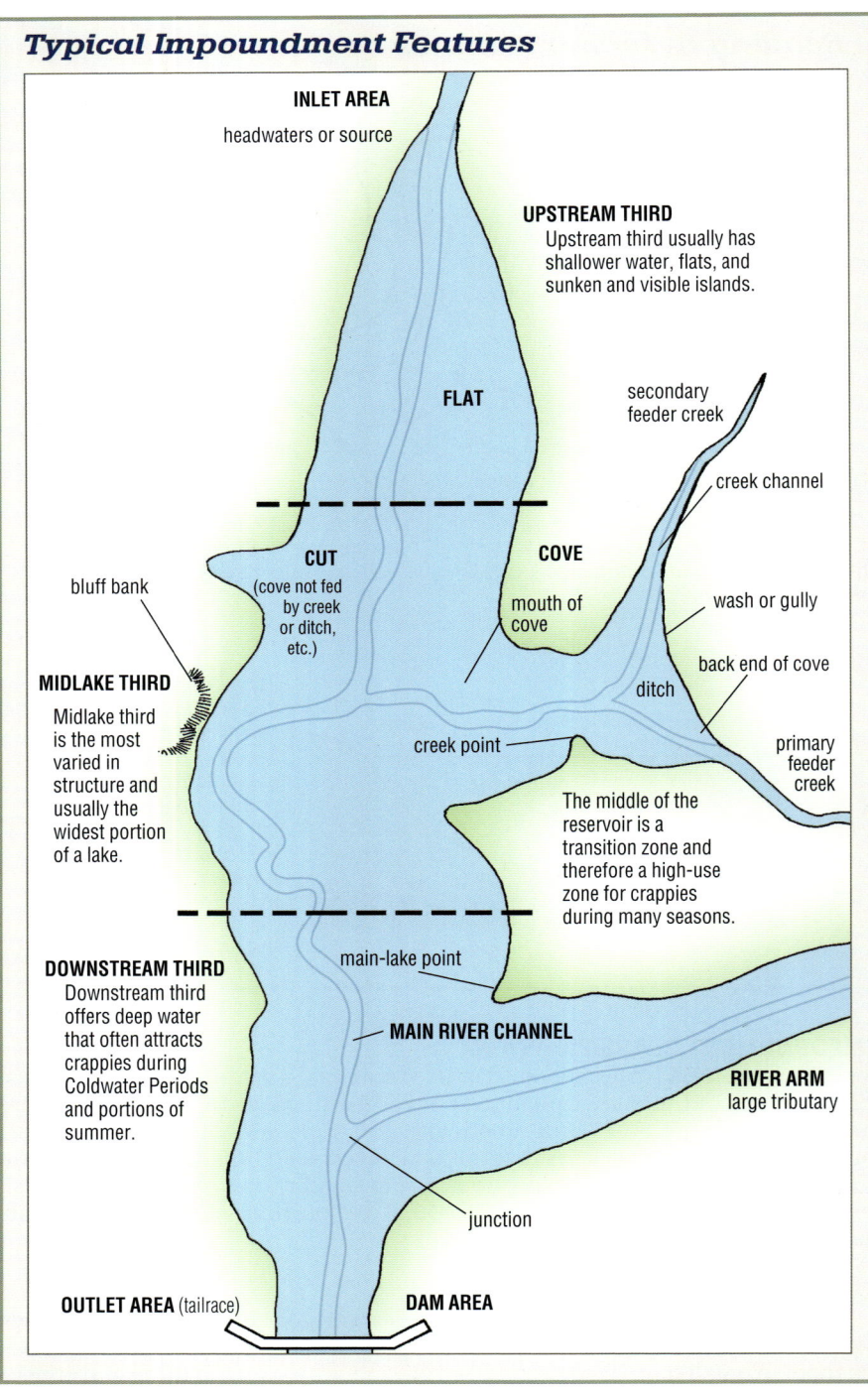

greatly due to the low, flat terrain. In Wisconsin, lowland impoundments called *flowages* provide multispecies fisheries, as do lowland impoundments on bayous in Louisiana.

Lowland impoundments feature vast flats with cover provided by the flooded timber and thick vegetation that sometimes grows in rich soils. Some such waters have many small, low islands and may contain old pond dams in the basin, offering a bit of structure. Current is minimal and fishing patterns are typically similar to those in natural lakes.

FLATLAND IMPOUNDMENTS

Many of the nation's most notable crappie fisheries fall into the flatland classification. Waters like Barkley Lake, Kentucky-Tennessee; Lake Seminole on the Georgia-Florida border; and Santee-Cooper in South Carolina offer a broad, shallow basin extending from a main river channel that meanders through farmland and low hills. Several broad arms define former tributary creeks that may run only during the rainy season.

Because of the shallow, fertile basin, aquatic plants may thrive in clear impoundments, sometimes covering 50 percent or ever more of the surface area of the reservoir. Weed-fishing patterns predominate in these waters, though flooded timber, brushy banks, and stumps also offer cover for crappies, particularly in flatland impoundments that are murky and thus have little plant growth. River channel ledges in the 12- to 20-foot range also hold crappies. Bass are abundant, too, and other species including white bass, hybrid stripers, and catfish are also common. These older reservoirs continue to offer excellent fishing.

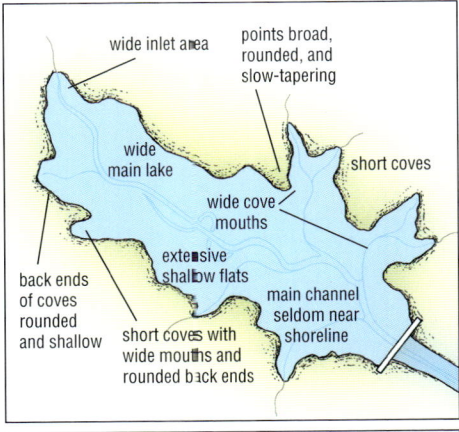

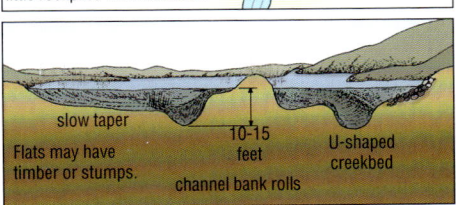

HILL-LAND IMPOUNDMENTS

Hill-land impoundments provide the classic reservoir shape, with many small fingers branching from a main basin that surrounds a major river channel. These impoundments are deeper than flatland impoundments but not as wide, because hills on either side of the river constrict them. Creek arms are narrower and deeper, with extensive submerged timber, though this form of cover has been declining over the many decades since most of these reservoirs were built.

Water color ranges from fairly clear with a greenish tinge to stained. The color may vary seasonally, with spring rains making the water murky and summer plant growth fostering clear water in creek arms. The upper end of the reservoir tends to be murkier where the main river enters, with silt gradually falling out as water approaches the deep basin near the dam. Crappies often undertake seasonal shifts in location, particularly during the Prespawn and Postspawn Periods, and prior to the Coldwater Period.

HIGHLAND IMPOUNDMENTS

Dams on highland impoundments usually are constructed in steep, narrow ravines. This category of reservoir is therefore narrow but very deep, where high bluff walls border long, narrow, deep-creek channels. The basin itself is also narrow and extends from higher elevations down to the dam. The deep basin offers few or no islands, but tributary creek arms may include islands and underwater humps. Most crappie fishing in spring occurs in the upper end of creek arms as fish move from deep structure to spawning areas.

Clear water with little cover can be a challenge for anglers. Crappies may live in available shallow cover or hold in water deeper than most anglers are accustomed to fish. Preyfish are not abundant, which limits crappie numbers.

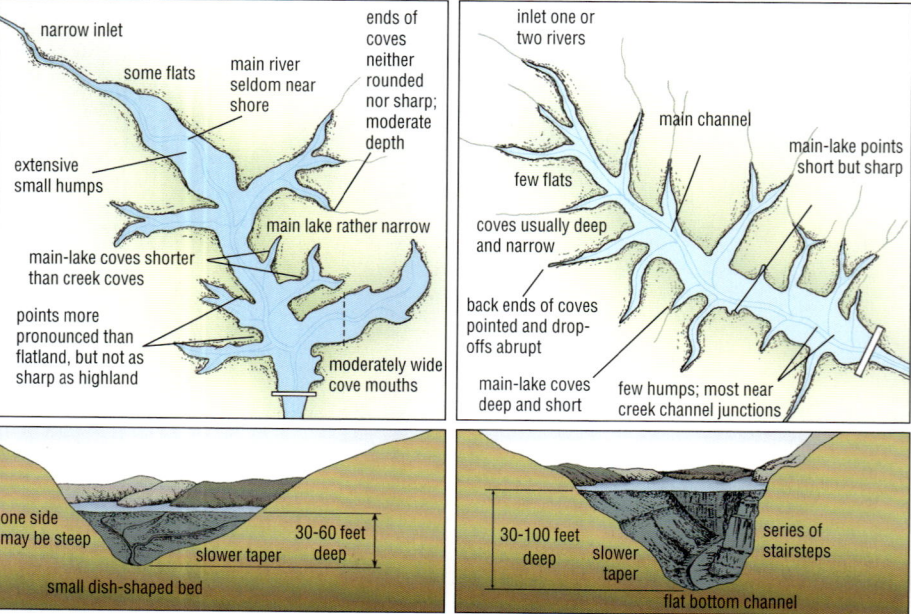

Dawn, twilight, and night-fishing are popular on these waters, because crappies roam shallower and seem to feed more actively in low-light conditions.

CANYON IMPOUNDMENTS

Huge concrete dams across steep, narrow canyons form canyon impoundments, the dominant type in the Southwest and West. These waters are the most capacious and deepest reservoirs, often over 200 feet. They're also ultraclear, a result of the sand and rock that form the basin. These substrates yield little plant life, so cover is in the form of sparse stick-ups, boulders, and sheer canyon walls with occasional rock slides. Canyon impoundments are narrow and very long, with long tributary arms.

These oligotrophic impoundments typically feature a deep, oxygenated hypolimnion that supports stocked rainbow trout. Warmwater species like crappies usually inhabit shallow bays and tributary arms, but also may roam the open water to feed.

PLATEAU IMPOUNDMENTS

In the high plains and low plateau regions from the Missouri River west to the eastern base of the Rockies, plateau impoundments prevail. These long, windswept reservoirs have a maximum depth in the 50- to 90-foot range. Though they may have long tributary arms, most coves are short and wide, not providing much protection from wind and waves. Due to wind, wave action, and loose substrate, vegetation is sparse. Plateau impoundments can offer good fishing in sections of the impoundment that contain hill- and or flatland characteristics. Where pelagic preyfish like shad, smelt, or alewives are found, crappies suspend consistently, except during the Spawn Period.

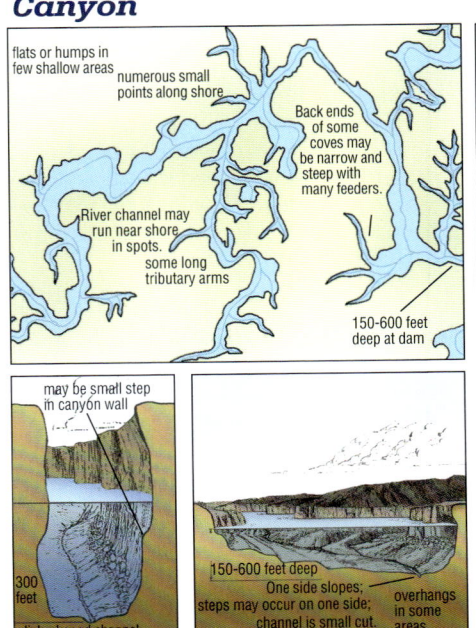

Classifying Crappie Waters

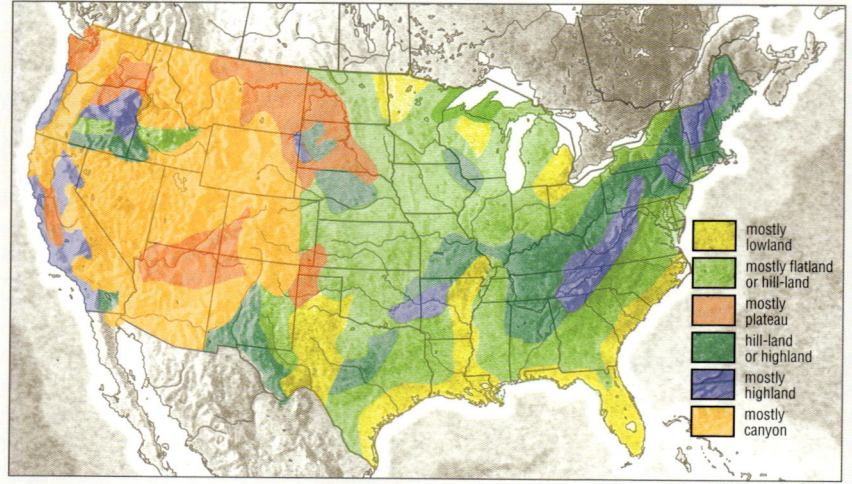

Impoundment Range Map

Legend: mostly lowland; mostly flatland or hill-land; mostly plateau; hill-land or highland; mostly highland; mostly canyon

Reservoirs constructed in similar landforms, even when they're in different parts of the country, are enough alike to fit into six basic groups: canyon, plateau, highland, hill-land, flatland, and lowland.

PONDS

Building a dam across a low area creates a pond if the watershed and soil type are adequate. The dam backs up runoff, forming a pond from 1 to 50 or more acres. Ponds typically are deepest near the dam, with gradually shallower water toward the upper end.

Cuts, points, humps, and flats with weeds or timber attract bass, sunfish, crappie, and catfish. In summer, bluegills and crappies may cruise open water to feed on zooplankton or small shad, or hold near willows or other overhanging trees to nab falling insects. Emergent vegetation and submerged weedlines also are good fishing areas. Particularly in southern latitudes, crappies tend to overpopulate small ponds, resulting in small, slow-growing fish. They should not be added to ponds managed for bass and bluegill for this reason.

DAMMED CREEKS

Creeks are dammed to power mills, to irrigate, and for fishing. These ponds can cover from 10 to over 100 acres. Standing timber and stumps near deep water attract crappies. When creeks prevent ponds from stratifying, crappies may move deep in summer. Structure and cover are diverse, and often many species are present as wild fish enter from the creek.

Low fishing pressure can mean superb angling, but competition with wild fish may inhibit crappie growth. Dammed creeks usually aren't fertilized, because water quickly passes through them.

PITS

Pits created by mining operations often fill with rainwater, springwater, or groundwater from the water table. Where water chemistry is suitable, crappie and

Built Pond and Dammed Creek

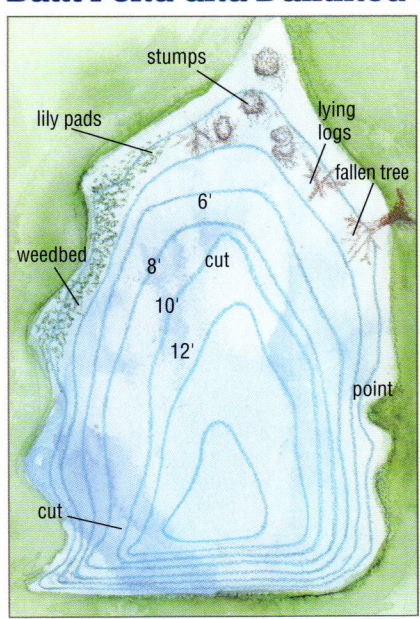
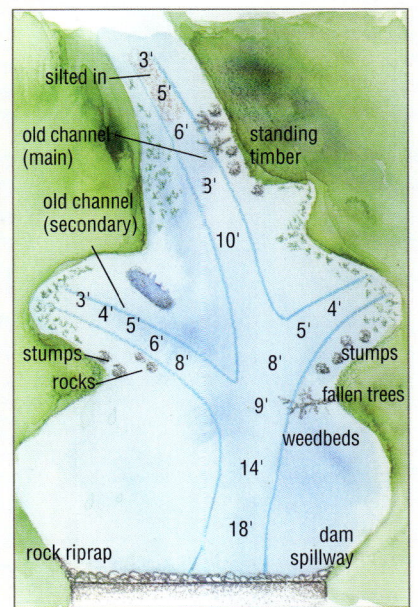

many other species thrive. Pits are typically deep and clear, with manmade structure such as shelves, roadbeds, mine shafts, and spoil piles. Clear water fosters weedgrowth if soft sediments and shallow flats are present. Stumps and flooded timber also hold fish.

Pits range from a couple of acres to over 1,000, and the fish composition varies from only bullheads to dozens of species. Check with property owners or fishery agencies to learn about stockings and management strategies.

Explore pits during the day, but expect best results during low-light periods and at night. Biomass is usually low due to infertile conditions, but trophy fish are possible. Some Florida phosphate pits are fertile and produce extraordinary fishing. The world-record, 4-pound 2-ounce bluegill was caught in Ketona Lake, a flooded limestone mine in Alabama. Presently, it's a poor fishery, which shows the importance of releasing large fish—and of fishing pits when they're producing big fish, before masses of anglers discover them.

THE ADAPTABLE CRAPPIE

Black and white crappie have adapted to and have thrived in a great variety of waters; they do best when these environments offer moderately clear, fairly warm water with plenty of oxygen. But they turn up in brackish estuaries, mucky prairie lakes, and stone-walled mining pits. They thrive among alligators in tropical lakes, and in water that's frozen over five months a year.

This adaptability is one of the most attractive attributes of the crappie. Wherever you are, a slab isn't far away. Thanks to stocking, they occur in every state but Alaska and Hawaii, absent only in the Rocky Mountains and some arid regions of the Great Plains.

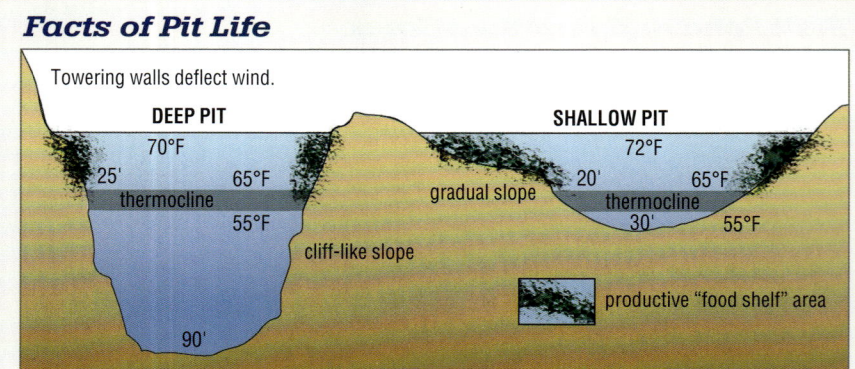

Facts of Pit Life

The clifflike walls of most deep pits provide little productive shelf. They're infertile compared to most shallow pits.

Towering walls surrounding many deep pits deflect wind. You can comfortably fish them even on windy days; but without wind, the depths don't reoxygenate to support much aquatic life below the thermocline. These pits may look like deep Canadian trout lakes. But despite their wilderness appearance, they're often infertile, with limited ability to produce fish.

Locating and catching crappies within these various waters depends upon understanding details of the kinds of structure and cover each offers. How crappies relate to them and feed in these diverse environments are the subjects of the next three chapters.

Chapter 3
Understanding Seasonal Movements—I

Crappies in Natural Lakes

SPRING — Crappie fishing and the rites of spring go hand in hand. When crappie fishing peaks, the dogwoods are in bloom and forsythia are bright gold. Wildflowers punctuate the gray forests and the songbirds return. Crappies lead us into the midst of these spring events, just as they flock shallow in vast numbers to create some of the best fishing of the year in natural lakes.

That opening may sound a bit biased toward the northern experience. And well it should. The great majority of all natural lakes in the United States are found in the North. Michigan, Minnesota, and Wisconsin lead the way, averaging well over 10,000 lakes apiece. The Dakotas, New York, and Maine come next, for sheer number of lakes, followed by Vermont, Connecticut, and New Hampshire. But natural lakes can be found in most states and exist from Florida to Oregon. If we tallied up all the lakes and took a census of the creatures that live within them, we would probably find that crappies inhabit about 70 to 80 percent within the contiguous 48 states. The southern rim of Canada is dotted with crappie lakes as well, and some of the continent's best crappie fishing can be found there.

Crappies living in natural lakes from Okeechobee in Florida up to Rainy on Minnesota's northern border share many common bonds and travails. Studies reveal that crappies, while well suited to relatively cold climates, do not perform well in extremely cold water and begin to lose essential motor function in the low 30°F range. Those two facts—living in cold climates, with loss of function in the coldest water—point to the need for depth in winter, down where the water is at its warmest (water is most dense around 39°F, and water at that temperature drops to the lake's bottom). And crappies do tend to drop deeper during the cold months throughout their range.

Latitude and lake types have a lot to do with how deep crappies winter. When the ice is leaving in spring, they can already be found shallow in many lakes, but most are still found near wintering habitat. In big, sprawling, mesotrophic lakes with a complex depth profile, crappies tend to winter in depths similar to those used in big reservoirs—at 40 to 50 feet. In smaller lakes and shallower lakes, even near the northern fringe of their range, they tend to winter in depths of 20 to 36 feet. In Lake of the Woods, which crosses the U.S.-Canadian border in Minnesota, most seem to winter at 40 to 46 feet. In nearby Rainy Lake, the fish move during late fall to enclosed basins with a maximum depth of 24 to 36 feet. Though both are very large lakes at the same latitude, Rainy is quite a bit shallower than Lake of the Woods. Yet both lakes maintain healthy populations of crappies that include significant numbers of 2-pound individuals.

Ice-out water temperatures at the surface of a lake tend to register right around 40°F by the time anybody gets out in a boat. As mentioned, some crappies—the vanguard of the spring foraging run—already are shallow. The first shallow crappies almost always show up in black-bottomed bays, marinas, boat canals, and other shallow, sheltered waters on the north side of a lake, where sun exposure is longest throughout the day and where the strongest winds can't quickly push that water back out into the main lake. Wintering crappies will migrate toward some of these areas in waves as the water warms into the 50°F range, and many stage outside these areas. Staging crappies typically suspend in 10 to 25 feet of water off a point, hump, or other structural element.

Similar movements take place in bays, canals, and marinas on the south side of a lake and toward main-lake areas, but these movements might be delayed or slower for a week or two. When cold fronts pass, crappies may move back to staging positions outside the bay or whatever area they're in, and suspend. These fish can be very difficult to catch, but it can be accomplished by jigging vertically with patience, long poles, light line, and sensitive gear. The most active crappies tend to be shallow, on flats 2 to 8 feet deep, and a wider variety of tactics can be employed to catch them.

Protected, shallow bays and canals with dark, soft substrates warm fastest and harbor a variety of tiny lifeforms crappies may use for food, such as plankton, burrowing insect larvae, and aquatic worms. These life forms also provide forage for the many minnows that gather in these areas, which can properly be called solar collectors. Crappies find warmth and a bounty of food in shallow, protected waters with a dark, soft bottom during spring. Within six weeks or so, they may abandon these areas as the water warms and chokes with weeds—and not return until the following spring.

CRAPPIE CHARACTERISTICS

Crappies often suspend but are not true open-water fish. They frequently suspend in what we call "confined open water." True open water involves large expanses of water where fish relate to light penetration, water stratification, and forage more than they relate to structure. True open-water fish, like salmon and striped bass, are streamlined and powerfully built.

Confined open water operates on a smaller scale. For instance, the open water that forms the center of a small bay (maybe 50 acres) is easy to interpret as confined. But the water between two main-lake points bordering miles of open water could also be considered confined. Wherever a shoreline, weedline, or the bottom is relatively nearby, you're probably still in confined open water. That's the world of the crappie in suspension. The crappie's body construction is an exercise in moderation. Its flat, relatively compact body allows it to make quick, responsive turns and function in and around weeds and brush. Its moderately sleek head-to-tail hydrodynamic design allows successful but limited use of confined open water.

Suspension Tendencies

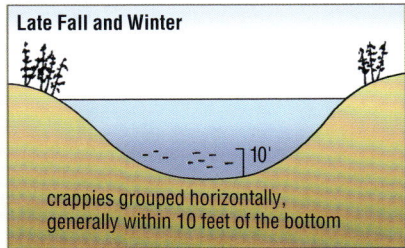

Late Fall and Winter

crappies grouped horizontally, generally within 10 feet of the bottom

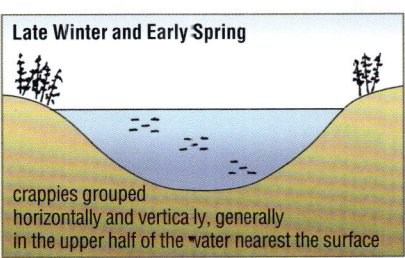

Late Winter and Early Spring

crappies grouped horizontally and vertically, generally in the upper half of the water nearest the surface

During late fall or winter, crappies begin to occupy deeper lake areas as well as weedy flats and drop-offs. Although it's impossible to make hard rules about how crappies suspend when they're in deeper water, here are two general tendencies.

When crappies first begin to use deep water, they suspend horizontally and usually near bottom. As a rule, during fall and through most of winter, crappies are within 10 feet of bottom.

During late winter, especially as ice-out approaches, this may change. While crappies may still be found near bottom, they tend to suspend both horizontally and vertically, often in the upper half of the water.

After ice-out, begin fishing in the upper layers. Remember that fish may be grouped horizontally. In spring, however, expect to find crappies at many depths.

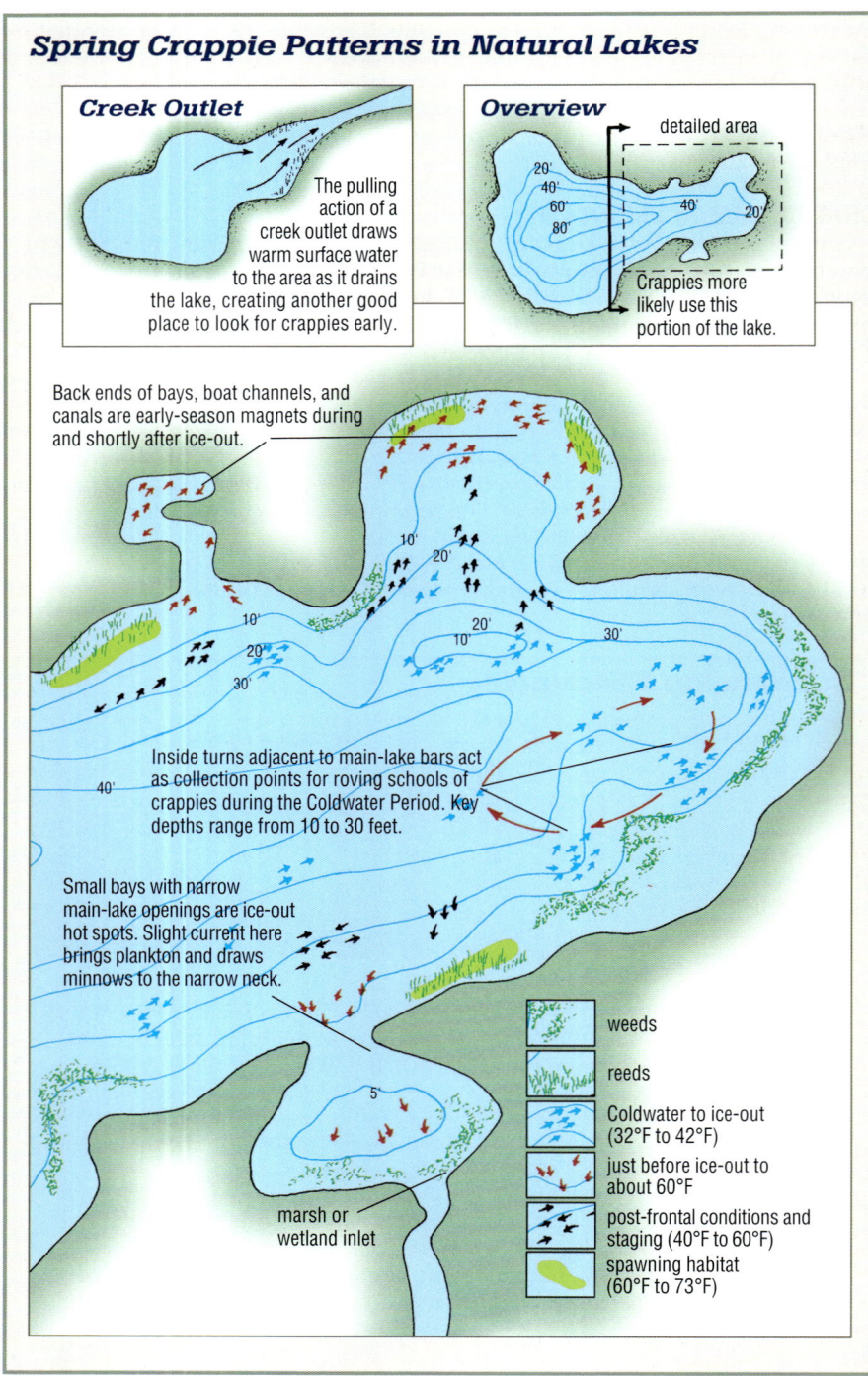

Much like bass, crappies are ambush predators only when at rest and in a negative or neutral feeding mood. When actively feeding, crappies are hunters. The hunt often takes them where minnows are, and they are adept at tracking minnows in relatively open water or in cover like brush, rocks, or weeds. Resting crappies may suspend in open water, in heavy cover, or somewhere between. The fish are opportunists with a penchant for suspension and a body construction that allows them to function well in several fairly disparate arenas.

Crappies are light-sensitive but in early spring are attracted shallow, where the water is warmer and holds much more food. They may compromise their visual comfort to satisfy needs to forage and find warmer water. Understanding that compromise helps locate them. For instance, baitfish and crappies are attracted to canals in early spring because the water is protected, shallow, absorbs the sun's energy, and warms more quickly than the main lake. Clear canal water permits substantial light penetration, which is good because it warms the water. Expect crappies to shy from direct sunlight in clear water. So, expect a compromise. Expect crappies to shy away from confined open water in the middle of the canal. Instead, look for them suspended near obvious cover. Crappies use the shadows formed by docks, hoists, old cattails, deadheads, posts, and bluff banks to satisfy the needs of their sensitive eyes while maintaining a vantage where they can watch for prey during the brightest hours of the day. Expect crappies to move away from cover during low-light periods into small areas of confined open water. The big "C" (compromise) concentrates crappies and makes location a little more predictable.

CANALS

Canals are man-made extensions of a lake inland to create harbors, sanctuaries for boats, and access. Even prior to ice-out in some lakes, the water in some canals warms enough to draw minnows and activate many species of invertebrates. The best channels are well protected from the wind, have some water color, have only one inlet (as opposed to a "flow-through" canal), and several secondary arms. All these characteristics allow the water to warm faster. The best canals are somewhat complex, providing side channels and an extensive overall area that can hold more baitfish and more crappies. Good canals also provide cover so crappies can make the big "C."

Generally speaking, good spring crappie fishing is not an early morning affair. Yet, especially in clear-water canals where crappies relate to easily recognized cover, lack of fishing pressure allows you to move from one cover option to the next, picking off fish at each one—crappies that won't be there later in the day.

If the canal is a "dead end," the warmest water seems to invariably linger near the back end—the farthest point inland. But, if you rush all the way to the back, it's possible to miss some good fishing on the way in and spook the biggest fish as you pass by. Whenever possible, fish your way into a canal. Or, in the case of very long canals, start 1/2 to 3/4 of the way to the back end. As you progress toward the back of the canal, keep an eye on your water temperature gauge. It's always possible that the best fishing is not in the warmest water, in which case you want to know what the water temperature is at all times, to try and recreate the best fishing in days to come.

Because most canals tend to average somewhere between 3 and 5 feet deep, with a few key areas of greater depth, it pays to keep an eye on the depth-finder, too. Crappies might be relating to the deepest water, the water with the most cover, the warmest, or the water where forage is thickest. Pay attention to all the

The Perfect Canal

The perfect canal? It's well protected from wind, has some water color, only one inlet as opposed to flow-through canals with two or more, and has secondary arms. Because prevailing spring winds are usually west, northwest, or north throughout most of the northern natural lake region, many of the best canals are tucked away in the northwest corner of a lake. The canal pictured here is further protected by trees on the north, and with the sun low in the southern sky, there aren't many trees on the southern shore to block the sunlight. Radiant energy is probably the most important factor in warming water and turning fish on.

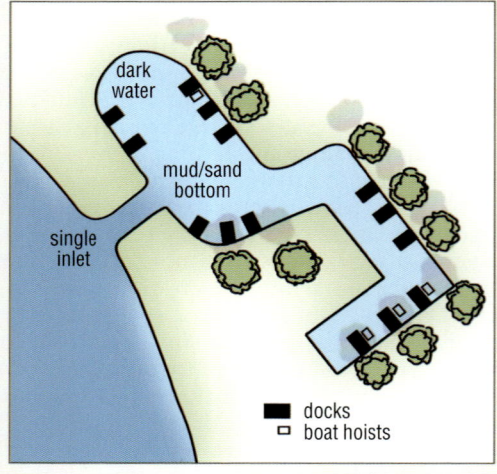

Good canals also offer cover, often in the form of boat docks and boat hoists. All things considered, the best docks also protrude from the north, west, or northwest portion of a canal bank. These docks gather the most sunlight and warmth, but the docks (cover) allow the "compromise" mentioned in this chapter. Early in the season, the best docks are also those farthest away from the canal opening.

clues, and you begin to piece together a reliable pattern that will help you catch crappies in that canal and others for years to come. And, because canals are so shallow, it's often possible to visually locate them. Move slowly and stare deep into the brush, grass, or under the dock pilings as you pass. Even a very subtle swirl or the appearance of any "nervous water" should be probed with a bait before moving the boat through the area.

As water temperatures in the surrounding bays climbs into the mid-50°F range, crappies inhabit canals less and less and soon vacate them, not returning until ice-out the following year.

BAYS

About a week to 10 days after canals begin to attract Cold Water and Prespawn Period crappies, main-lake-connected bays may also warm enough to draw fish. Bay location can be more perplexing than canal location. No set water temperature can guarantee crappie activity or location, but the 50°F mark can be highly indicative that crappies are in the bay—if it's a bay they traditionally use at all. Some bays never have crappies in spring and some are inconsistent.

The best warm most quickly, have multiple cover options (weeds, wood, docks, rockpiles), and have at least one hole with 8 feet of depth or more for crappies to retreat to during cold fronts. The bigger and more complex a bay like that is, the better—up to a point. Small bays warm fastest, but big, complex bays typically draw more fish in the long run. Bays with only the first two prerequisites are not as consistent as bays with all three. Once you find a bay that attracts crappies, it's likely to attract them each year. However, some attract crappies for a short time during the Cold Water and Prespawn periods before fish quickly vacate them. These tend to be strictly foraging sites without adequate spawning habitat. Often these bays are of the soft, dark-bottomed, mucky variety that warm fastest in spring—speeding up the development of a food chain. Crappies can spawn on mud if they have to, but not on silt or muck. They tend not to probe deep into such bays, so confine your fishing to areas directly adjacent to the mouth area of such bays—where they open into the main lake. Fishing can be especially productive near necked-down mouth areas where current can develop.

Bays can be fished from shore—on foot or in waders—or from a boat or smaller craft like a canoe. When searching for spring crappies in a bay, be systematic. Start where the wind is blowing into shore, where the water is likely to be warmest. From that point, move along slowly, controlling the boat with an electric motor, anchoring and casting out ahead. Or, if on foot, make a series of casts from short to long, then move down the shoreline about one cast length to start all over. Crappies can move quite a bit in spring. Don't let them slip right past you!

In early spring, a one-degree water temperature change can be a very big deal for a crappie. It's a much bigger deal than it will be later, during summer. If 90 percent of a bay is 48°F in spring, it will have no crappies at all if the remaining 10 percent is 50°F or warmer. That's where all the crappies are—in the water that's just one or two degrees warmer. It's especially true in early spring that the best locational tool for crappies is a good temperature gauge.

Bay fishing usually begins about midday, gets progressively better during the afternoon, and peaks as the sun begins to sink below the treetops. Until later in the spring, calm, sunny days are generally better than dark days. The best daily period is usually late afternoon to sunset because the water remains warm enough to stimulate fish activity, yet decreasing light penetration allows the big "C" to take full effect.

Many bays have smaller feeder creeks running in. These areas are crappie magnets, unless the incoming water is extremely cold. Bay fishing will continue to produce for half a month to six weeks with adequate spawning habitat such as reedbeds, pebble-sand substrates around weedbeds, or other soft-to-hard bottom transitions around docks, fallen trees, other woodcover, or rocks. Crappies prefer to spawn around cover whenever possible.

MAIN-LAKE REEDBEDS

Some of the most exciting spring crappie fishing in natural lakes takes place around main-lake spawning areas. Reedbeds on the main lake produce some of the largest crappies caught in natural lakes during this time frame, and the fishing can be highly visual. Spotting crappies with the naked eye then dapping baits in front of them with a long, extended pole continues to be the prime method for catching them in main-lake reedbeds during spring.

An entire chapter could revolve around how crappies relate to reedbeds and adjacent drop-offs. We've distinguished four patterns of progression into these areas that will keep you on crappies throughout spring. It's possible to find reedbed crappies before they move into the reeds but it's easier to take advantage of better concentrations in canals and bays until main-lake temperatures broach 50°F.

Reedbeds are easy to find, the old tan and brown stalks protruding above the water like signposts, in spring. The only way to be certain crappies are in a main-lake reedbed is to move very slowly through it with an electric motor or pushpole and look for fish with your polarized sunglasses. The first groups that move in, usually sparse in number, are spooky in a normal year. Reedbeds are typically too large and too tough to fish through by making long casts when you only suspect the area is holding fish. It's too time-consuming, with better fishing, perhaps, waiting in a nearby bay or series of canals.

Be stealthy. Don't take the boat through large clumps of reeds, drag the hull across shallow spots, or bang around in it. Move slowly. Fish into the wind so that once you spot crappies, you don't drift over them before getting the boat turned around. Once crappies are spotted, cast beyond them or to the windward side. Casts that land right on them make them scatter. When big numbers of fish finally enter a reedbed, they spook less easily.

The best reedbeds are like the best bays and canals: Size and complexity are positives, and wind-protected beds attract the most fish. Prevailing spring winds are north-by-northwest throughout most of the range of natural-lake crappies. Thus, the best-protected reedbeds tend to appear on the north and west sides

Patterns in Spring—Where to Find Crappies

	Shallow Patterns			Deep Patterns	
				Pivot Point	Open
	Canals	Bays	Reeds	(drop-off)	Water
Week 1	y	n	n	y	y
Week 2	y	y/n	n	y	y
Week 3	y	y	y/n	y	y/n
Week 4	y/n	y	y	y/n	n
Week 5	y/n	y	y	y/n	n
				y = yes	n = no

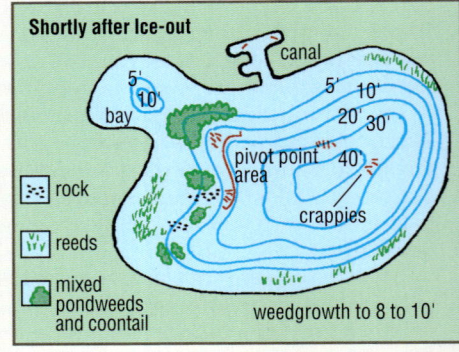

Shortly after Ice-out — weedgrowth to 8 to 10'

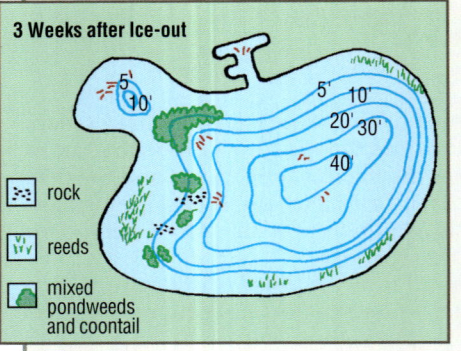

3 Weeks after Ice-out

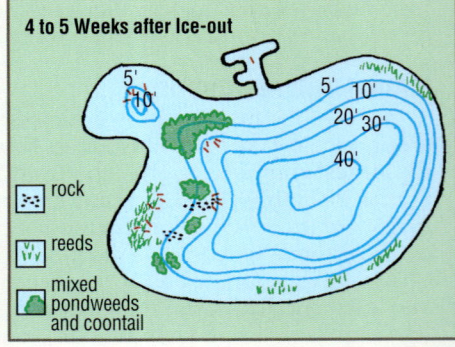

4 to 5 Weeks after Ice-out

of a lake. How the wind, sun, and other factors warm the water during spring continues to be misunderstood. Many assume winds blow warm surface water into areas and good fishing is the result, though that's sometimes true. Warm rain, gentle breezes blowing into shore on a warm day, and run-off can help warm certain specific areas of a lake. But the main generator in the warming process is the sun and its radiant energy. The more light penetration, the better the possibility for radiant absorption. Waves hinder light penetration. Calm water absorbs more heat.

On a calm spring morning, the warmest water is on the lake's surface. When the wind picks up, this warm water is pushed to the windward shore, raising the water temperature in this area. This effect can only last as long as warm water is being generated. The water shift causes cooler water to be pulled to the opposite side of the lake. Again, this is only temporary, especially in a big wind. The calmest areas in the lake should be absorbing more radiant energy, thereby warming faster. By mid-afternoon, when the best crappie fishing usually takes place this time of year, water on the calm side of the lake can be warmer on windy, cloudy days. It depends on the strength and duration of the wind and how long it blows in one direction. Gentle breezes and slight winds can continue to push warmer surface water into certain areas all day, especially on sunny days. But the best way to make certain is to keep checking that water temperature gauge. Until surface water

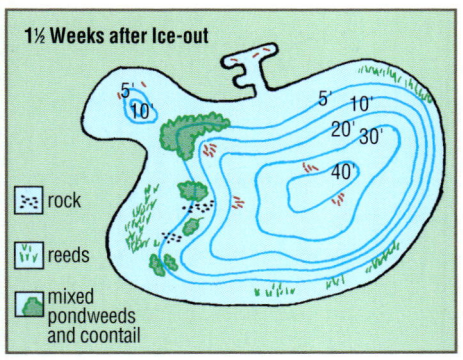

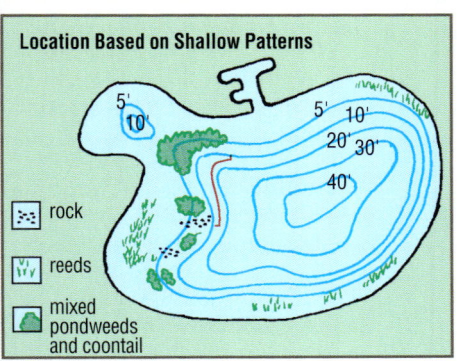

Take three shallow patterns—canals, bays, and reedbeds; throw in an intermediate pattern—the weedline drop-off; add crappies suspended in open water over a deep hole. And what do you have? Confused anglers.

Figuring where crappies are, and when, in small lakes isn't difficult. It depends on available options. At ice-out, expect crappies to school mainly along drop-offs or in open water. If canals are available, expect some pivot-point (drop-off) crappies to move to canals, and some open-water fish to move to the pivot point. Later, if bays are also available, expect more pivot-point crappies to move to them, and still more open-water fish to move to the pivot point.

Still later, if reedbeds are available, expect most of the remaining pivot-point and open-water crappies to move into them. This progression may take 3 to 5 weeks. If shallow-water options aren't available, the fish hold in the two deep-water patterns longer.

on a lake or in its bays broaches about 60°F, the most active crappies appear in the greatest numbers in the warmest areas you can find.

The first groups of crappies to come into reedbeds tend to hang around the fringes of the bed. Expect them to appear first in the deepest reeds on the outer rim of the bed near the sharpest drop-offs. Later on, very active fish might push into water only one foot deep, but the biggest fish tend to prefer proximity to sanctuary and use the deepest portions of the reedbed. Big fish also like cover, and cover is relative in a reedbed. As in bass fishing, comparatively thick sections of reeds tend to attract the most fish. Larger reedbeds do attract the most, but don't ignore smaller, isolated patches of reeds, which sometimes hold relatively small groups of big fish.

SHORELINE-CONNECTED HUMPS

The final piece of the spring puzzle is the most difficult to identify but consistently produces slab crappies. It involves main-lake humps, though even that description can be somewhat deceiving. These are not to be confused with true main-lake humps that rise out of a deeper basin and can be vast in area, shallow on top and not connected in any way to shore. The natural-lake humps crappies typically use in spring tend to be adjacent to shoreline-connected structure. Often these areas are adjacent to or connected to other key spawning areas, like reedbeds.

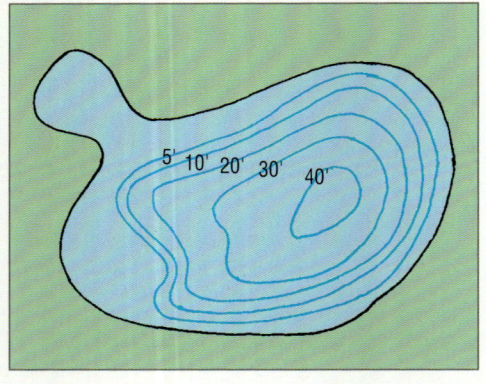

4-Pattern Lake (no canals)

	Shallow Patterns			Deep Patterns	
	Canals	Bays	Reeds	Pivot Point (drop-off)	Open Water
Week 1	n	n	n	y	y
Week 2	n	y/n	n	y	y
Week 3	n	y	y/n	y	y
Week 4	n	y	y	y	n
Week 5	n	y	y	y/n	n

Key areas must provide the following:
• Some reasonably shallow (2- to 4-foot) water;
• Hard bottom, usually including some gravel and rock, as well as sand;
• Some weedgrowth;
• Access to confined open water.

When working a bay, series of canals, or a reedbed, look at the lake map and thoroughly explore any bars, points, or humps that connect to or saddle up to these zones, using sonar and an underwater camera, watching for connected but somewhat isolated rises topped with hard bottom or rocks.

Timing is the key with shoreline-connected humps. Consider a typical reedbed that crappies spawn in: It's 3 to 4 feet deep throughout. Leading up to the reedbed is a large, shallow flat only 5 to 6 feet deep. On the outer edge of the flat the bottom rises to within 2 or 3 feet of the surface, topped with rock or gravel mixed with sand. It's logical to assume that most crappies that spawn in the reedbed stage on or otherwise relate to this outer rim of the flat at some point after ice-out. Some of those crappies stay on the outer rim of the flat and use the shallow rise or hump for spawning needs, and they tend to be some of the biggest crappies in the lake.

This is not a numbers pattern, but a big-fish pattern. Crappies prevail on the outer rim of those shallow flats and shoreline points in spring, but they're tough to find and even tougher, at times, to catch. Crappie activity is much more predictable and consistent in bays and canals, but those are typically not big-fish patterns. A true, hardcore, big-crappie addict is better off spending a significant portion of time each spring probing these main-lake areas on the outer frontier of crappie spawning habitat.

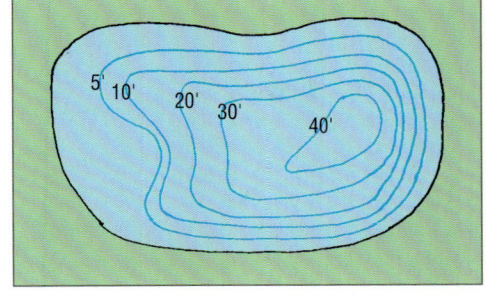

3-Pattern Lake (no canals or bays)

	Shallow Patterns			Deep Patterns	
	Canals	Bays	Reeds	Pivot Point (drop-off)	Open Water
Week 1	n	n	n	y	y
Week 2	n	n	n	y	y
Week 3	n	n	y/n	y	y
Week 4	n	n	y	y	y/n
Week 5	n	n	y	y	n

Fewer shallow water patterns mean crappies spend more time in deep water.

As main-lake temperatures warm into the 50°F range, some crappies, many of them large, are attracted to reedbeds. Later, still more fish move in. At some point it seems a commitment is made. Many crappies make a definite commitment to reedbeds, while others remain on the fringe of the flat around isolated spawning habitat. At this point, the fish are mostly quite active and catchable—and quite large. But, on any natural lake, this is the last "spring" pattern to take advantage of. When main-lake temperatures approach 60°F, just as reedbed fish are going strong and hump fish are just getting going, the bite in canals and shallow bays already may have tapered off to almost nothing. With all these patterns, timing is key, and water temperature is a pretty solid indicator of what's going on.

SUMMARY

These four key spring crappie patterns in natural lakes are progressive. Fish canals first, bays second, reedbeds next, and finally main-lake humps. Each natural lake may not be able to provide all four patterns, but other patterns exist as well. Crappie lakes vary quite a bit. Shallow, ancient eutrophic lakes with dark water warm quickly and may progress through these patterns faster than mesotrophic lakes. When reedbed patterns are red hot on eutrophic lakes, canal patterns on nearby mesotrophic lakes might be just getting started.

The Pivot Point— A Shallow and Deep Water Pattern

A "pivot point" is a key transition between deep and shallow-water habitats. This area may be the gathering point for deep crappies before they penetrate the shallows, as well as for shallow fish that drop back deeper due to weather changes.

Look for parts of flats connected or adjacent to other crappie spawning areas such as reedbeds.

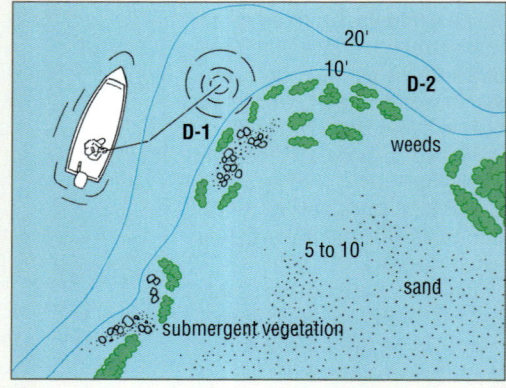

Top areas offer: 1/ reasonably shallow water (2 to 10 feet); 2/ hard bottom, usually including some gravel and rock, as well as sand; 3/ weedgrowth; and 4/ access to open water.

The tips of points (**D-1** in this example—especially the rocky areas) or inside turns (**D-2**) in a bar qualify if they have these characteristics. This pattern occurs along certain parts of the deep-water edge of an emerging weedline on a bar. Key spots have weeds and rock dropping into deep open water.

Crappies may use a pivot point shallow or deep. They may suspend along the weedline or penetrate it and move up on the adjacent flat, and may also suspend along or off the weedline, either deep or shallow.

Main-lake crappies offer the most consistent trophy patterns. But if you're taking some kids out for a day of spring crappie fishing, best to take them to a canal or shallow bay when the weather is stable and where the water temperatures are hovering around 52°F to 56°F. Fishing can be fast and furious in these solar generators, and often the best fishing is on foot from shore and docks, where kids can run around on the banks and enjoy the warming environment. At any rate, these four progressive patterns represent the most productive we've found for spring crappies in natural lakes. With regard to the spawn, location is already 80 percent solved. Crappies on foraging forays in early spring won't be far from spawning habitat. They often choose spawning locations involving wood, weedcover, or reeds in locations protected from wind and wave action. The earliest spawners often pass through channels to connected bays or ponds. These areas warm quickly into that 70°F window crappies tend to spawn in, and offer abundant minnow forage. The latest spawners use main-lake areas protected by points of land. For a detailed description of timing the spawn and finding essential habitat, including substrates and cover that spawning crappies use, refer to Chapter 1.

TRANSITION TO SUMMER

On the way out of spawning areas, back toward the main lake, crappies move across flats and tend to hold on or near the first major drop-off they come across. Water flowing out of the spawning area (bay, channel, creek, or pond) often holds higher plankton counts than the main lake, attracting hordes of shiners, shad, chubs, and other minnows. Adjacent cover in the form of newly emerging cabbage, deep bulrushes, stumps, or brushpiles attracts large groups of crappies and holds them for a time, before they eventually filter off to summer habitat. But there is no universal manner in which crappies behave at any time of year. Much depends on lake type, water clarity, latitude, primary forage options, and a host of other factors.

Studies suggest that, during spring and through the spawning period, crappies increase their activity during the day, peaking at dusk, then become less active at night. After the spawn, however, crappies that have moved from spawning sites into confined open water feed heavily after dark. On both murky and clear South Dakota natural lakes studied by Dr. Chris Guy at South Dakota State University, using radio telemetry, he recorded substantial movements of crappies beginning at dusk and lasting through the night. During the day, they were less active, but moved closer to shallow cover at dusk and remained there until dawn.

"After the spawning period, the crappies we tracked in two lakes didn't move nearly as much," Guy said. "Black crappies in a clear natural lake shifted into deeper water after the spawn, though most remained at the same end of the 1,000-acre lake. In the rather murky impoundment, where we studied white crappies, some moved off shore while others remained in shallow cover. The differences may have been due more to environmental conditions than to differences between the species."

Transition Position

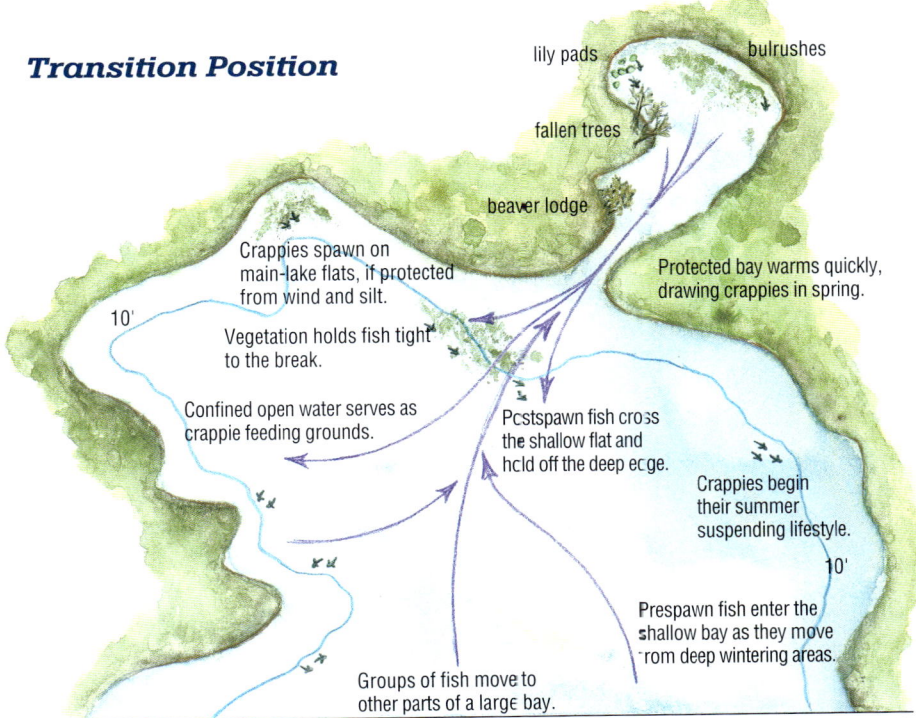

Crappies in Natural Lakes

Crappies in Natural Lakes

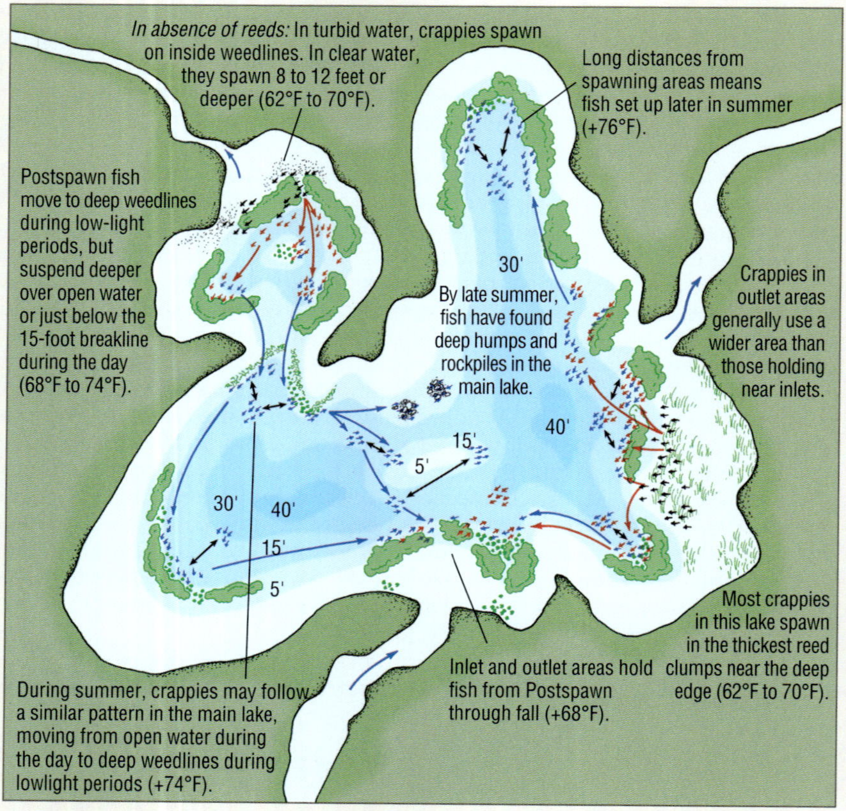

In absence of reeds: In turbid water, crappies spawn on inside weedlines. In clear water, they spawn 8 to 12 feet or deeper (62°F to 70°F).

Long distances from spawning areas means fish set up later in summer (+76°F).

Postspawn fish move to deep weedlines during low-light periods, but suspend deeper over open water or just below the 15-foot breakline during the day (68°F to 74°F).

By late summer, fish have found deep humps and rockpiles in the main lake.

Crappies in outlet areas generally use a wider area than those holding near inlets.

During summer, crappies may follow a similar pattern in the main lake, moving from open water during the day to deep weedlines during lowlight periods (+74°F).

Inlet and outlet areas hold fish from Postspawn through fall (+68°F).

Most crappies in this lake spawn in the thickest reed clumps near the deep edge (62°F to 70°F).

- spawning fish
- postspawn
- summer
- postspawn movements
- summer movements
- daily movements

Crappies often suspend off a deep breakline, around humps, or along deep weedlines from Postspawn through the Summer Period. Look for them deeper on bright sunny days **(Position 1)**. They may suspend higher on cloudy or windy days **(Position 2)**. By late afternoon (earlier on cloudy days), they use the base of the weeds **(Position 3)**. By sunset, often they're over the weeds, feeding on or near the surface **(Position 4)**.

Postspawn crappies in natural lakes switch rather swiftly from shallow cover to "nowhere land," and all the popular spots suddenly fall flat. Many anglers lose track of transition crappies in lakes they fish because of the diurnal shift described above. Crappies that fed during the day and during low-light periods all through spring may suddenly begin feeding almost exclusively at night in waters considered clear, off-clear, or of average visibility.

Even in water considered cloudy, the night bite can be exceptional during the transition from Postspawn to summer. Crappie fishermen along the Georgia-Alabama border have long known this to be true in West Point Lake on the Chattahoochee River, where the water is far from clear and secchi disks are visible only down to 3 feet or less. During the May crappie run there, a brightly lit flotilla of boats can be seen every night from the Route 219 Bridge. Anglers arrive in droves every evening and anchor along the edge of submerged creek channels with brush, waiting for crappies to go on their nightly feeding binge. In almost all environments, nocturnal crappies move shallower to feed at night. This schedule can persist into early summer and, in some cases, continues until the following spring.

West Point crappie enthusiasts used a variety of fishing lights both to see better and as fish attractors. During the day, small shad form tight schools offshore, feeding on plankton. After dark, shad schools disperse, generally moving shallower and toward the bank. Scattered formations, positioned along shallower edges, are far easier for crappies to intercept than the tight balls that form during the day, in open water with no barriers to stop them. At night in all environments, crappies often move into very shallow water in search of minnows that occupy open water during the day, or minnows that become much more vulnerable around cover at night. The crappie has the largest eyes (as a percentage of body size) of any North American freshwater fish, probably providing them an advantage over their prey in darkness. They are uniquely adapted to foraging at night.

As mentioned, crappies move out of the shallow spawning habitats of spring toward summer haunts. In most natural-lake environments, they suspend during the day in summer—shifting vertically from day to night, seeking shade, depth, or cover during the day and shallower, plankton-rich areas, foraging during low-light periods and at night.

The postspawn transition is one of the trickiest moves crappies pull all year (except for the times, of course, when they just refuse to bite). During the Postspawn Period, plan to do lots of searching—first with maps, then with sonar. If you know where crappies spawn, and you know where they can be caught in summer, finding them during the transition can be as easy as using a straightedge on a map between those two points (but

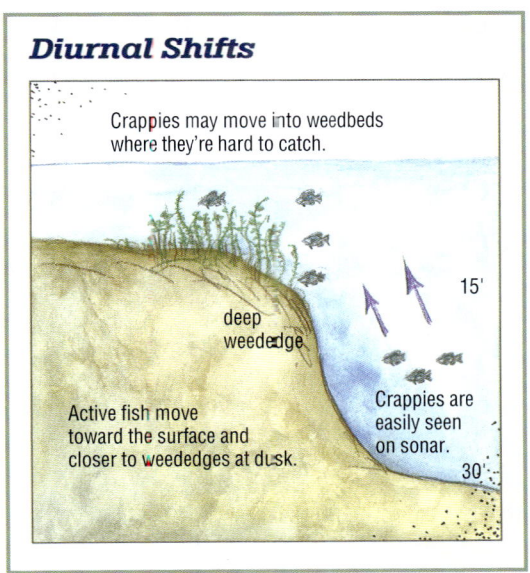

Diurnal Shifts

Crappies may move into weedbeds where they're hard to catch.

deep weededge

Active fish move toward the surface and closer to weededges at dusk.

Crappies are easily seen on sonar.

15'

30'

rarely is). Drawing as straight a line as landforms will allow, search the first drop-offs into main or secondary basins that you come to, following the line away from spawning habitat. This, at the very least, is a good area to begin searching with sonar.

On new or unfamiliar lakes, choose a general area that includes spawning habitat, extensive shallow flats (early-season food production) and confined open water. Idle in a serpentine pattern over the breaks, scanning for cover and schools of fish. Crappies often suspend off breaks in classic "Christmas-tree" patterns, scattered vertically from 5 or 10 feet under the surface down to 15 or 20 feet. Crappies tend to be most visible with sonar during the middle of the day, when they hold deepest and farthest from the break. Once a school is located in a transition area, count on them using it for several weeks in most cases—or as long as prey is available. General patterns may hold until turnover in fall, or when vegetation begins to decay.

In other words, you already may have a found a "summer" area.

SUMMER

Some lakes maintain more patterns than others, due to variations in size, depth, and complexity between waters. In most lakes, crappies scatter into a variety of patterns. A lot of folks give up on crappies during summer, for this and other reasons. Down South, many anglers feel the weather is just too hot to get out. Some say warm-water crappies don't provide good tablefare. A number wait for the cooler waters of fall, thinking crappies will concentrate more. That can be a logical error in many lakes, as crappies will set up and become more predictable and more concentrated during summer than in spring or fall. Fishing at night provides another option for Southern anglers. And, hopefully, filling the freezer isn't everybody's only reason to go fishing for crappies.

As crappies spawn most prolifically after surface temperatures reach the 70°F to 75°F range, then spend several weeks in transition, true summer patterns often won't set up until main-lake surface temperatures have broached 80°F. Surface temperatures, however, have little to do with the establishment of summer patterns. It's more about timing. If you know when crappies spawned, count on most summer patterns beginning to appear within 2 to 3 weeks afterward.

WEEDLINES

One of the first to establish is the weedline pattern. Many of the crappies that begin the summer on weedlines may disperse into a variety of other patterns as the season progresses, depending on the complexity of the lake and the availability of other patterns.

The weedline pattern tends to be cyclic and involves elements of other patterns. During the transition, the cyclic nature of the crappie's daily activities begins to come to light. During the day, crappies tend to move out, away from the weedline, to suspend in confined open water or to hold on or above slightly deeper structure, like a rockpile in 20 feet of water. As light intensity decreases during evening, crappies often move up to the deep weededge. As light levels continue to decrease, crappies may move into cups and pockets in the weedbed, the most active fish cruising through the very top of the vegetation. During the night these fish may move quite shallow, into and around the heaviest and densest weeds, where they are sometimes difficult to approach or catch.

At daybreak or sometime prior, the cycle begins to reverse itself. Good catches can be made along deep weededges in the early hours, but the bite typically slows

Of Crappies, Summer and Weedlines

To catch crappies, timing is critical. Dawn and dusk are key times to intercept active crappies in the most predictable locations. To predict movements and intercept crappies along a weedline, find irregularities.

Area A is an inside turn (cup) in the weedline where two different weed types (cabbage and coontail) meet. If crappies happen to appear on this spot early (as shown), most will be suspended somewhere between the surface and 6 feet down. If a hatch is occurring (particularly a mayfly hatch), crappies might be feeding on top, right over the weeds. If crappies are here late in the morning or early in the evening, they might relate differently, holding tighter to or inside the edge, or suspending adjacent to the weedline.

Crappies tend to move along a weedline as morning progresses, holding near breaks in the weedwall like **Area B**, where hard bottom (in this case a finger of gravel) interrupts the weedline. Some fish penetrate the weededge and find pockets, such as **Area C**, where the edge triples in size over a small area—hiding more minnows, nymphs, and zooplankton than do straight sections of the weedline. On cloudy days, other crappies at this point might suspend over the weeds or just outside the weededge.

Area D is a weedwall. By this time (7 a.m. to 8 a.m.), shallow crappies might be hugging the outside edge for shade on bright or calm days. Most continue to suspend about halfway between top and bottom, and fewer fish penetrate into the wall here, where weeds are too thick to afford easy movement for foraging. Crappies scatter along weedwalls, so it pays to probe the edge while moving slowly along.

As the sun climbs in the sky, some fish tend to move slowly away from the weedline **(Position E)**, suspending slightly deeper. Activity levels are declining, but crappies are still catchable while slightly scattered or moving in a loosely associated manner. By noon, they have regrouped, suspending over deeper water **(Area F)**. These fish are tougher to catch.

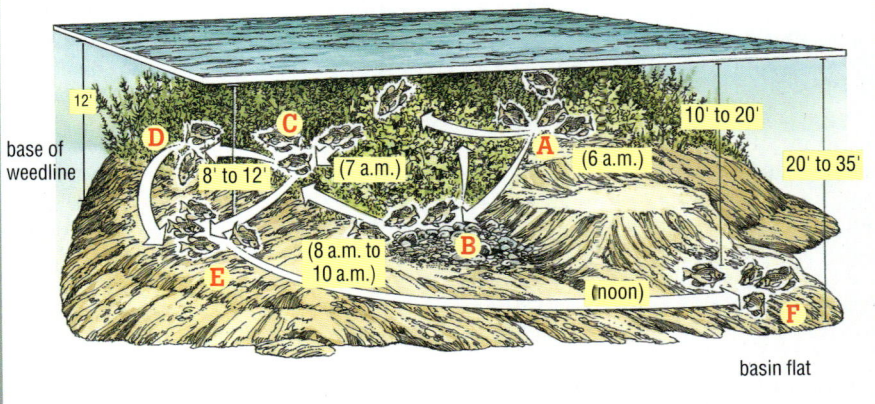

as light intensity increases. By mid-morning, the fish might be found suspended 5 to 15 feet down over 20- to 30-foot depths, depending on wave action and water clarity. And, if structural elements exist like the rockpile mentioned above, crappies may position on the shaded side during the brightest hours of the day. By late afternoon, they begin to rise again.

Like most fish, crappies reach their metabolic peak in summer when the water is warmest, meaning they need to ingest more food per day than during other parts of the year to keep up with their increasing energy expenditures. So, crappies can be active and fishable during all phases of these daily cycles. Of course, the best techniques to employ might change every few hours or so. Pitching jig-plastic combos or small lures and swimming them horizontally along the weedline tends to excel early and late in the day, while jigging vertically with bait might score best during the middle of the day.

Weeds and the rich, organic substrates they grow in harbor lots of life. From weed-clinging epiphytes such as scuds or grass shrimp to burrowing mayfly nymphs to rich fields of plankton, baitfish find a smorgasbord of forage items in and around weedbeds. Each plant and substrate type nurtures a unique community of insect larvae and invertebrates. If shad, shiner, and chub populations die back later in summer, crappies can easily transit to a diet of invertebrates along a healthy weedline. So, logically, the best weededges are diverse. Where various substrate types and disparate weed varieties all come together in one area, and where the weeds are thick and healthy, baitfish and crappies find the most diverse and heavily populated supply of invertebrate forage.

As weeds reach their zenith during early summer, look for areas where various types come together. For instance, healthy stands of cabbage, coontail, and curlyleaf pondweed all found in a relatively small area, bordered on the shallow side by a field of lily pads, might be a key spot. It's a good place to start looking. Diverse weed types coming together tend to form lots of pockets and open areas that crappies (and anglers) can use to their advantage. Even cruising past a shoreline at high speed, it's possible to spot some of these biologically diverse areas. If a homogeneous shoreline of all cattails, all bulrushes, or all maiden cane suddenly breaks into a diverse mix of all those types with scattered pad fields just beyond, it often pays to slow down and take a closer look at the deep weededge.

Another key element is the surrounding structure. Weedline crappies tend to prefer confined open water to true open water. One example of confined open water would be an expanse between two underwater points that are relatively close together, say 100 yards to a quarter mile. If each of these points harbors a healthy deep weedline, it would be hard to imagine crappies not using the area in a good lake for that species, if it's not extremely deep between the two underwater points. Crappies typically prefer to have some "deep" options in the area, like brushpiles, rock humps, weed humps, or reefs. Having these elements rising out of 15- to 35-foot depths is far preferable to having them at 50 feet or deeper. Confined open water might be found between islands, between sunken humps, or in the middle of a large, structurally diverse bay.

Confined open water can be a pattern in itself, as some baitfish increasingly suspend out among the developing fields of plankton. Many open-water or entirely pelagic species of baitfish, like threadfin shad, emerald shiners, and ciscoes, suspend all summer to take advantage of this bounty. Eventually, in a variety of lake types, some crappies are drawn to this developing food chain far off-shore.

OPEN WATER AND WIND PATTERNS

Weedline patterns eventually lead to other patterns as the environment continues to blossom with life. As veils of plankton explode into thick, viscous green veils visible to the naked eye, some crappies and bluegills take to the open seas and can be found scattered over depths of 80 feet or deeper at times.

The tiniest forms of plankton are made up of plant life called phytoplankton. Larger specimens include animals called zooplankton. Even the largest zooplankton remain barely visible to the human eye, but not to the eyes of crappies or bluegills, which often feed on large zooplankters. Plankton of both varieties undertake vertical diurnal movements in the water column, moving up as the light intensity decreases late in the day, and moving deeper again as light levels increase the following morning. Open-water schools of crappies tend to hover just below the thickest accumulations of plankton—and just below feeding schools of baitfish. Depths that open-water crappies use depend on cloud cover, wave action, water clarity, and color and time of day, but it's most typical to find active, suspending, open-water crappies within 2 to 15 feet of the surface. Less active fish tend to be deeper than 12 feet.

The primary key to locating an open-water panfish bite is wind direction. The second most valuable bit of information is wind history. Plankton can pile up along a shoreline where the wind is blowing in. The bite builds exponentially for every day the wind blows in that direction. Where it's blowing into a thick, healthy weedline, nomadic fish following the wind can mix with resident fish that stay on that weedline all summer, creating a double whammy accumulation of crappies.

In glassy conditions, nomadic schools of baitfish and crappies can be located by various means. Bluegills often broach and porpoise, giving themselves away. Crappies more often dimple the surface. Look for any kind of surface activity, however. Wherever small minnows are jumping out of the water over depths of 30 feet or more, chances are good that feeding crappies are the cause. And, quite often, the thickest, greenest veils of plankton can be seen in the water during calmer spells. These areas can be quite productive. It's not uncommon to find big schools of open-water crappies hovering high in the water column over 50- to 100-foot depths during long calm spells, though it's more common to find them over depths

Microscopic Zooplankton

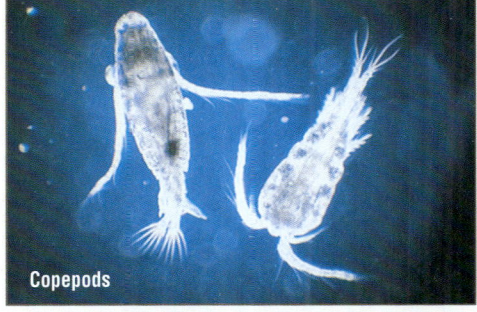
Copepods

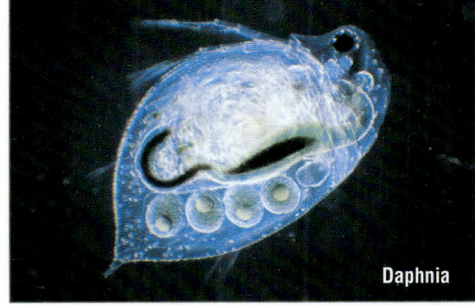
Daphnia

Zooplankton, like these, are at the base of the food chain and critical to panfish. Find dense veils of them and panfish won't be far away.

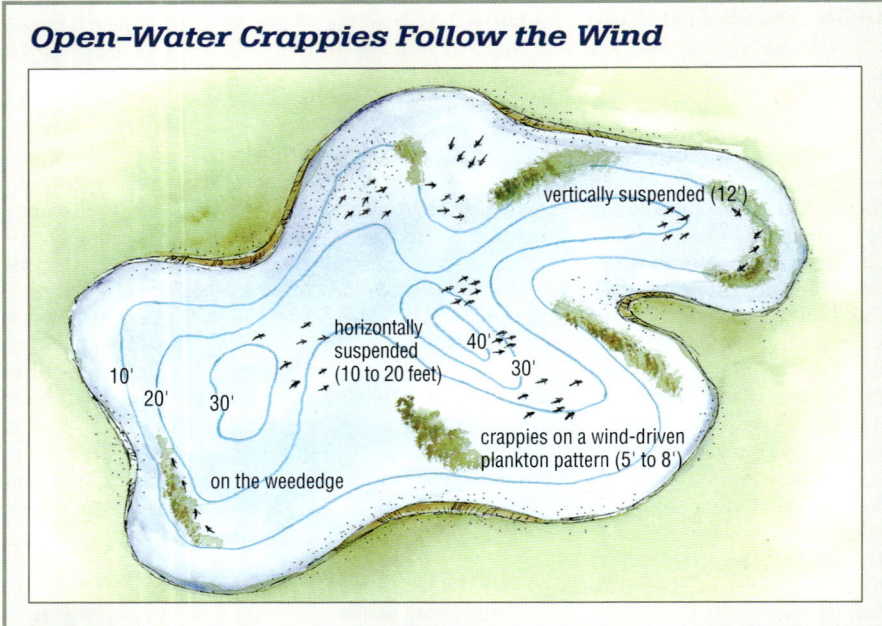

Open-Water Crappies Follow the Wind

of 20 to 40 feet in those portions of lakes or basins harboring extensive shallow flats. It can be difficult to locate schools with sonar when crappies cruise just beneath the surface, but areas where sonar indicates lots of baitfish should always be checked. These open-water areas can be covered by side trolling, drifting, or spider-rigging, while slowly trolling forward. Any tactic that keeps the boat easing along is more likely to intercept these roaming schools of fish that aren't held to a specific area by any kind of physical structure.

For suspended crappies, water temperature can be a better guide to good fishing. Especially on large lakes, surface temperature can vary by 4 or 5 degrees from one area to the next. The warmest water tends to hold the most plankton (though that's not always true), and the edges where colder masses of water meet warmer masses can create a plow effect, concentrating plankton and baitfish along the edge. In open water, several acres of the surface might read 74°F, while several adjacent acres might read 69°F. Using a surface-temperature gauge, look for that transition zone where the temperature begins to change and scout it for plankton veils, surface activity, and schools of baitfish.

When the wind changes direction often over a three- or four-day period, patterns can dissipate. Some crappies remain in open water but scatter to the point where it becomes difficult to locate fishable concentrations. Crappies may begin to concentrate on deeper structural items or on existing cover on those structural items, suggesting a switch to a different pattern.

HUMPS, BRUSHPILES, ROCKPILES AND REEFS

One of the most overlooked summer patterns for crappies in natural lakes involves deep cover, and this pattern has a lot to do with thermoclines. Natural lakes tend to set up thermoclines somewhere between early and mid-summer, depending on weather patterns. The thermocline is a transition zone between an upper layer of warmer, highly oxygenated water (epilimnion) and a lower layer of cooler, less-oxygenated water (hypolimnion). Thermoclines can establish as shallow as 8 feet down or can be pushed as deep as 100 feet or more (especially in very large bodies of water like the Great Lakes); but a more typical range for thermoclines is between 20 and 40 feet.

The thermocline is a band of water that typically extends 6 to 10 feet from top to bottom. Within that band, temperatures decline quickly from top to bottom. The epilimnion may read 74°F on the surface and the temperature may only drop 10°F, to 64°F, at 30 feet. But within the thermocline, temperatures can drop another 10°F in a span of only 10 feet—1°F per foot or, in some cases, even faster. Where thermoclines establish in a lake has to do with overall depth, natural currents, wind-driven currents, atmospheric pressure, mineral content of the water, and a host of other factors.

Thermoclines can be located by a variety of means. The most popular method for anglers involves the use of sonar. With the gain turned up on a good depthfinder, the water-density change within a thermocline can be detected as a band of gray or indeterminate color, or (on color monitors) as a distinct band of light green or blue well above the bottom reading in deep water. The thermocline can be pushed deeper on the windward side of a lake, and can rise toward the surface of the lee side of a lake during periods of extended and consistent wind patterns.

Areas where thermoclines intercept structure can be important spots for crappies in natural lakes during summer. Because of the lake's low oxygen content, crappies can only descend beneath the thermocline for very short periods of time. This serves to concentrate fish just above the zone of rapid temperature change. Rockpiles, humps, reefs, brushpiles, fallen trees—and anything else crappies can use for cover—that extend above the thermocline become key areas, if the thermocline is shallower than 40 feet.

A rock- or brushpile on an otherwise featureless flat in 20- to 25-foot depths can become a prime summer haunt for crappies in natural lakes as well as reservoirs, especially when found in close proximity to diverse forms of shallow cover and structure crappies tend to use, like weedlines on points and shallow humps in areas with large shallow flats near an archipelago of islands or series of mainlake points. The best "deep" cover in natural lakes is rarely far from an extensive and diverse weedline or rocky shoreline with added cover (fallen trees, etc.) and rarely far from some example of confined open water.

Deep rockpiles, rock flats, and reefs can provide plenty of crayfish, insect larvae, and other forms of invertebrates for crappies to prey upon when baitfish numbers decline or recede temporarily to open water. One reason we refer so often to rockpiles is the documented preference crappies have for transition zones, where some soft substrates surround areas of rock or gravel. Just as areas where diverse soils and bottom types coming together can provide a greater mix of plant and invertebrate life, so, too, can the meeting of hard and soft bottom in deeper areas provide a wider variety of forage options. Transitions from soft to hard bottom can, in fact, be key areas for most species of fish living in natural lakes for the same reasons. Such areas consistently draw more baitfish over the course of time.

The intersection of the thermocline with these types of structure or cover can serve to concentrate crappies at a certain depth level, making them easier to locate vertically, in some cases. The "deep" bite on a rockpile or hump is often hottest during mid-morning and afternoon hours, and often dematerializes as the sun approaches the horizon later in the day. As light levels decrease, crappies tend to rise and suspend off nearby weedlines, fallen trees, rows of docks, and other forms of shallower cover. By sunset, they might move right into the weedline or fallen trees and concentrate along outside edges and branches, with some fish cruising over and among the wood or weeds.

As described in the segment on weedlines, this pattern often reverses at dawn, with crappies moving out to suspend off the breaks or over their deep cover before settling back down to rockpiles, humps, and deep reefs sometime around mid-morning.

FALL/WINTER

During late summer, crappies spend increasing amounts of time suspending off main-lake breaks in natural lakes. The portion of the water column they suspend in tends to become gradually deeper as summer draws to a close. If the break is from 15 to 25 feet, crappies tend to hover at 20, below the lip of the break.

When the leaves begin to brighten, the air clears, and the mornings become brisk, change becomes the norm within the aquatic world. But crappies love stability and move until they find it. With autumn comes another period of transition for them, in this case from summer habitat toward and into wintering habitat. In

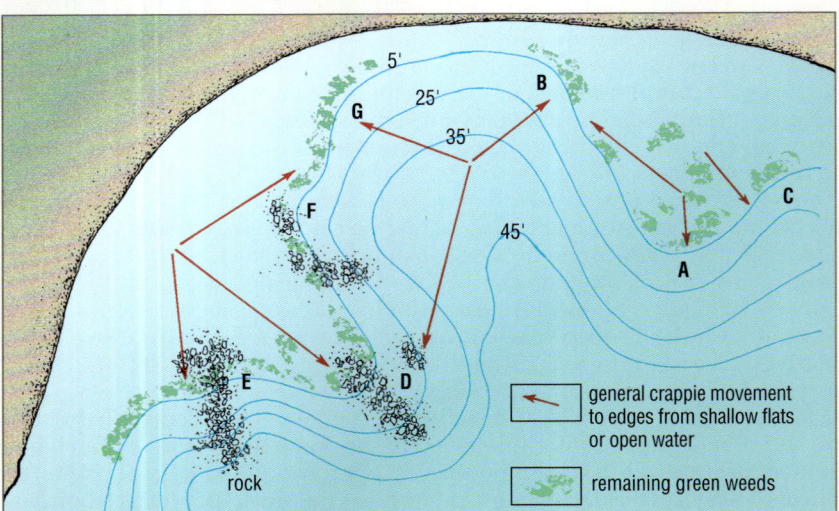

Natural Lake Shifts

As water cools in natural lakes, much of the weedgrowth on flats dies, although some deep-lying weeds usually remain along the deep edge of weedgrowth along drop-offs. Crappies holding on shallow flats shift to join those already holding along drop-off edges. Fish holding in open water do the same.

Once along edges, they may continue to hold along the deep edge of remaining weedgrowth or drop much deeper when rock cover lies in deeper water.

Point A and **Inside Bends B** and **C**—larger points with rock and weeds and distinct drop-offs—attract more crappies than smaller points without prime cover. This small point is secondary to the larger adjoining point.

Other problems include lack of a distinct point or inside bend. Crappies tend to scatter and groups of fish may never form.

many cases, especially in small lakes and ponds, this "transition" means nothing more than crappies eventually moving deeper and suspending closer to bottom, very near the areas they occupy all summer. In larger mesotrophic and oligotrophic lakes, the fall transition can entail actual migrations over considerable distances.

As the water cools, crappie metabolism slows, yet nature encourages fish to feed quite aggressively to build energy reserves for approaching winter. The stress of extreme cold takes a toll on crappies. The fact that their natural range ends in the southern extremes of Canada suggests how much cold water crappies are willing to put up with. Studies reveal that, when caught in water reading 35°F or less, they begin to lose fine-motor control, making it difficult for them to remain upright and swim straight.

Summer patterns tend to remain in place until the onset of turnover, though crappies may increasingly concentrate on weedlines, deep weedflats, rockpiles, and larger structural elements during late summer into early fall. Turnover represents a major change in the crappie's world. When surface temperatures descend to about 60°F, the difference in density between the upper layer of the water column (epilimnion) and the top of the thermocline begins to disintegrate.

Point D and *Inside Bends E, F,* and *G*—prime territory. Concentrate on *Point D* and the more distinct *Bends E* and *F*. Bend E looks particularly good, not only because it's so distinct, but because it offers a rocky drop-off into deep water. As is also the case on *Point D* or *Bend F*, crappies could hold along the deep weededge, slightly up on the flat, or deeper along rocks on the drop-off.

During fall and winter, crappies in natural lakes spread horizontally along weededges so long as weeds continue to provide cover. Rockpiles and humps attract fish, too. But overlooked schools also hold at the base of sloping points that drop into the lake basin.

In natural lakes, they usually hold within 5 feet of bottom during fall, but move shallower under mild, stable conditions. Of course, it's rare to find all three structural elements so close together on a real lake.

As weedbeds decay, crappies move to mid-depth breaklines or deep points. Deep points are most productive on lakes with few humps and breaklines because the fish have fewer options.

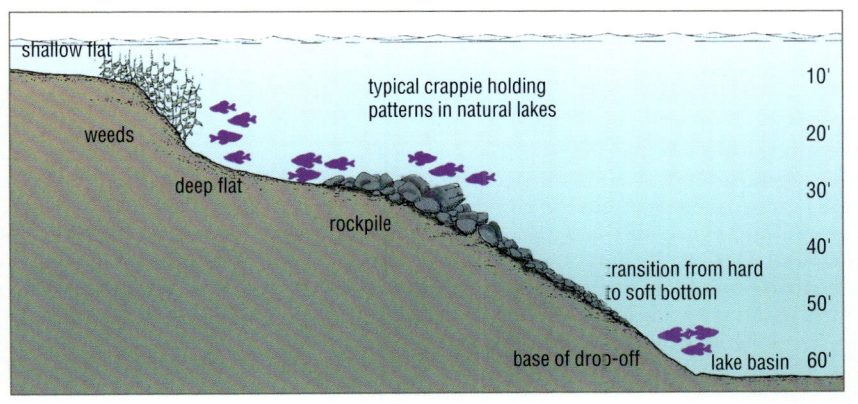

A big wind can churn the water at that point and begin the mixing process called "turnover" that eventually drives oxygenated water into the deepest portions of the lake. This period of circular, vertical currents, punctuated by odd smells and the sight of bottom detritus floating on the surface, lasts about 5 days. It can be a poor time to go fishing. The key to location at this point is to find a different type of lake—a deeper, larger one still weeks away from turnover, or a shallower lake that has already turned over and stabilized.

TRANSITION ZONES

Once a lake stabilizes, crappies can find oxygenated water on deeper flats that were, just weeks ago, out of reach. Down on those flats they find fields of invertebrates that may have remained uncropped by any kind of fish life for several months. The emergence of new feeding grounds attracts various species of baitfish, which in turn draw crappies—all predictably structure-oriented. As pointed out earlier, a variety of substrates coming together in one area offers a more diverse selection of invertebrates—one of the primary reasons "transition zones," where hard bottom meets soft, attract a variety of species in fall, including walleyes, bass, perch, and bluegills, as well as crappies.

Hard-to-soft transition zones ring the basins of most lakes. Basins are another piece to the puzzle, offering the best winter habitat for crappies in most natural lakes. As the water continues to cool in fall, crappies move closer and closer to areas of the greatest environmental stability. Needs for stable temperatures, stable ph factors, stable food supplies, and protection from wind-driven currents begin to corral the fish in predictable locations. Crappies are not well equipped to handle benthic depths of 80 feet or greater, so they tend to prefer enclosed basins of moderate depth—basins no deeper than about 50 feet. In many lakes, they concentrate in basins found in bays. In other lakes, they find large depressions on otherwise shallow flats. These basins and depressions tend to max out between 20 and 45 feet in depth in most cases. However, some lakes have no such basin areas and crappies are forced to find flats in that 20- to 45-foot depth range that borders much greater depths.

Odds are good that the bottom of an enclosed basin or of a large depression on a flat is soft—made up of muck, silt, or some composite of other soft substrates. Structural elements that hold crappies most of the year—points, humps, islands, rockpiles—tend to be composed of some combination of bedrock and/or broken rock blending into gravel, then sand, clay, or similar "hard" substrates. Where these substrates blend into the softer types carpeting the basin itself, crappies can concentrate. But it's a linear concentration, spread out along a narrow, snaking transition zone between hard and soft bottom types.

Bottom transition zones can be located quite easily, in most cases, with sonar. Hard bottom produces a "hard" reading on a depthfinder screen, and soft bottom produces a thinner, more diffuse signal. The sound emitted by the transducer on a depthfinder doesn't "bounce" off muck very well. Much of the energy of the signal is absorbed. So, with the gain turned up on a sonar unit, it's possible to visually see (and place markers along) the demarcation between hard and soft bottom types. An underwater camera can further clarify precisely what types of bottom are actually coming together below the boat. It can be important, when trying to develop angling patterns for crappies, to know whether they're holding on clay or sand, muck or gravel, and so on.

Bottom transition zones around these basins and flats can exist anywhere from 8 to 70 feet down, or even deeper. More commonly, the transition zone (which is only a few feet wide, in most cases) occurs somewhere between depths of 15 to

40 feet. It's common, too, to find transition zones along edges where the bottom begins to flatten out. Where the breaks (drop-offs) leading down from structures crappies use in summer—such as main-lake humps, shoreline points, islands, and rockpiles—meet the softer substrates of a basin, they become principle holding zones. Crappies can become structure-oriented, and often hold so close to bottom they cannot be marked with sonar—especially when active along transition lines. Active fish can be right on bottom when feeding, while inactive crappies may suspend within 2 to 10 feet of bottom.

Key areas also include the mouths of bays and openings to sloughs, backwaters, or any protected, shallower area crappies use during the summer months. Places to look include the widest areas between 20- to 40-foot contours outside the mouth

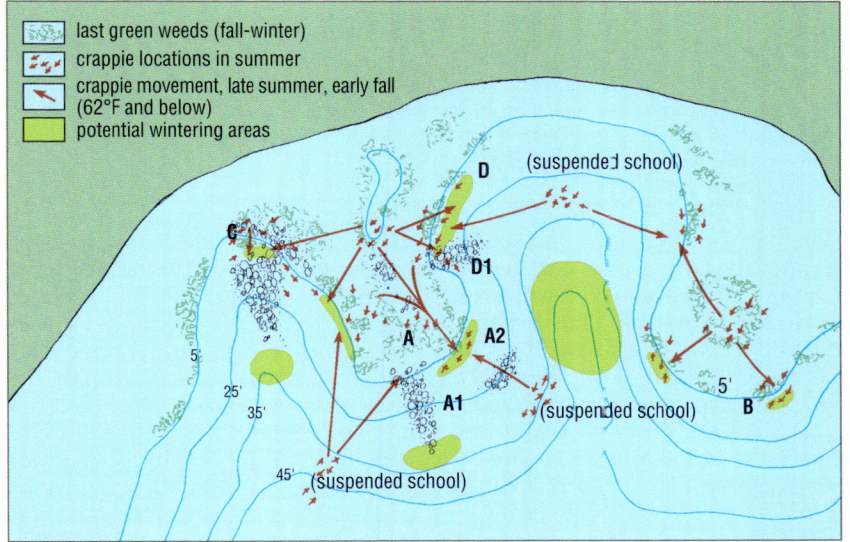

Transition from Summer to Fall

During summer, some crappies suspend, some use deep weededges, and some hold on weedy flats. As water cools, all these various groups tend to converge along the deep edge of remaining green weeds.

Larger points with some rocks and good weedgrowth (like **Area A**) attract more crappies throughout the year than smaller points or points with less diverse cover (such as **Area B**). **Point A** and its inside turns (**C** and **D**) are prime habitat when water temperatures slip below 60°F and crappies congregate on weededges. Immediately after turnover, check these spots first. Deep, healthy weeds along **Point B** will hold some fish but they're second-best options. Cast tube jigs or present small jigs and minnows under slipfloats.

As winter approaches, some crappies continue to slip deeper along the bar, holding on rockpiles and outcroppings in intermediate depths (12 to 25 feet, depending on water clarity and temperature) in areas like **A1, A2, B1, C1,** and **D1**. Vertically jig with jigs and minnows. By late fall, some or most of the crappies in this area will group in fairly loose schools along transitions from hard to soft bottom in deep water (30 to 45 feet). Some crappies may remain along deep weededges by first-ice, but most will be within 5 feet of bottom in basin areas like **E** or **F**.

The Right Spots

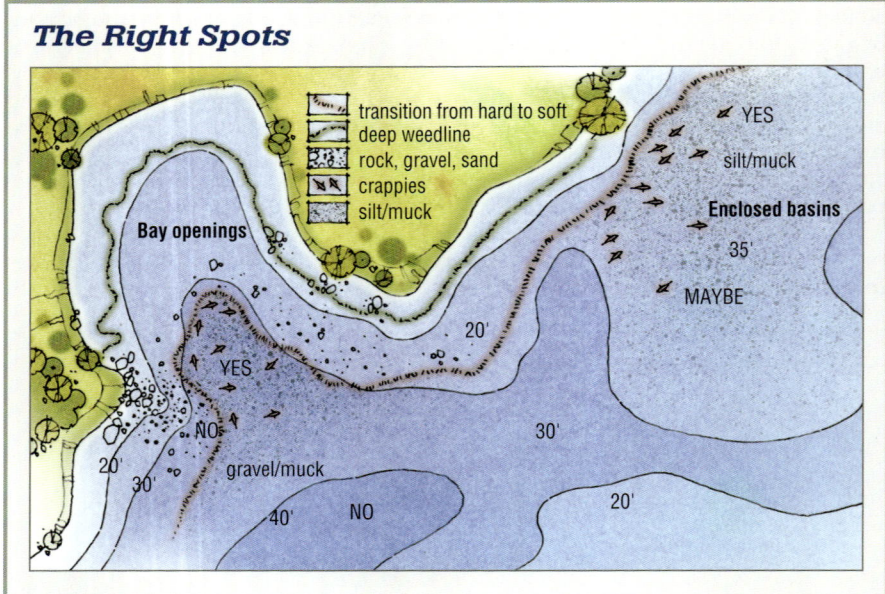

of a bay on the main lake. If the contours form a cup or crease of slightly deeper water pointing toward the embayment area, the entire area can become important for crappies. Here detritus from weeds tumbling down slopes during turnover in past years has mixed with the varying bottom contents to create rich fields for aquatic life. Surrounding structure and depth serve to stabilize the environs as well.

Transition bites almost always take place over the softer substrates on the basin side of the zone, but the best bites seldom occur far from areas where breaks meet the basin. Bloodworms, insect larvae, and other invertebrates are the targets, so the softer side of the substrate divide tends to hold the most active fish. In some cases, transition-zone crappies can be marked 1 to 3 feet off bottom with sonar, but they often peg themselves to the muck. Anything that looks like a bump on the bottom reading could be a crappie, a perch, or another variety of panfish during fall. Underwater cameras can be very useful in determining what these areas look like and what the bottom is composed of, so no rocks or other anomalies can be mistaken for feeding fish during future sweeps through the area.

OTHER FALL PATTERNS

Crappies in many systems react differently to the same set of circumstances. Canadian Shield lakes, the northernmost frontier for giant crappies, cool soonest within their natural range and serve as a model for many deep lakes that hold the fish far to the south of these rocky, wilderness-enshrouded lakes.

Cooling water slows crappie metabolism here, as everywhere else. They tend to locate in huge bays during summer, occupying the shallow water that's denied to them for half the year in these harsh, northern environments. As the water begins to cool (in August, most years) fish move slowly toward winter habitat, generally within the bay itself, or outside a smaller bay into a larger one. They move slowly within a general area, foraging. Once found, they generally remain in the vicinity for a week to several weeks.

Fall location centers around quick access to deep water. Sharp drop-offs that eventually break into 20 to 40 feet of water tend to concentrate the most fish. Gradually tapering flats are less appealing. The "elevator theory" of autumn location holds for many species of fish in Shield lakes, including crappies, which seem to prefer to descend straight down 10 to 25 feet when conditions get rough, rather than be forced to travel horizontally for several hundred yards or more to reach preferred depths. And conditions can get rough in a hurry on the Shield.

The sharp-dropping edges of shoreline points, the steep edges of deep (20 to 25 feet down) rock humps, and the saddles between reefs or small islands situated within or just outside bays that provide good summer habitat are the most logical places to begin hunting for crappies in late August and September. As in other natural lakes, the transition zone from soft to hard bottom at the base of the drop-off surrounding these and other structures is a key area. A school of crappies using a sunken hump, for example, might slowly circle the base of the hump, foraging on invertebrates or on baitfish attracted to the area for the same reasons. Crappies follow the transition zones around structure like a trail. They can be anywhere in relatively close proximity to the transition zone—feeding on bottom 25 feet away (usually on the soft-substrate side of the transition), suspended 2 to 10 feet above the transition, or anywhere just off the structure.

Crappies can, in fact, locate anywhere over the deeper flat (20 to 40 feet deep, in most instances) around the structure. When they suspend, they won't be in the middle of the bay a mile from structure but generally within 200 feet of it. Crappies can be found suspending in saddle areas between two islands, or between the tip of a shoreline point and an adjacent sunken hump, or off a deep cabbage bed, or between two rockpiles on a 20-foot flat, or within any other example of confined open water in the bay. In other types of lakes—shallower prairie lakes, mid-latitude mesotrophic lakes—crappies can be found suspending in very similar (if not identical) areas in fall, but these areas tend to be within the main lake on those other bodies of water.

Suspended crappies generally can be caught in fall, even within a day or so after a cold front passes. (Cold fronts can have the opposite effect in fall, actually inspiring fish to feed more aggressively.) Contact can be made with these fish by drifting, control-drifting, or slow-trolling with small spinner rigs, ultralight crankbaits, or suspending baits while keeping an eye on the depthfinder. They may position near bottom or suspend 5 to 15 feet above it.

Crappies tend to be closer to drop-offs by early evening. During morning and evening, fish tend to hold fairly tight to structure and close to bottom. On dark, cloudy days, Shield crappies tend to hug the bottom tighter for longer periods throughout the day and bite more aggressively. They tend to move less on sunny days in these environments. On sunny mornings and evenings, and during most sunny afternoons, crappies tend to rise up, and it's typical to find them 5 to 15 feet from bottom in 25- to 40-foot depths. In this position, they become extremely active and catchable, especially when it's calm or a slight chop breaks up the surface.

The midday, sun-related activity is probably due to the stained, tea-colored water common to Shield lakes. Sunlight makes it easier for crappies to see their food. The increased light penetration generates more activity among zooplankton, resulting in actively feeding baitfish. By late afternoon or early evening, crappies tend to move back to those drop-off areas surrounding points, humps, islands, or rockpiles, where the action can be fast for the last hour or so before the sun sets. This describes the same, roughly circular pattern of daily activities they follow in summer, from structure to suspending in confined open water, back to structure—except everything happens 5 to 15 feet deeper in most cases during fall.

WINTER

The best way to locate winter crappies is to stay on them throughout autumn, because wherever they end up by late fall (mid-October Up North to late December down South) is where they'll be for the next 3 to 5 months.

Crappies are forced to subsist on things other than minnows during winter in many natural-lake environments—another reason they're drawn to basin areas with soft substrates harboring large supplies of invertebrate life. If enough baitfish persist through winter to keep crappies satisfied, they, too, will be drawn to basin areas, where water temperatures and food supplies remain most stable through the cold months. Water is most dense at approximately 39°F, and the densest water sinks to bottom. It's least dense at 32°F (ice stage) and this floating layer serves to insulate both the lake and its inhabitants. Extreme atmospheric cold serves to thicken the ice from the bottom of the ice layer. But the thicker the ice, and the more snow that packs on top, the greater the degree of

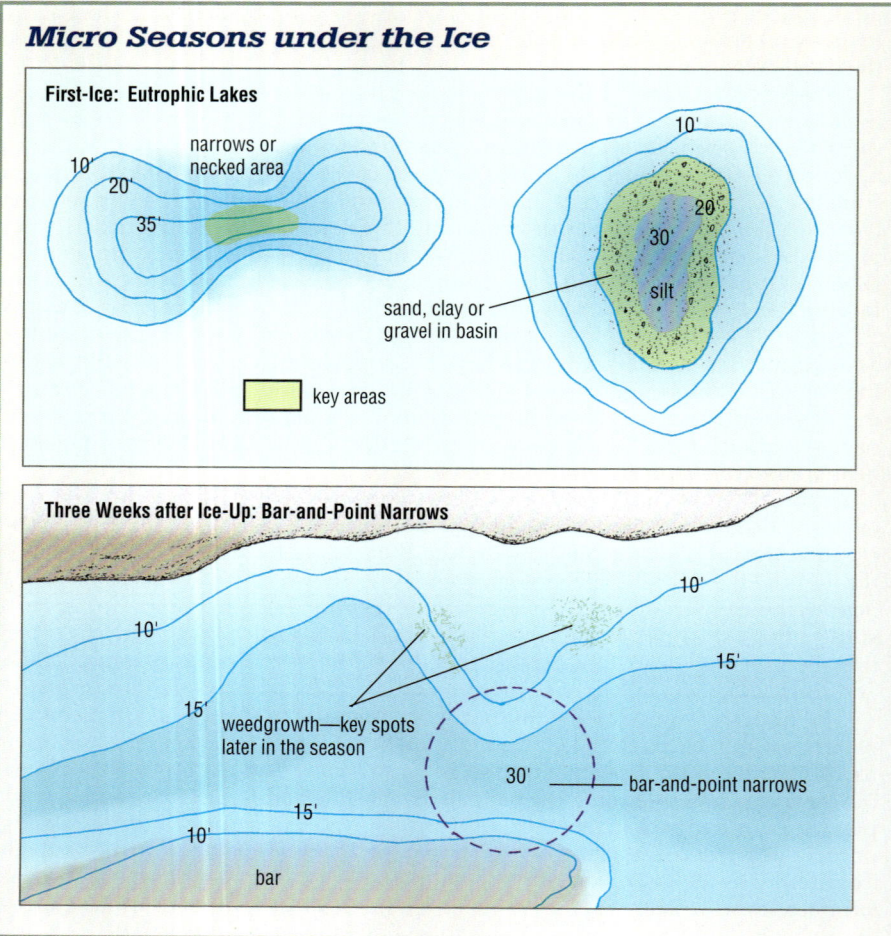

Micro Seasons under the Ice

First-Ice: Eutrophic Lakes

Three Weeks after Ice-Up: Bar-and-Point Narrows

62 Critical Concepts . . . All About Finding Crappies

insulation and the more constant the water temperatures below the ice. The surface water is coldest; the bottom water, warmest.

In shallow lakes and ponds, crappies may not have the option of spending the winter any deeper than 12 to 18 feet. In shallow eutrophic lakes, crappies tend to settle in and near the deepest portion of the main-lake basin, and may continue to relate to any remaining deep, healthy green weeds. In larger, deeper lakes with more options, crappies tend to winter on basin flats or wide main-lake flats in depths of 20 to 45 feet. Though crappies can winter at 50 feet or deeper, it's rare.

One of the most interesting things to note about wintering crappies toward the far northern end of their range is their seeming ability to predict just how severe the winter is going to be. Picture a chain of lakes, all connected by a large stream or canal. At the top of this watershed is a shallow lake only 12 feet deep, where "fish kills" occur due to oxygen depletion during the harshest winters. In the middle of the chain is another shallow lake, but with a slightly deeper

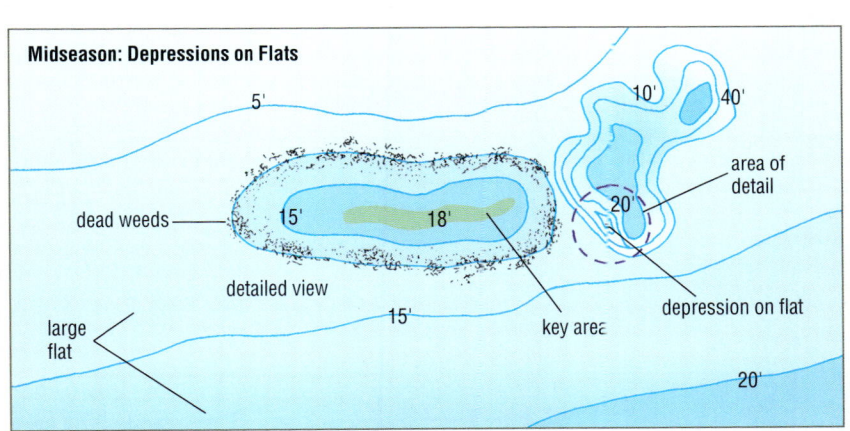

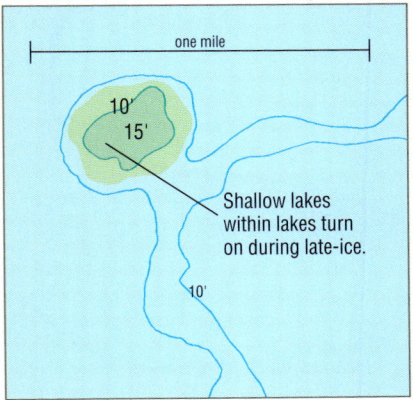 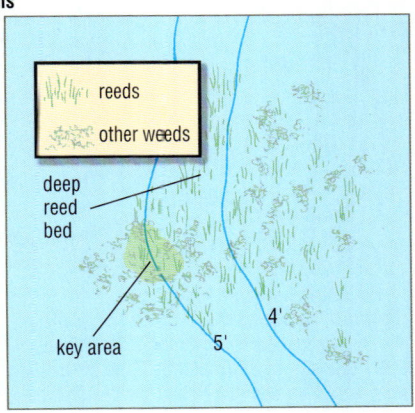

basin of 15 feet. At the bottom of this chain is a large mesotrophic lake with some basins over 50 feet deep. Crappies can pass freely between the lakes. During late autumn just prior to a very harsh winter, we find no crappies in the top two lakes, even though they used these waters all spring and summer. Ice fishing for crappie is a waste of time on the top two lakes. But, during late fall before a mild winter, crappies can be found in the top two lakes of the chain and will remain all winter. This scenario has played itself out for us many times over a variety of chains in Michigan, Minnesota, and the Dakotas. This is just one more thing about crappies that makes you say, "Hmm," reminding us that the more we learn about living things, the more we realize how far away we are from completely understanding them.

SUSPENDED CRAPPIES

During winter, suspended crappies are a bonus in natural lakes. High-flying crappies, those big, buttery, golden slabs that float under your ice hole 5, 10, 15 feet or more off bottom, are the easiest ones to catch. When they scratch their bellies on bottom, micro-suspending one or two inches above the mud, they become harder to find.

So, why do we find crappies suspending one day and out of sight the next? To better understand when, where, and why crappies suspend in winter, consider the types of lakes we find them in. At one end of the spectrum we find shallow eutrophic and late-mesotrophic lakes. Drain the water from one of these ancient lakes and you reveal a basin that resembles a giant saucer, with very few reefs, points, humps, or other forms of fish-holding structure. You might be pressed to find double-digit depths, as well.

At the other end of the spectrum are the big, sprawling early- to mid-stage mesotrophic lakes and even some very deep oligotrophic lakes. Drain one of these monsters and, wow—structure everywhere. Shallow flats surrounded by steep

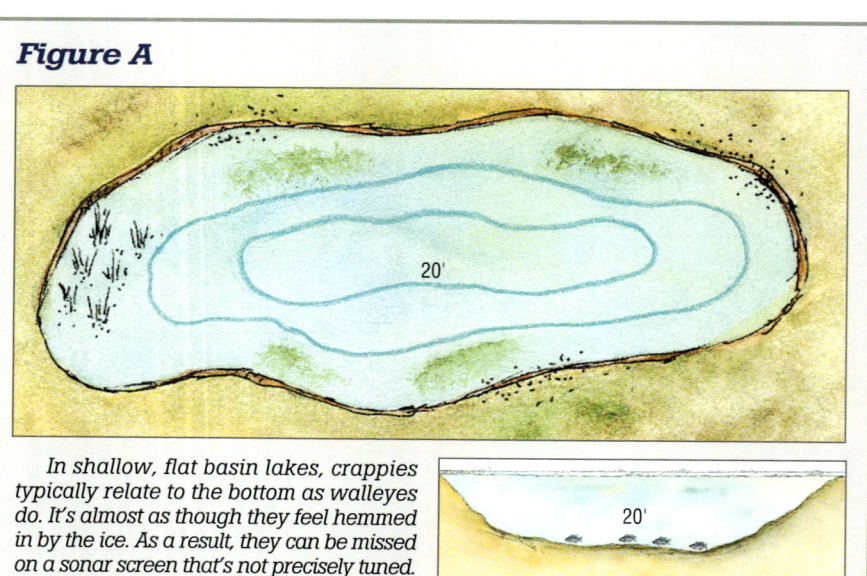

Figure A

In shallow, flat basin lakes, crappies typically relate to the bottom as walleyes do. It's almost as though they feel hemmed in by the ice. As a result, they can be missed on a sonar screen that's not precisely tuned.

Figure B

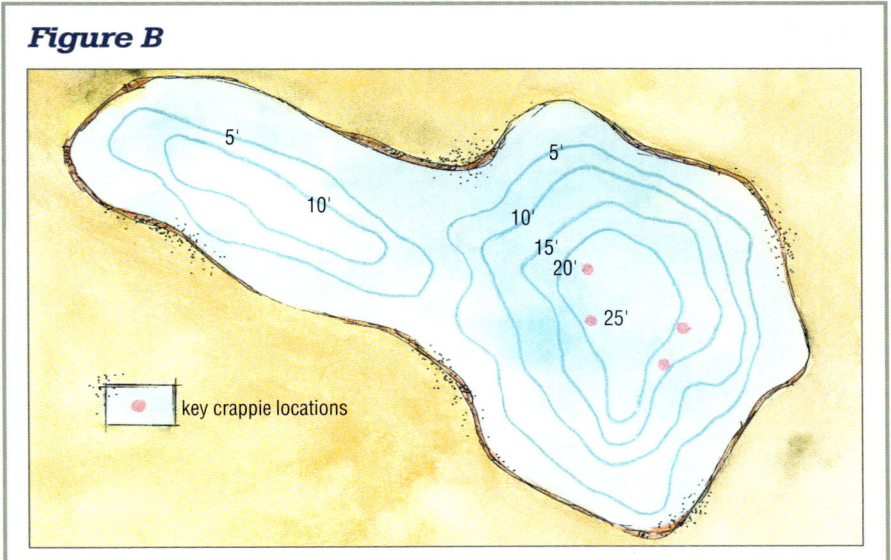

key crappie locations

drop-offs, reefs, benthic zones, chains of submerged islands, and humps, and more vertical structure, by far, than found in our eutrophic lake.

Between these two extremes exists a third type of crappie lake—one more difficult to label because it exhibits characteristics of both extremes. For the most part, these lakes lack an abundance of structure and cover. While the basins are simple and mostly featureless, they exhibit more ups and downs than a standard, bowl-shaped eutrophic lake. These lakes have stretches of moderately deep water, but nothing beyond 30 to 35 feet.

Whether or not crappies suspend has a lot to do with the layout of the lake. Crappies hug bottom to feed on invertebrates until they become satisfied. Then, they might suspend. That's why basin shape, structure, and water depth are such important locational tools in natural lakes. Combine these with plankton migrations, and the picture unfolds.

Basin-Shaped Lakes—In structural terms, *Figure A* is a typically shallow, fertile, dishpan-shaped basin. Though exceptions always exist, crappies rarely suspend in these types of lakes. Mostly, they remain glued to within a foot of bottom during winter. Without fine-tuning your sonar or straining your eyes, it's very difficult to find crappies with sonar in these lakes. But when these lakes are small and lightly fished, they represent a crappie angler's dream come true. When large and pressured, dishpan lakes can become the opposite—a crappie angler's nightmare.

It's not that crappies can't suspend in such lakes, but likely that the water simply isn't deep enough for them to feel comfortable in suspension most of the time—which is why night-fishing can produce an entirely different result. Of course, crappies sometimes have no choice but to suspend in these types of lakes. By mid- to late winter, these lakes can suffer oxygen deficits from biological activity within the relatively shallow substrates. Oxygen deficits are most common in lakes that are shallower than 15 feet at the deepest point, and/or have heavy weedgrowth or heavy algae blooms during summer. In late fall, aquatic weeds wither and die.

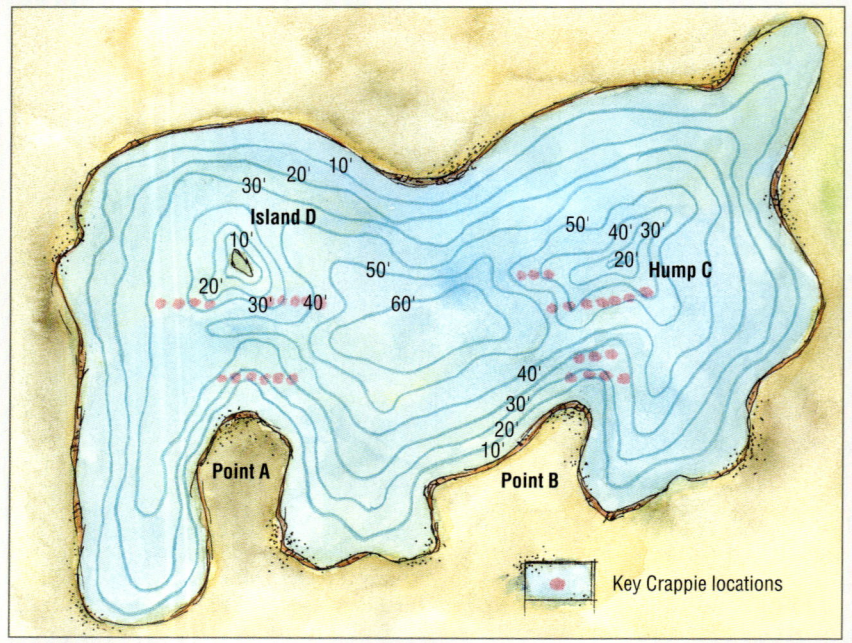

Figure C

Crappies suspend in confined open water adjacent to structure. When distance between structures (**Point A** and **B** and **Hump C** and **Island D**) is short, crappie schools trade back and forth. When distances are large, they remain more or less discrete. When pressure is exerted on discrete schools, crappies slide toward and reposition themselves in secondary locations.

Algae dies, also, and blankets the bottom. As this organic material decomposes throughout winter, it steals oxygen from the water. Without a great deal of water volume to begin with, dishpan-lake oxygen levels can quickly drop to levels where crappies find survival difficult. At that point, they suspend to find more highly oxygenated water closer to the surface.

Dishpan-Plus Lakes—Now add an appendage to the basic dishpan-shaped lake and several feet of depth, so it resembles *Figure B*. In winter, the deeper eastern basin becomes the key crappie location. Though the western basin will attract crappies in spring, anglers could fish it all winter and struggle to put together one meal of crappie fillets. It's as if all the fish swam downhill.

Crappies in the eastern basin of this lake will suspend in winter, but not in the manner we often picture crappies suspending, 5 to 10 feet off bottom. In lakes of this type they tend to hover only 1 to 3 feet off bottom. After a cold front, it may not be possible to mark them with sonar, as they tuck close to bottom. On such lakes, it pays to prospect with underwater cameras and tiny jig-and-maggot combinations, as the fish are hard to mark with sonar and tend to be feeding on insect larvae, aquatic worms, or tiny crustaceans when pinned to bottom.

Lower a bait into a likely spot and often a mushroom cloud of crappies suddenly rises from bottom to intercept it. If the lake is lightly pressured, after catching several fish it can be possible to coax the school into hovering higher than usual—6 or 7 feet off bottom, waiting for more food to descend from above.

Like the shallow, fertile crappie lake in Figure A, however, some of these lakes are prone to oxygen deficits late in winter. When this happens, crappies can be spotted much higher in the water column. In fact, if oxygen counts become dangerously low, they sometimes mill right under the ice over the deepest part of the basin, where the snow and ice is likely thinnest and whatever sunlight can penetrate continues to fuel the only oxygen-producing agents left in the lake—phytoplankton.

Best for Last—We've saved the best type of lake for winter crappies for last—at least, it's the easiest one for most anglers to figure out, with a slightly increased amount of recruitment every spring. The lakes illustrated in **Figure C** could also be viewed as bays, or portions of much larger lakes that have several equally good areas. That's why these lakes are ideal, if you don't lose the trees for the forest. Some anglers are intimidated by a big-water scenario, but it's simply a matter of breaking down the lake into sections—each section containing every type of habitat crappies need throughout the year, including mid-depth basins (20 to 45 feet deep) for wintering purposes. Each section could represent the total area used by a population of crappies that rarely (if ever) coexists with other populations in other sections.

Each bay, cove, or segment of a large, sprawling lake functions as a single entity, offering plenty of opportunities for anglers to spread out and explore. The key is finding deeper water, especially in the Far North. In mesotrophic bays and lakes like these, crappies often choose to winter in basins or on flats between 40 and 50 feet deep. Find a variety of structural features (sunken islands, reefs, shallow flats, sharp drops, shoreline points, saddles between islands, etc.) associated with the deep hole or flat, and you've probably isolated a "crappie section." Deep basins draw crappies in winter, and diverse structural features hold them through the remainder of the year.

Shiners, perch, young-of-the-year perch, and other forage-sized baitfish for crappies can be abundant in lakes of this type, allowing crappies to prey on minnows all year—an important consideration for anglers trying to determine what the fish might bite. In the smaller lakes discussed earlier, minnow forage can be thinned quickly, before midwinter in many instances, and anglers are better off switching to tiny jigs, plastics, and livebaits that imitate aquatic invertebrates. In fact, minnows don't work as well in such lakes. Conversely, in the bays or lakes similar to Figure C, minnows and minnow imitations tend to produce best all winter long.

In lakes like this, crappies react in many different ways to winter—reactions as diverse as the environment they live in. The most typical reaction involves crappies suspending 4 to 12 feet or more off bottom much of the time. This is due, in part, to the larger populations of baitfish found here. The crappie's entire energy source is no longer pinned to bottom. And it's also likely that larger perch, sauger, walleyes, or possibly bass rule the bottom. Typically, when crappies suspend here, they can be found in confined open water adjacent to structure, especially main-lake and island points, sunken reefs, and saddles connecting two structures. Pelagic baitfish like shad, smelt, ciscoes, and emerald shiners, relating to open water most of the winter, become the primary source of food for crappies.

Crappies typically mill around in these expansive environments, even during winter. When the distance between structures is short, crappies generally swim slowly back and forth from one to the next. When the distance is large (say, a mile or more), they remain in the same general area between the structures all winter. It's not unusual to locate them, catch a few, and suddenly find no fish visible on sonar. To stay on them, you have to keep moving. Crappies won't move far or fast, but the tendency for them to circle the area they have defined as their winter home is almost universal during the cold months. And, as mentioned, these are some of the easiest crappies to locate with sonar in winter, because they tend to stay off bottom more of the time.

The Zooplankton Connection—In these large, deep, multi-structured environments, plankton also plays a key role in crappie location. No need for a science course, but it pays to remember several key points. Most importantly, crappies are well connected to the bottom of the food chain—by sunlight and plankton. They routinely gobble up quantities of zooplankton—and not just as fingerlings, but all through their lives. Though the human eye may not be able to see them, zooplankters remain visible to crappies throughout the plankton's lifespan.

Plankton is light-sensitive. In summer during daylight hours, herds of zooplankton (and the veils of phytoplankton they feed upon) hang deeper, suspended in the water column. At night, they rise toward the surface. In winter, however—especially when the lake is covered with a layer of ice 2 to 4 feet thick—light penetration is greatly reduced during the day. Zooplankton can be fooled into thinking it's nighttime all day long, so the herds rise and suspend high during the day. Baitfish respond accordingly and crappies may rise with them, holding higher as winter wears on. Ice and snow are light-limiting factors, and during the harshest winters you're likely to find crappies suspending higher in the water column in classic Figure C lakes—higher, even, than you might be able to visualize with sonar.

What You See Is What You Get—Ironically, all of the above is pretty much the reason crappie hunting makes anglers scratch their heads in winter. If they go to a **Figure C** lake, finding suspended crappies on the screen all day, then visit a lake more representative of **Figure A** or **B** a few days later, they might fail to find any crappies at all if they continue to hunt for suspended fish, without simply prospecting across the most likely areas. Failure to consider basin type, light penetration, and plankton movement can lead to one of the oldest fallacies in fishing: "If you can't see them, don't waste time fishing there." And that, inevitably, leads to a second fallacy: "Few or no crappies exist here."

While it may not look like it, the crappies in each of the three lake types mentioned here generally exhibit very similar behavior during winter. But it's in Lake C that crappies are most visible to us most of the time. On the other hand, adventuresome crappie anglers who understand these lakes may discover relatively untapped crappie-fishing opportunities in lakes like **A** or **B**. These lakes tend to have fewer access points, few if any boat ramps, and can often be found surrounded only by forests or open prairie. And, on these lakes, what you see isn't necessarily what you're going to catch.

It's not uncommon for crappies to move shallow during winter in natural lakes, especially during late winter. Those same reedbeds, weedy flats, canals, sloughs, and dark-bottomed bays that attract crappies in early spring can attract them for weeks prior to ice-out. In fact, shallow (3 to 7 feet deep), late-winter patterns comprise one of the most overlooked programs going for big winter crappies in every type of lake they inhabit.

Chapter 4
Understanding Seasonal Movements—II

Understanding Movements in Reservoirs

RESERVOIRS Reservoirs come in all shapes and sizes, with myriad depth profiles. Depth and structure, of course, are dependent upon the lay of the land before an impoundment is filled. Mountainous regions tend to have deep, clear reservoirs loaded with rocky, vertical structure, while flatlands tend to have shallow, relatively featureless reservoirs with gradual breaks. Between these extremes, reservoirs take on every imaginable shape and depth profile, with structure formed by everything from muck to rock.

Crappies exist in every type of reservoir. While the overall environment may vary considerably from one reservoir to the next, crappies locate and behave in a very similar manner across the board. In most cases, crappies indigenous to reservoirs descended from populations of river crappies, and river fish are notorious for making seasonal migrations. This age-old habit does not change simply because the environment does.

Reservoir crappies typically move to deeper areas, toward the main lake or main basin of a reservoir, just prior to winter.

Reservoir crappies typically move to deeper areas, toward the main lake or main basin of a reservoir, just prior to winter. During spring, this migration reverses itself as crappies once again move shallow. During summer and early fall, crappies make use of the best cover options available while hunting the most prolific forage items the reservoir has to offer. When migrating, they use the same "roads" they used before the reservoir was created: old creek and river channels. Most of the time, they can be found on or just off this road.

Reservoir crappies also tend to suspend over creek and river channels a lot during every season of the year. And, because river crappies are often far more dynamic in terms of movement than lake crappies, overall location patterns can be much trickier to develop—especially during the transition periods of winter-to-spring and fall-to-winter. The following chapter outlines the fundamentals for finding crappies within each season and within each of the main types of reservoirs they inhabit.

WINTER TO SPRING

FLATLAND AND LOWLAND RESERVOIRS AND FLOWAGES

Flatland impoundments typically fluctuate less than 10 feet annually; tend to have cloudy, murky, or stained water; and arise in broad, sprawling flatlands. Creek arms are usually wide but shallow, and creek channels are sometimes silted over, indistinct, and difficult to find. Water depth at the dam is typically in the 40-foot range, with increasingly shallower contours upstream. In most parts of the country, white crappies tend to dominate this type of habitat. Unlike their cousins in other types of impoundments, crappies in flatland reservoirs often use the main-basin area near the dam, especially in winter. A classic example of a flatland reservoir might be Santee-Cooper in South Carolina.

Lowland reservoirs are flooded marshes or bayous. A classic example of a lowland reservoir would be Black Lake in Louisiana. Lowland reservoirs often have dams on small, narrow creeks. The main river channel is seldom near shore, and 50 percent or more of the surrounding shoreline can be composed of marshland. Channel bends are often long and gradual, and the surrounding flats tend to be quite large. Bays and coves are usually very shallow and are often choked with weeds. The seasonal movements of crappies in lowland reservoirs are all but identical to those in flatland reservoirs.

There is no classic definition of a "flowage." Most lakes called flowages arise in the North (most, in fact, are in Wisconsin, though some exist in Michigan, Minnesota, and other states). Some have all or most of the attributes of a lowland or flatland reservoir. But some occur in hilly country, employing relatively small dams that affect far less of the landscape than a hill-land reservoir. In

Flatland Reservoirs Winter to Spring

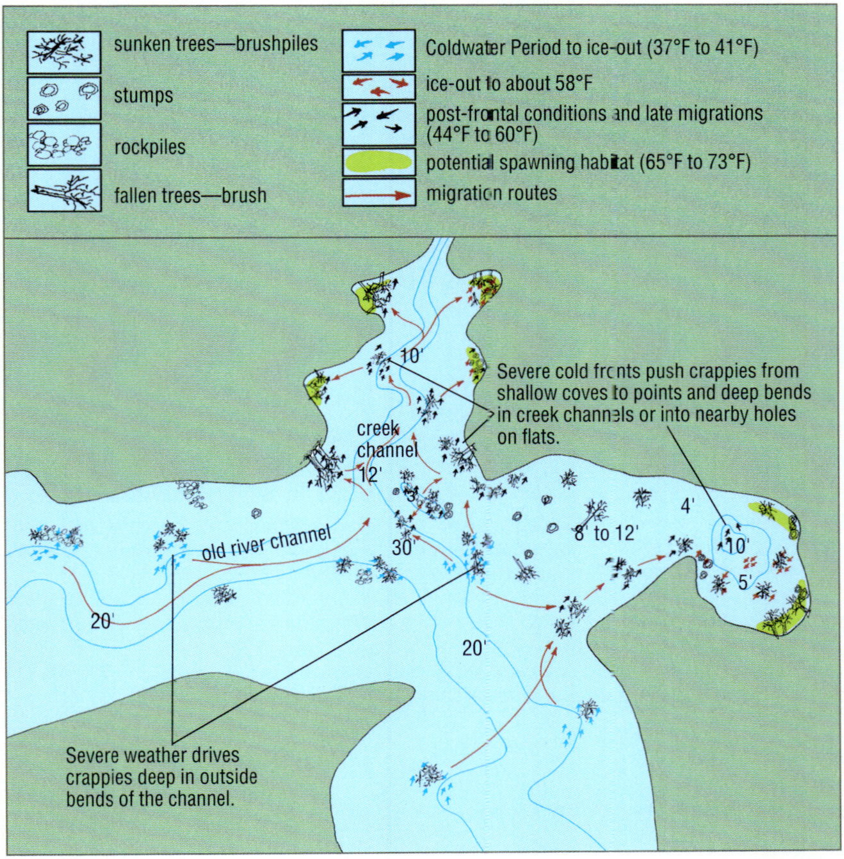

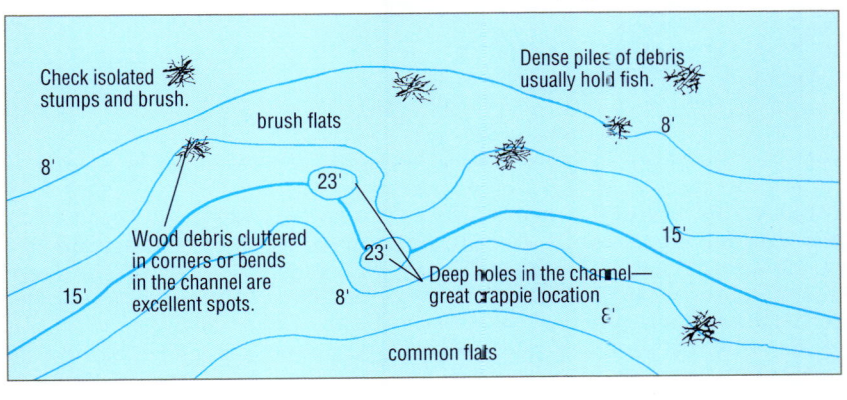

Channel Curves and Turns—Holding Areas

Understanding Movements in Reservoirs   71

Drifting for Suspended Fish

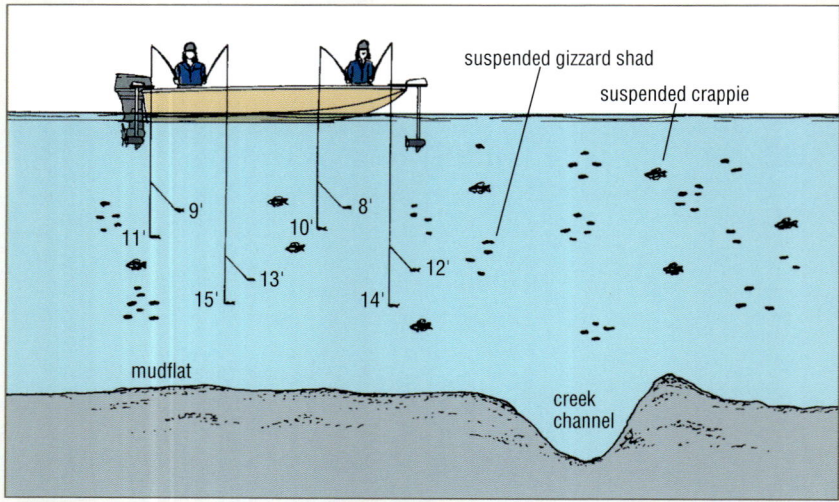

During the postwinter period, crappies and gizzard shad scatter over the lake, with localized concentrations. Use sonar to locate spots with the most crappies and shad milling about. Some of these areas are as big as five football fields.

The most effective way to catch postwinter crappies is to drift. In Kansas, anglers can use only two rods and no more than two hooks or lures per rod, so most drift with two rods rigged with two jigs each.

Electric trolling motors are used to control the speed and direction of the drift. On windy days, use a sea anchor to slow the boat.

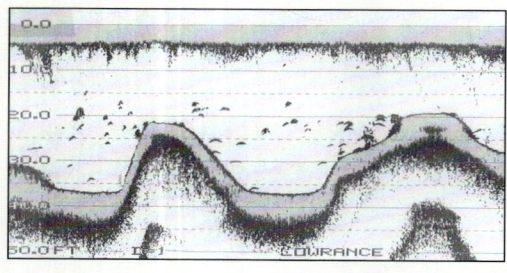

schools of crappies and shad in midwinter

Kentucky, this type of flowage is called a "river-run reservoir." These are typically long and narrow with an easily distinguishable creek channel and lots of woodcover. Maximum depths at the dam may exceed 40 feet, but the deepest areas along the main river channel are in the 20- to 25-foot range. Flowages often harbor excellent crappie fisheries.

Somewhere between 1980 and 1995, most crappie anglers across North America's flatlands gradually arrived at the same conclusion: Winter is usually the best time to pursue crappies in flatland reservoirs, because all the locational patterns

Drifting Bottom

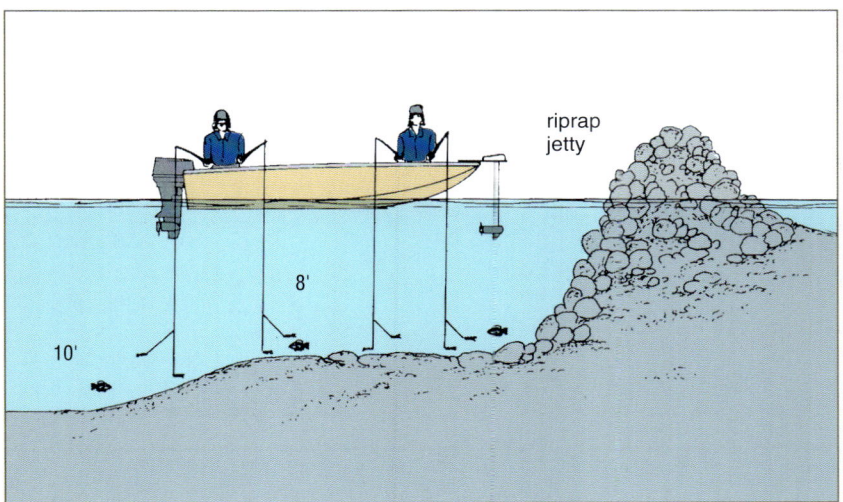

Toward the end of the postwinter doldrums, drift fishermen catch more crappies on the bottom in 8 to 10 feet of water than suspended over deep water. The most productive spots are mudflats close to riprap causeways or jetties.

Early in the day, however, drifters do best over deeper sections of mudflats and creek channels. After midday, crappies move shallower on mudflats and lie on or near bottom in 8 to 10 feet of water. They frequently favor riprap 8 to 10 feet deep. Once they hit the rocks, their prespawn antics are about to begin.

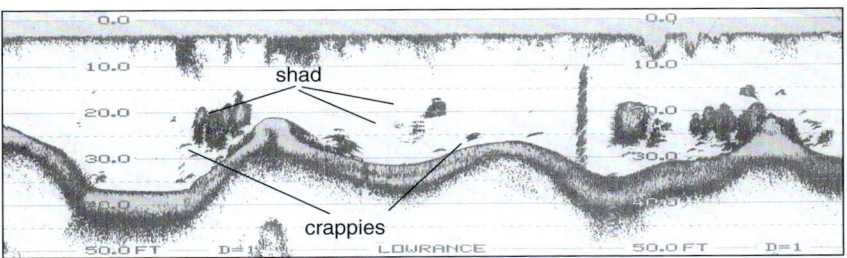

When water temperature rises above 42°F in winter, schools of crappies and shad break up and scatter across the lake.

merge into one. They coalesce into tighter groups during winter than at any other time of year. Because crappies everywhere seem to locate and suspend thickest in areas less than 50 feet deep, shallower flatland reservoirs offer the most habitat for them to spread out across. And their seasonal migrations in these types of impoundments tend to be longer than anywhere else.

In the latitudes of northeastern Kansas, winter fishing generally begins about three weeks prior to the winter solstice, which occurs 4 to 6 days before Christmas in most years. During late November in Kansas, crappies and their primary prey—

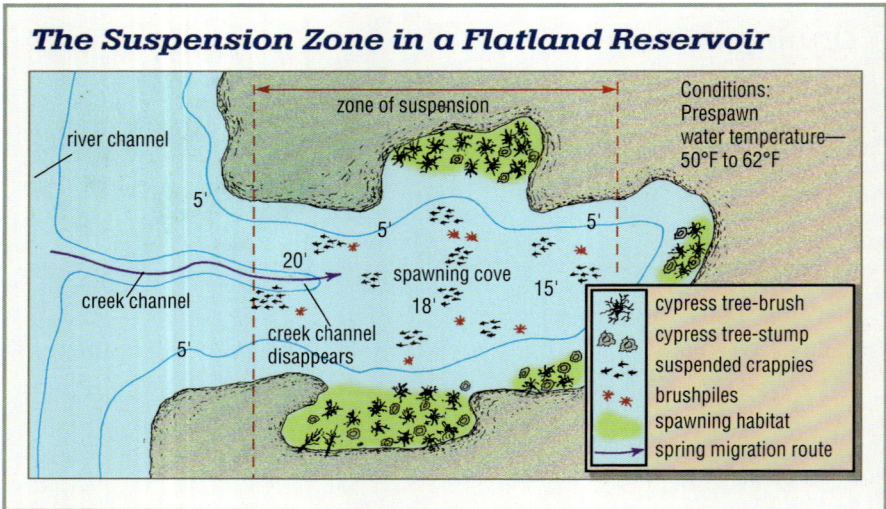

gizzard shad—begin congregating in giant schools that gradually become even larger as winter progresses. By February, some schools of shad and crappies are 3 to 5 feet thick and 30 feet in diameter, suspended over submerged creek channels.

From such massive schools, anglers routinely extract 100 or more crappies per day. Perhaps crappies form such schools to increase predatory efficiency, just as the shad gather in tight schools for protection. Many Kansas anglers contend that such schools are more vulnerable to fishing pressure than they are during the spawn, and further contend that more restrictive creel limits need to be established for winter fishing.

Fishing can be so extraordinary in winter that a few crappie specialists shun big schools that suspend over creek channels, contending that suspended crappies are too easy to catch and rarely include the system's biggest specimens. These anglers are looking for 2-pounders, which they believe assemble in smaller, looser groups. And bigger fish do tend to segregate themselves, spending more time near bottom, where a properly tuned depth finder is required to find them.

Schools of flatland-reservoir crappies can range from the dam to the upper reaches of feeder creeks and rivers. In lower Michigan, this behavior often ends during October, while it may continue until December in Kansas. As winter progresses, schools tighten and coalesce in the middle and upper third of the reservoir, leaving most of the waterway barren of crappies. During an unusual winter in Kansas, some schools of crappies and shad continue to hold less than a mile from the dam, suspended over depths of 30 to 35 feet. This typically occurs when crappie and shad populations are extremely high. In Michigan, lakes lack shad and may be iced over by early December. There it's more typical for flatland crappies to remain in the lower third of the reservoir (closer to the dam) all winter. Latitude, climate, and forage all play a role in ultimately determining where crappies might spend the winter in flatland reservoirs, yet in all of these shallow lakes continent-wide, crappies group tighter during the cold months.

In Kansas, shad and crappies often remain in confined areas for days. Occasionally, schools move several miles in a day or two, sometimes merging with other large schools to form a megaschool. In Michigan, where conditions are harsher, it's unusual for crappies to move several miles in any direction in a day or two at any point during winter—but they do move. A "migration" of 500 yards or so, however, is more likely in colder climates.

During the coldest spells of winter in Kansas, most can be found gathered in tight groups along river or creek channels. But whenever the water temperature is above 38°F, a substantial aggregation of crappie and shad will likely meander slowly across mudflats that stretch hundreds of yards from the edge of the channel. Schools on the flats in winter tend to be smaller than those along creek channels. An isolated brushpile on a flat in 14 to 17 feet of water can hold a wandering school of crappies for extended periods of time. As long as the water temperature remains below 42°F, the winter scenario just described remains intact. But as it climbs to 45°F, schools of shad and crappies begin to disperse, spelling the end of the winter bonanza. This usually takes place about 10 days to 2 weeks prior to the March equinox.

In Michigan, water temperatures on the surface often read about 40°F the first day a boat can get out after the ice breaks up. By then, crappies have already begun to disperse—often earlier than they might in Kansas. When the ice leaves in late March or early April, some crappies can already be found lingering in shallow coves where the water warms fastest. (Northern fish of many species react earlier to the approach of spring, in terms of water temperatures, than southern fish.)

Transition to Spring: As March and early April days pass in Kansas, schools of shad and crappies diminish in size. Eventually, countless single crappies and random bunches of five or six fish wander after small, loosely knit schools of shad as both species begin a slow journey to spawning sites. During the 50 to 65 days required for crappies to shift from winter feeding grounds to breeding grounds, inclement weather often erupts. Spiteful north winds usher in one cold front after another. A bit of snow flies now and then. Temperatures become

frosty enough to ice rod-tips. Cold fronts may barrel across the Kansas prairie every five to six days, usually turning crappies sullen and making them reluctant to feed.

Most crappies and shad suspend across the mudflats and creek channels, ignoring structure like humps, drop-offs, and channel edges. Sonar shows countless black specks, and flashers display orange blips that should be interpreted as single crappies and small balls of shad suspended from 4 to 25 feet.

As this transition period from the end of winter to the beginning of spring unfolds, crappies and shad spread lakewide again. No longer do we find stretches of barren water. During this 50- to 65-day spell, crappies exceeding 12 inches become scarce, and the whereabouts of big crappies has most anglers puzzled. When asked about it, one veteran of many frustrating March fishing trips in Kansas reckoned that big crappies scatter so widely over thousands of square acres of water that finding them becomes an impossible task. In fact, crappie fishing in general becomes a pretty tough chore. Consider this common scenario: On any given afternoon in late April, a group of 10- to 12-inch crappies might be found in a foot of 50°F water along a rocky shoreline inside a cove. A small, inconspicuous spot like that might be the only shoreline holding catchable crappies in the entire lake. The next afternoon, that shoreline could become like every other bank in the lake—devoid of crappies, with no discernable reason anglers can deduce for the crappies to move.

One dynamic pattern stands out during the Prespawn Period. It involves what we call the Suspension Zone.

In Michigan, larger crappies may mix with smaller ones in those same kinds of shallow venues, usually relating to shoreline cover like brush, reeds, bulrushes, and fallen trees in shallow, dark-bottomed coves. When these coves are fairly large, it's possible that crappies may use the entire cove, if sufficient shoreline cover is available. Crappies can become concentrated in small areas when the wind blows in one direction for several days, warming the area where the wind is cracking directly into shore a few degrees more than all surrounding areas. As with bays in natural lakes, wind-driven current patterns can determine your final step when tracking spring crappies in water temperatures ranging within the low 40°F to high 50°F range.

Crappies can also become concentrated in small coves that have no shoreline cover. In this spring scenario, crappies tend to suspend right in the middle of the cove when it's calm, or concentrate near the shoreline where a sufficient wind is causing waves to slap the shore. Of course, that's assuming the weather has been stable and warming.

In most areas of the country, in both lowland and flatland reservoirs, one dynamic pattern stands out during the Prespawn Period. It involves what we call the Suspension Zone. Typically, crappies begin to move toward spawning habitat as the surface of the water approaches 50°F. In most flatland and lowland reservoirs, classic crappie spawning habitat is found in shallow embayments and coves. In the absence of anything resembling those options, crappies spawn in brush, woodcover, reeds, or weeds along main-lake shorelines. Before moving into shoreline cover to spawn in any of these habitats, when water temperatures at the surface read somewhere between 50°F and 59°F, they stage and suspend in open or somewhat open water away from shore.

In classic spawning bays or coves, crappies wander like nomads across featureless flats. When they hold for any appreciable length of time, they often loosely relate to brushpiles, cribs, or some other form of cover. It's common to find prespawn crappies, scattered but in groups, suspended 5 to 10 feet down in 10 to 18 feet of water within spawning bays or coves (old creek arms that have silted in), in both lowland and flatland reservoirs. As the water warms above 60°F, you can find them with increasing regularity associated with shoreline cover until they finish spawning.

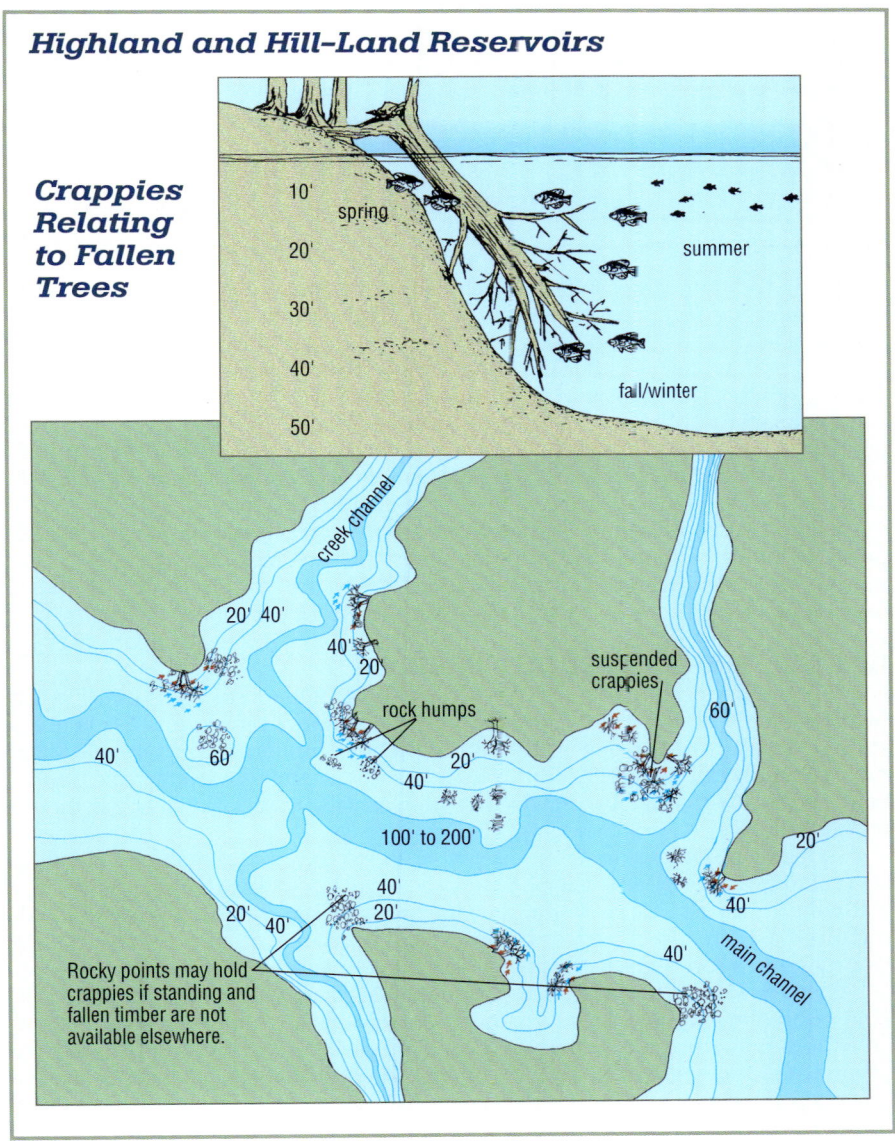

Highland and Hill-Land Reservoirs

Crappies Relating to Fallen Trees

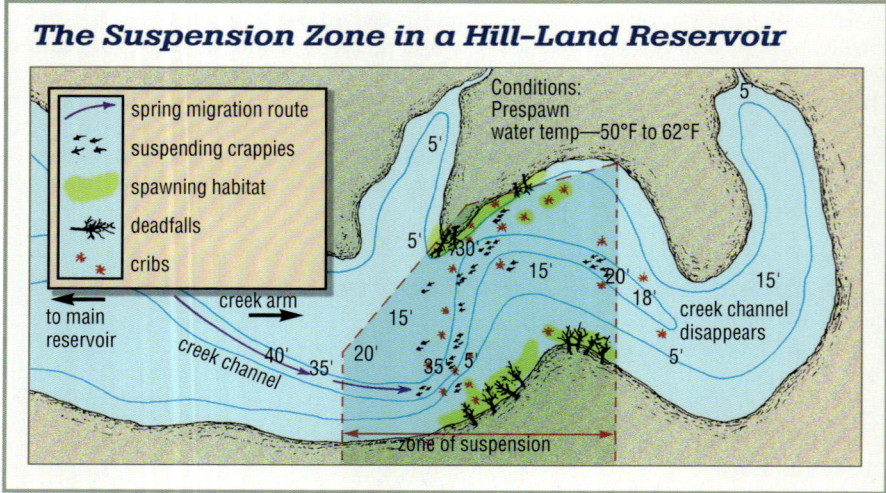

Spring weather can be harsh in the northern states, and crappies move out of coves entirely during nasty cold spells. The creek channels entering these coves may be silted in and indistinct. Crappies may move to the most precipitous drop-off they can find, which might be hundreds of yards away within the main lake, and suspend there. The most precipitous drop might be from 8 to 10 feet, but they seem to prefer depths in the 12- to 17-foot range to ride out a cold front. These particular suspended crappies, driven off by cold fronts, can be very tough to catch. As with natural lakes, the best bites usually occur during stretches of warm, stable weather.

Perhaps the most common spring pattern in all reservoirs involves the Suspension Zone. It's common for crappies to move upstream from main-lake or near main-lake wintering spots into creek arms of flatland, highland, and hill-land reservoirs until they reach an area of maximum environmental stability.

HILL-LAND AND HIGHLAND IMPOUNDMENTS

Hill-land impoundments are typically clearer than flatland reservoirs. Depths near the dam tend to be in the 100-foot range. Contours throughout the lake are steeper. Creek arms are longer, narrower, and more numerous, and are the places most crappies call home most of the year in these deeper environments. Depths near the mouth of a creek arm, where it intersects the main lake, can be in the 40- to 50-foot range.

Highland reservoirs are even deeper, with maximum depths often reaching several hundred feet. Creek arms tend to be 60 feet or deeper at the mouth. Typically the water is quite clear and the lake has little standing timber, with lower fertility—which equates to fewer pounds of predatory fish. But potential for trophy-sized specimens of all species seems to increase.

When the subject turns to seasonal migrations, crappies in highland and hill-land reservoirs may be nothing like their nomadic cousins of the flatlands. In these environments, they may remain within the general area of a single main-lake point, cove, or creek arm all year. Habitat in the depth ranges crappies prefer (50 feet at the deepest, most of the year) is limited in these environments, compared to shallower flatland impoundments.

Or crappies may be true to their river heritage and move many miles to spawn. It is quite typical for hill-land crappies to winter in and around timber on primary points (a primary point being one at the mouth of a creek arm, where it intersects the main river channel). When the water at the surface approaches 50°F, they may pack up and move upstream within the adjacent creek arm.

Little scientific observation in the form of tracking studies exists on this topic, but some professional anglers and guides from various parts of the country have described the movement like this: As the surface water warms to about 47°F, crappies rise straight up out of their wintering habitat. They linger within 5 feet of the surface for about 24 to 48 hours, then suddenly make like bees for the upstream sections of the creek arm. They don't hold or stage anywhere until they reach the point where the maximum depth of the creek channel tapers up to about 35 feet. At that point they spread out and stage for several weeks, sometimes for more than a month. The area they inhabit continues from that point, where the maximum depth in the creek arm is 35 feet, upstream to a point where the maximum depth is about 20 feet.

During the time it takes for the water to warm from about 50°F to 60°F, crappies spend a lot of time suspending throughout this staging area, which is why we call the upper one third of a major creek arm the Prespawn Suspension Zone. Guide Bill Fletcher of Arkansas theorizes that this zone represents one of the most environmentally stable areas in the reservoir during early spring. "The nights can be quite cold in early spring," he said. "In water shallower than 20 feet, like the back ends of bays and coves, where crappies eventually spawn, water temperature can fluctuate quite a bit over a 24-hour period. Crappies don't like to yo-yo around much. Water needs enough volume to provide stability for them. But they apparently don't like too much water volume, either. Back up the creek arm, where the water is 45 to 55 feet deep, crappies just move through in spring. They never hold on anything long enough to be caught until they reach that magic depth range."

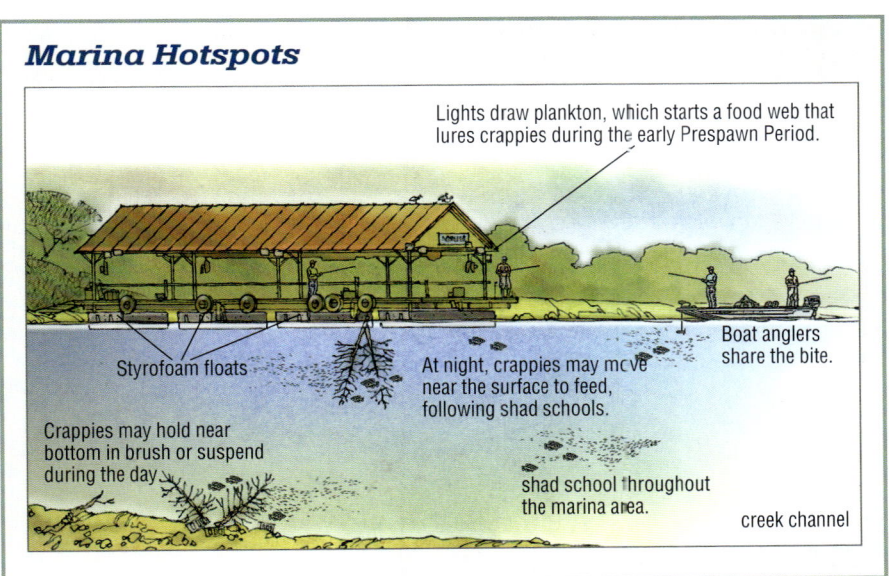

Marina Hotspots

When crappies first appear in that range, they tend to hover a long distance from shore for days, typically holding right over the creek channel in the top half of the water column. Forage species like shad and shiners prefer stability, too, and often hold in the upper part of the water column in the same areas. In all cases, they're moving closer to spring spawning sites during prespawn movements. Warm, stable weather extended over several days eventually triggers shallow movements into fallen trees, submerged brush, reeds, and other shoreline-related cover. Cold fronts, however, send them back out into the Suspension Zone.

How deep crappies suspend depends primarily on water clarity and available light. In low light, on cloudy days, or in cloudy water, crappies tend to hover within 6 feet of the surface over depths of 15 to 25 feet. On bright days in clear water, they can hold 10 to 15 feet down over depths of 25 to 35 feet. Crappies have sensitive eyes, and they seek comfort levels with respect to light penetration. Suspended crappies at this time of year can be highly active, easily caught by trolling crankbaits or spider rigging most of the time. The most active fish suspend at the same level throughout the Suspension Zone.

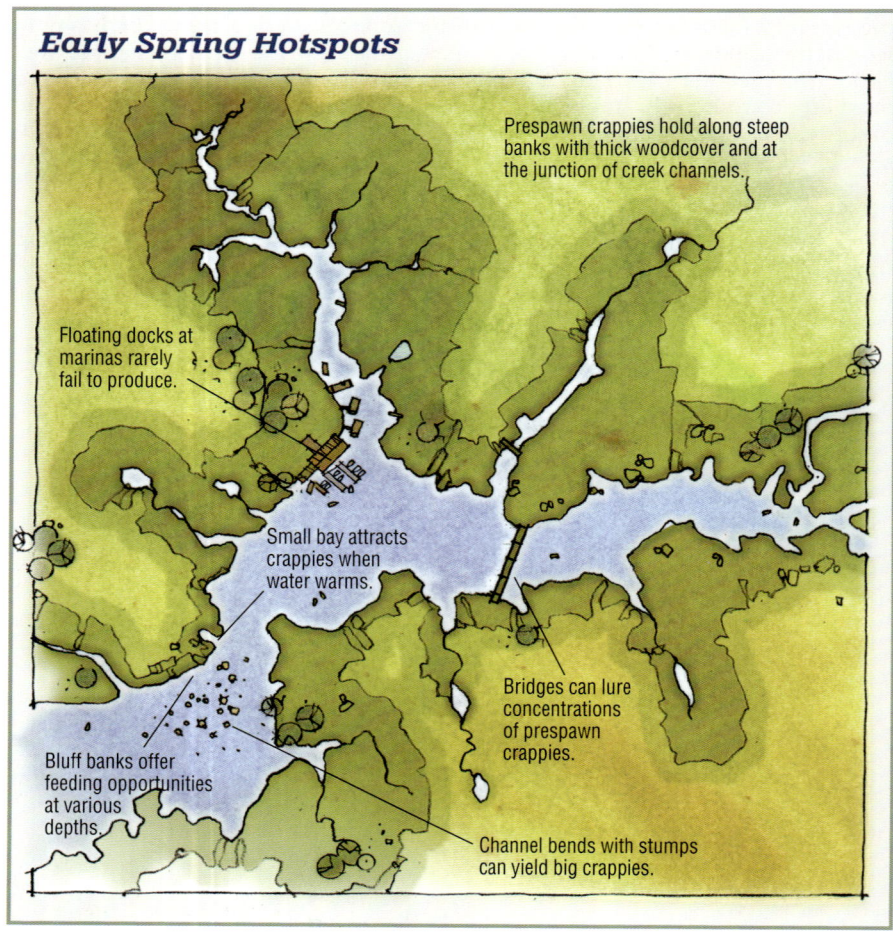

Early Spring Hotspots

Prespawn crappies hold along steep banks with thick woodcover and at the junction of creek channels.

Floating docks at marinas rarely fail to produce.

Small bay attracts crappies when water warms.

Bluff banks offer feeding opportunities at various depths.

Bridges can lure concentrations of prespawn crappies.

Channel bends with stumps can yield big crappies.

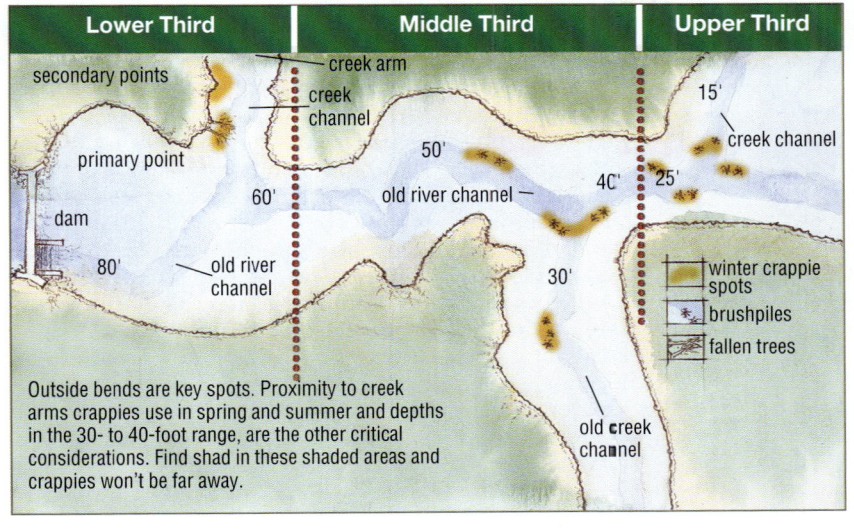

Typical Winter Spots for Crappies in Southern Reservoirs

Outside bends are key spots. Proximity to creek arms crappies use in spring and summer and depths in the 30- to 40-foot range, are the other critical considerations. Find shad in these shaded areas and crappies won't be far away.

Brushpile, crib, stake bed, old discarded Christmas trees with cement galoshes—whatever form it takes, a manmade fish attractor provides crucial habitat in these often barren zones of spring activity. "A brushpile is like a McDonald's," Fletcher says. "Put it in the right spot and crappies show up in numbers to eat there." Since the subject here has been open-water suspended crappies, you may reasonably wonder how brushpiles factor in. Well, if crappies hold 5 feet down over 35 feet of water 100 yards from shore, chances are good that a tree or brushpile is somewhere nearby. Knowing where key brushpiles are and marking them on GPS can be crucial, even when crappies are suspending.

"Crappies follow river and creek channels like highways," Fletcher said. "Brushpiles placed in strategic spots along those highways hold fish. Crappies may not be on or in the brushpile itself, but it's a baitfish magnet. If they can't find forage in the open water, crappies crash the brushpiles this time of year and chase baitfish out. When you see crappies suspended anywhere near a brushpile, they're actively feeding."

During the Prespawn Period at Lake Norfork, a classic highland impoundment in Arkansas, the Suspension Zone in one of the major creek arms will be several miles long. With so much territory to search it pays to have a good starting point. One of the best is a "channel crossing," where the creek channel bends close to one shoreline, then bends again and runs over to the other. "It's an absolute," Fletcher said. "Put a brushpile anywhere on a channel crossing and prespawn crappies will hold there. Absolutely always."

Crappies at this time of year often turn on during the afternoon. Look for a creek arm, cove, or finger that lies north-south. The fish tend to use the east side in the morning and the west side in the afternoon.

In addition to large expanses of excessively deep water, hill-land and highland reservoir banks can be markedly devoid of cover. Shallow bays, backwaters, coves, and inlets are scarce and often limited to the upper reaches of impoundments. These limited shallow areas that provide spawning grounds for crappies often must be shared with bass, bluegills, catfish, and sunfish. Highland reservoirs, in particular, warm late, simultaneously sending several species of fish to compete for limited spawning habitat at the same time.

During winter, crappies use deep cover on main-lake points. Brushpiles, fallen trees, and standing timber become magnets, holding crappies most of the year in some cases. Rocky points tend not to attract many of them unless timber and brush are present. Shorelines are generally steep, and points may not extend far from shore. Crappies winter among the branches of fallen trees or the limbs of brushpiles in depths of 30 to 60 feet, or around rockpiles at the base of these quick-dropping points. The best points for locating wintering crappies are usually near intersections, where creek arms join the main lake. As spring approaches, crappies that will spawn there slowly ascend the slope, using increasingly shallower cover as the water warms.

In all reservoir types, crappies look for sand and marl bottom—soft but not mucky—to carry out their spawning activities.

While winter depths of 40 feet are most common, crappies in spring often hold 15 to 20 feet deep, depending on water clarity. In cloudy water, they may move much shallower and stay there for longer periods of time. Active fish often suspend near secondary elements like logs, trees, and brushpiles as the water warms from the low 40°F range into the low 50°F range. Where cover is scarce, crappies hold and suspend on breaklines from a shallow shelf into deeper water. Breakline fish often immediately move shallower into areas that warm most quickly—channels, canals, and shallow, dark-bottomed bays—in this temperature regime. Cold fronts can drive them out again in spring.

Crappies throughout their range spawn in temperatures of about 68°F up to about 74°F, though temperature is not the main determining factor. Day length, in fact, is probably more critical. Science is discovering that most fish, including crappies, have a sort of internal calendar triggered by the length of the day. As the days grow longer in spring, they spawn within a certain window. That window, which may be influenced by events like full or dark moon phases, falls between certain calendar dates each year and has been determined over time, as well as and through genetics. It's Mother Nature's way of ensuring survivability—of making certain young-of-the-year fish attain a safe size by autumn, leaving them better prepared to make it through the winter.

In all reservoirs types, crappies look for sand and marl bottom—soft but not mucky—to carry out their spawning activities. A mix of gravel and sand is preferred over silt and other fine particles that allow eggs to sink to levels where oxygen is deficient. Though crappies have been observed spawning on the branches of woodcover in some environments, they seem to prefer spawning right on bottom where proper substrates can be found. If such cover is available, crappies spawn in and around reeds, brush, bulrushes, cypress trees, stickups, stumps, or maidencane in 2 to 6 feet of water. If no cover is available, crappies may spawn a little deeper on open sand, sand-marl, or sand-gravel flats.

SPRING TO SUMMER

FLATLAND RESERVOIRS

As mentioned earlier, the genetic history of most reservoir crappies extends back to a time before the water was impounded and they were living in a river, where extensive migrations were required to find suitable habitat during each of the four seasons. In flatland reservoirs, the need to travel persists, and crappies may move miles between spawning grounds and summer haunts after the water warms into the low to mid-70°F range. During this migration phase, which can last days or weeks, crappies are often tough to locate and tougher to consistently pattern.

Even in summer, flatland reservoirs produce a breed of strawberry bass that amaze, amuse, and baffle most anglers. Call 'em papermouths, speckled bass, or calicos, if you prefer (someone once said that crappies have more aliases than a roomful of criminals). Point is, even crafty old locals who spend copious hours of free time chasing flatland crappies can come up blank during summer.

Ned Kehde, former archivist for the University of Kansas and a longtime *In-Fisherman* contributor, studies the stupefying ways of flatland crappies year 'round. In summer, he admits to spending most of his time hunting them on mudflats. "Most fishermen focus on channel edges," he says. "Lots of crappies cruise these drop-offs into 25 or 30 feet of water along the river channel during summer, but I'm finding larger fish on brushpiles in 14 to 20 feet of water in the middle of expansive, uneventful mudflats most years.

"Most crappies in the flatland reservoirs of Kansas evacuate coves sometime in June," Kehde says. "The water in the shallows becomes too warm. Though flatland reservoirs can have maximum depths ranging from 45 to 55 feet, the best flats are in mid-depth areas."

The best brushpiles are frequently the ones placed in the middle of nowhere, a long distance from any appreciable structure or depth change. Crappies also find a brushpile balanced along the edge of a minor drop of only 2 to 4 feet very appealing as well—as long as it's in the middle of an otherwise homogeneous mudflat. But some of the best spots coincide with shoreline points, where the widely spaced contours of a gently sloping mudflat bend out toward the main river channel.

Sometimes we're lucky enough to stumble onto an old brushpile out there, but (in states where it's legal) it's best

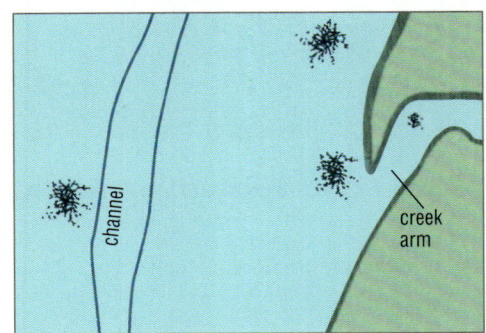

Postspawn Flatland Reservoir

On this reservoir section, the brushpile inside the creek arm leading to the spawning area is a likely place for the postspawn feeding frenzy. The larger brushpile just outside the cove probably is the most used cover element in this section throughout most of spring, especially if unsettled weather keeps crappies from venturing far from open water during early spring.

Crappie Spawning Sites and Summer Haunts on a Flatland Reservoir

Main-Lake Spawning Site and Summer Spots

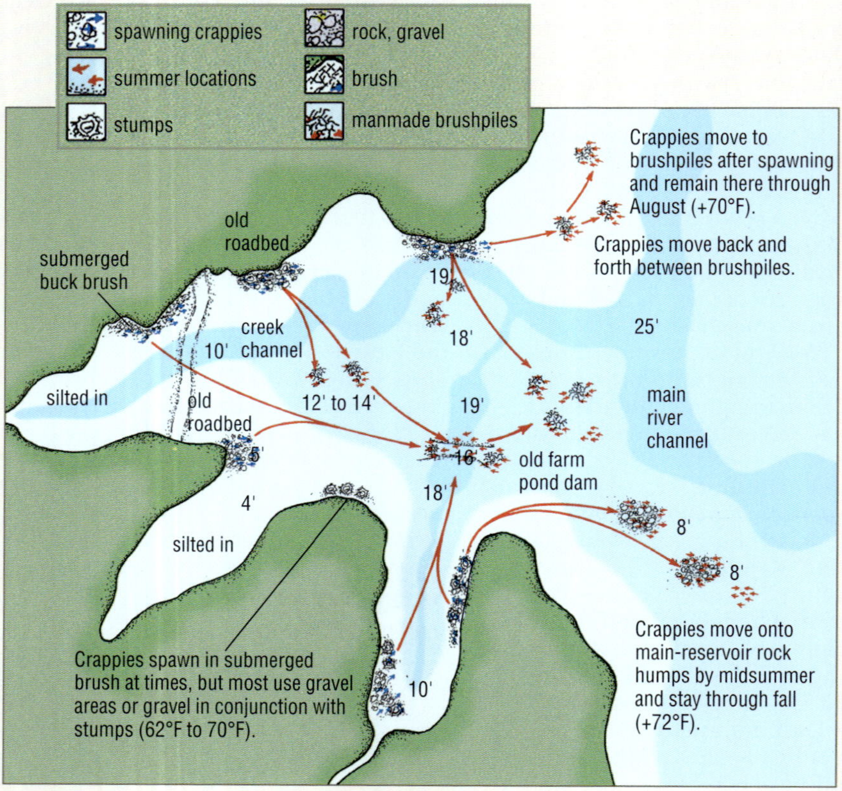

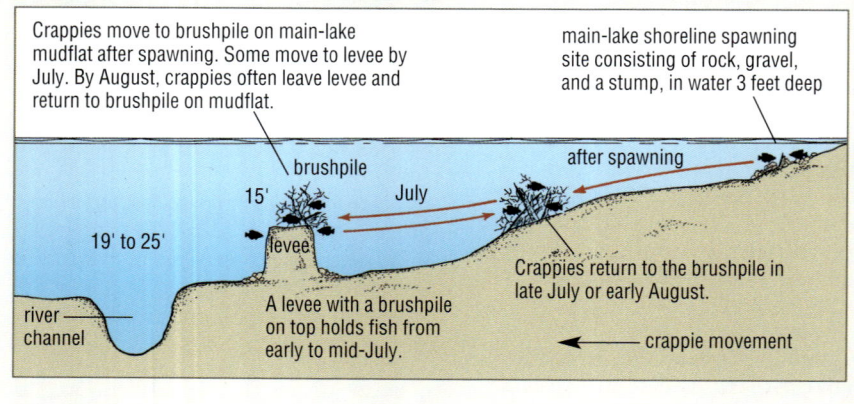

to place your own, made with hardwood and cinder blocks, buckets of brush filled with cement, or just a pile of limbs bundled together and weighted down with rocks. (Be certain to mark each one with your GPS, while also triangulating its location with shoreline objects or highlights.) "The best brushpiles are made of willow," Kehde notes, "though cedar or hedge lasts longer. I don't know why, but crappies seem to prefer willow."

Crappies often suspend vertically near the tops of brushpiles, but they might also be found suspended anywhere within 20 feet or so of the pile.

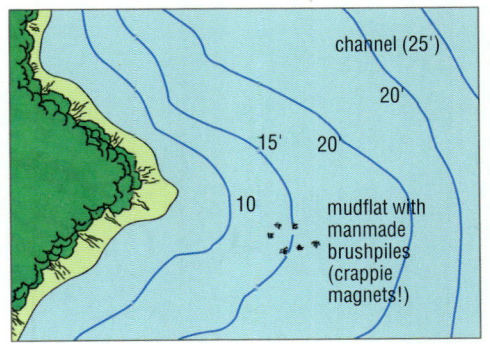

Mudflats produce best when summer weather's consistently hot and water levels don't fluctuate wildly.

When they're up high in clear, calm water, boats spook 'em. Under those conditions, Kehde likes to put a marker near a brushpile and anchor a short cast away. He then pitches jig/plastic combos and swims jigs horizontally over and around the cover. But most days and in most conditions, Kehde prefers to jig vertically with 1/16- to 1/8-ounce jigs tipped with 2- to 2½-inch tubes. "During summer, your presentation should be vertical about 80 percent of the time and horizontal about 20 percent," he adds.

Rising water in a flatland reservoir sends crappies shallow. Conversely, drawdown forces them to secondary drop-offs. In either case, the mudflat pattern can dissipate, so it tends to follow a stable-condition model. "Still, the mudflat pattern in 14- to 20-foot depths always ends up being the most consistent for bigger crappies over the course of the season," Kehde affirms. "But, if the reservoir is less than 15 years old, crappies can remain somewhat channel-bound, as if they don't trust things not to revert back to the way they were before the dam was built. But the real reason crappies in newer reservoirs continue to relate to river and creek channels is the fact that fewer brushpiles have been planted on the flats. Also, as a reservoir ages, the less distinct its channels become."

Most of the mudflat patterns Kehde talks about take place on the main lake away from the river channel. The most obvious summer patterns in flatland reservoirs involve crappies around brushpiles along the top lip of river and creek channels; but as Kehde insists, these are also the most commonly exploited patterns. Other patterns that persist through summer on flatland reservoirs include areas 10 to 20 feet deep, usually on brushpiles, logs, or submerged timber, in the backs of bays or the very back end of creek arms. These patterns hold until water temperatures at the surface drop below 60°F in fall.

Flowages: A type of reservoir similar to a flatland impoundment is the flowage, a riverine environment found mostly in Wisconsin, Minnesota, and some other upper midwestern states. A flowage is generally narrower than a flatland reservoir, with more current and created with a smaller dam. They're often located in rolling country with hills and valleys. Flowages are often filled with cover in the

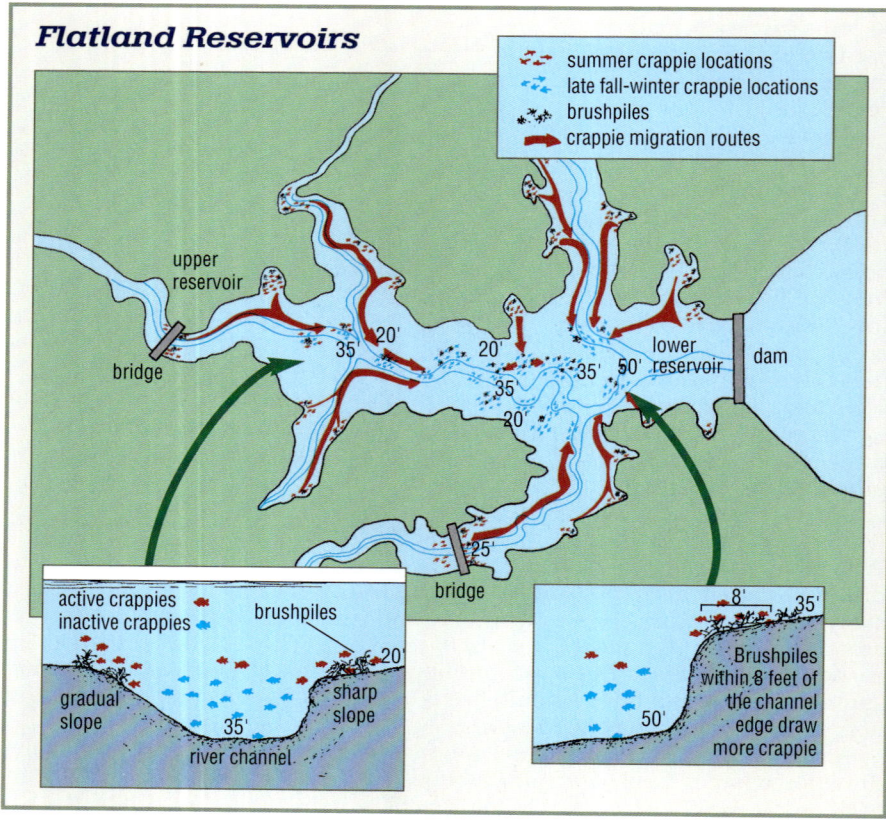

form of flooded and fallen timber, cribs, and submerged brush. Flowages also can be ideal for the recruitment of riverine chubs and shiners. The combination of cover and an apparently limitless food source in a flowage can produce an excellent trophy crappie fishery.

Flowages can be tough to pattern during the Postspawn Period, because the fish scatter and have almost unlimited cover options. Crappies settle into summer patterns late, usually sometime in August. In the latitudes where flowages exist, the nights are already beginning to cool, and water temperatures are slowly backing down from summer highs. Crappies begin to school more tightly at this time, in and around the densest cover available on 10- to 15-foot flats adjacent to the river channel. As the nights begin to cool the water in late August, these schools begin to group even more tightly and start to move deeper.

The best spots in flowages from late August through September are often the deepest holes in the old river channel—the same places crappies frequently inhabit during winter. These holes occur in bend areas, and typically range from 18 to 28 feet in depth. When highly active during late summer, crappies may spread back up onto the flat during feeding forays, into the densest cover available in depths of 10 to 15 feet. They may group heavily where combinations of cover come together—for instance, logs mixed with brushpiles and boulders, with a few stumps thrown in for good measure.

Choosing a Creek Arm

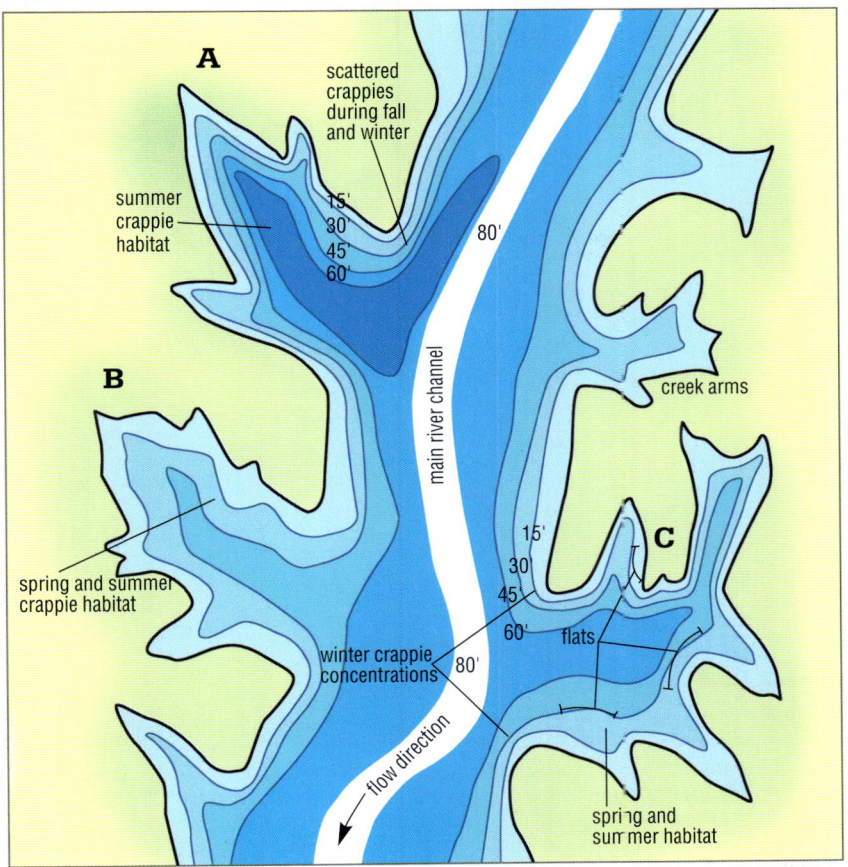

This map is based on an actual portion of a reservoir on the Georgia–Alabama border. Narrowly spaced contour lines indicate that **CREEK ARM A** is deep and lacks flats that serve as spawning habitat. Crappies hold here during summer, but the mouth of the creek arm is far from the main river channel. Crappies disperse from such areas in fall. The distinct point on the upstream side probably holds crappies, but not the huge schools you're after.

Prespawn and spawning crappies use **CREEK ARM B**, and it holds some fish year-round. The points at the mouth will not attract many crappies during fall and winter because they are shallow, and too far from the main river channel.

CREEK ARM C has extensive flats at varying depths and a defined creek channel that provides prespawn, spawning, and summer habitat. The points on the upstream and downstream sides of the creek mouth are long and slope distinctly, but not too steeply, into 60 feet of water. Crappies move to these points when the water temperature drops into the 50°F range.

Although you can't tell from this map, **CREEK ARM C** has lots of trees along the old creek channel and on the north point. Guess where most of the crappies will be!

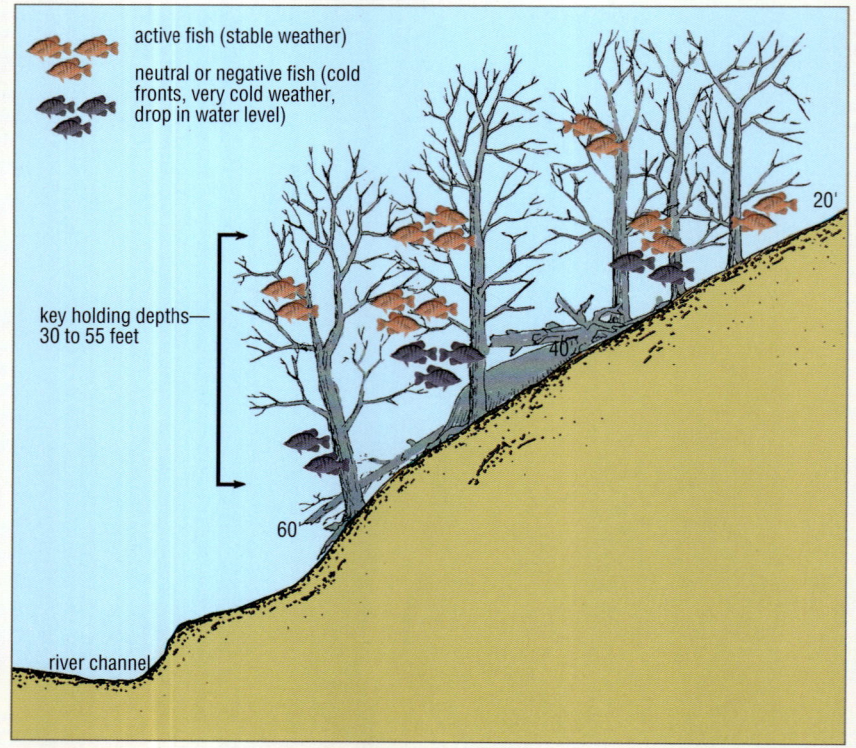

Environmental factors determine crappie position on a timbered point. Look for crappies to suspend high in the trees under mild, stable conditions. They may even move to shallower trees, but rarely in less than 20 feet of water.

Cold fronts, frigid water, or a drop in water level will shift crappies into deeper water and into the dense heart of the trees. Not only are they in a negative feeding mood, but they are more difficult to get at.

It can be difficult to tell what the cover is composed of when using only sonar. An underwater camera can reduce the amount of time spent looking for key spots. It's typical to fish 10 to 20 areas filled with dense cover before catching a single crappie, but the next spot could hide the mother lode concentrated in a small area of mixed cover. Once discovered, these spots ordinarily remain exemplary for the remainder of the season, and for many seasons to come during late summer and early fall.

Like their cousins in flatland reservoirs, crappies in flowages are most active during periods of stable weather with intermediate barometric pressure, and suspend in or near the tops of the branches of fallen timber and brushpiles. They may retreat into deeper holes and hug bottom after a cold front. But, as late summer gives way to fall, mild cold fronts may actually turn crappies on and precipitate a hot bite.

HILL-LAND AND HIGHLAND RESERVOIRS

In the expansive environments found in hill-land and highland reservoirs, crappies may remain in relatively shallow patterns all summer. Those in the upstream or upper third of hill-land reservoirs often spend the summer in shallow deadfalls, logs, beaver dens, and stumpfields. The key to finding them is to go upstream to a point where the river channel disappears. At some point, water carried into the impoundment by the river dumps its load of silt and sand

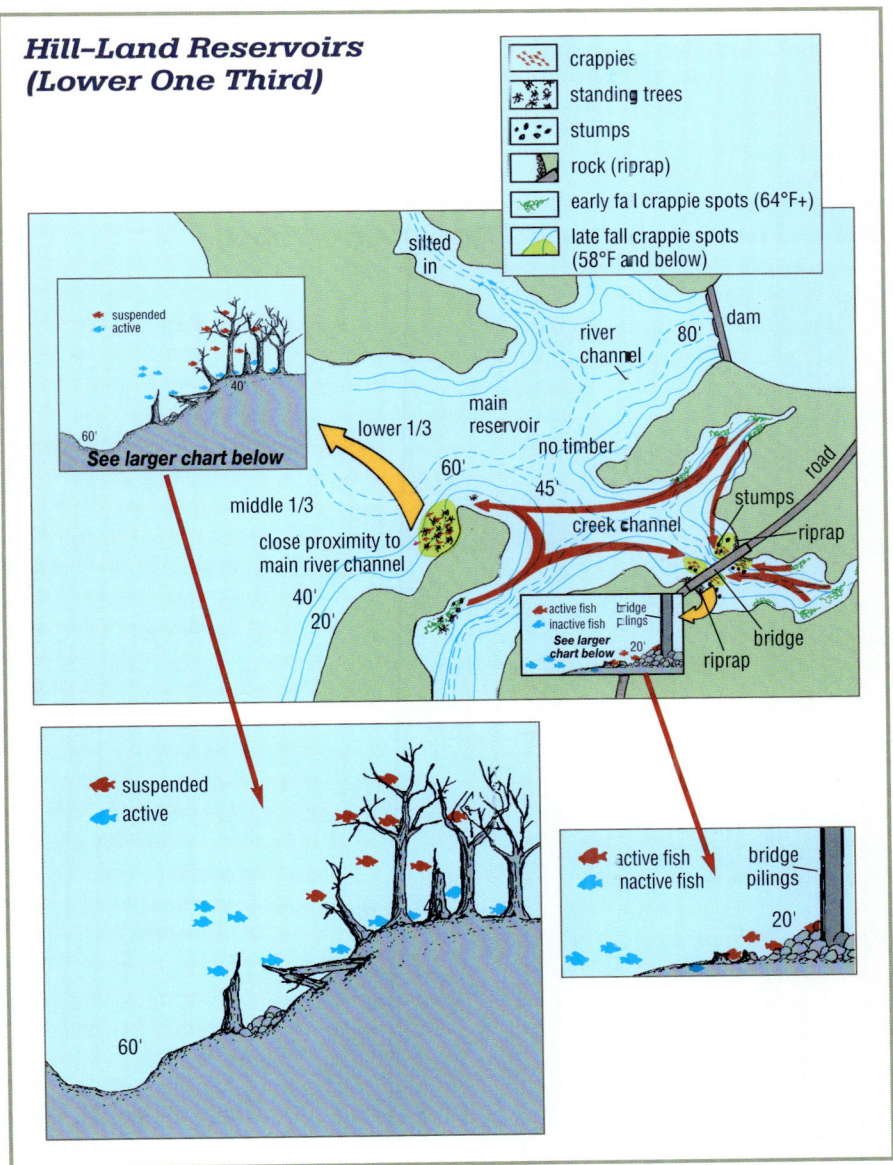

and eventually buries the river channel in the uppermost sections of the lake. Drop back from that point until you find a distinct channel, and begin your search there.

Hill-land reservoirs house some of the most prolific crappie bites in the United States. Places like Weiss Reservoir (Georgia-Alabama), Lake Fork, Toledo Bend (Texas), and Kentucky Lake are known for consistently producing numbers of slabs, with many topping 2 pounds. In the mid-sections of these reservoirs, crappies tend to inhabit larger creek arms during summer, and multiple patterns can be producing at the same time. It's not uncommon to find big crappies scattered throughout a shallow cove and feeding in the top foot or two of the water column during the evening and into the night, while at the same time others can be found in fallen trees, submerged timber, stumpfields, and along the edges of hydrilla beds in 5 to 20 feet of water near primary and shoreline points in the main body of the creek arm.

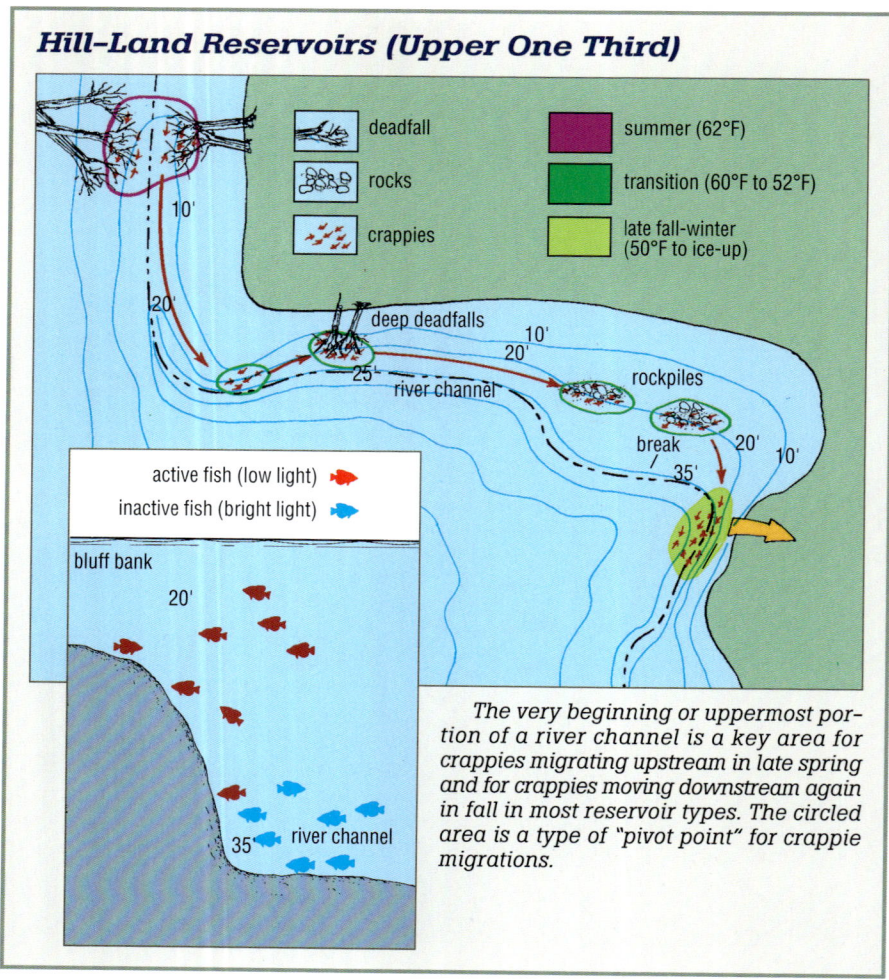

The very beginning or uppermost portion of a river channel is a key area for crappies migrating upstream in late spring and for crappies moving downstream again in fall in most reservoir types. The circled area is a type of "pivot point" for crappie migrations.

Creek Arm Shifts

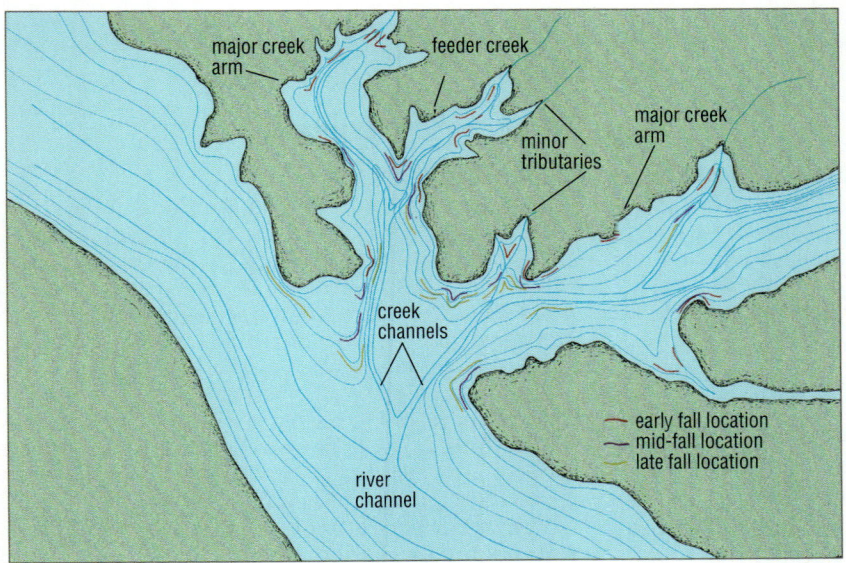

In early fall, many crappies are in the upper ends of major creek arms and feeder creeks, where mid-depth cover ranges 8 to 20 feet deep, and shad or other baitfish are abundant. Look for timbered points that slop toward the creek channel or brushy channel edges.

As water temperature falls into the upper 50oF range, crappies gradually shift downstream to deeper points along channels. In colder water, crappies prefer a greater range of depth options. Location shifts from tributaries and feeder creeks to main-lake points, particularly those at the mouth of major creek arms.

Not all creek arms hold crappies. The best bets are the larger ones, with some depths exceeding 45 feet in the main channel, and with good woodcover in the back ends of the connected coves and along the major shoreline points. It's not uncommon for anglers to leave crappies alone during the summer, especially in the huge, sprawling, hill-land venues of the South. Anglers in surveys claim the weather's too hot, or that crappies make less suitable table fare in summer, or that bass, striper, trout, or catfishing occupies most of their time. It's possible that most summer angling for crappies in the South takes place during nighttime hours.

Crappies inhabit the thickest timber, weedbeds, or stumpfields they can find along the banks of a major creek arm. When hunting creek-arm crappies on huge reservoirs, it helps to look at the year as a process. Think shallow and near the back end of coves, when crappies spawn. From that point on they move back out toward the main reservoir, and it takes them all summer to get there. Any dense, expansive cover between those spawning sites and the primary points at the intersection of the creek arm and the main lake could hold crappies in summer. The later in summer it gets, the closer to the main lake your search should start.

Crappies are not in the cover all the time. During low-light periods at the beginning and end of the day—or on a particularly dark or windy day—crappies will invade the cover. During the remainder of the daylight hours, they're typically suspended away from the cover or buried deep within it for shade.

FALL TO WINTER
HILL-LAND AND HIGHLAND RESERVOIRS

The most classic winter pattern involves submerged, standing timber on the slope of a shoreline point that drops to the edge of the main river channel. In essence, the best points are ones where the river or creek channel bends in fairly close to shore—but not too close. Crappies love trees in areas like this, especially those that rise from bottom to within 15 to 25 feet of the surface. Whole trees are better than rotted, pole-like trunks. Having no trees at all often equates to no crappies. Finding such trees often requires some on-the-water research, because most topographical maps fail to indicate where standing timber remains. And most of the trees in most Southern reservoirs are slowly rotting away. Placing a few tall brushpiles on these points eventually brings crappies back.

Crappies love trees in areas like this, especially those that rise from bottom to within 15 to 25 feet of the surface.

Another key late-fall-into-winter pattern on hill-land reservoirs involves bridge abutments. These areas are among the most popular targets for night fishermen. Most bridges on hill-land impoundments cross creek arms, because the main body of the reservoir is too wide. When these bridges cross the main reservoir, or cross a creek arm close enough to the mouth to span channels at least 40 feet deep, crappies often use the base of central abutments as wintering sites, especially where the lip of the channel is in close proximity to an abutment.

Key spots in this case include: The lips of the channel directly adjacent to bridge pilings; riprap banks dropping into depths of 20 feet or so; and stumpfields, brushpiles, or timber reaching out to the lip of the channel.

Crappies in the upper third of highland or hill-land reservoirs move downstream, away from the river and into the main lake. This movement takes them down the main river channel to a point where its maximum depth reaches at least 35 feet. From that point on, they seem to search for a bend hole with suitable habitat with respect to cover, depth, environmental stability, and forage.

Mid- to lower-reservoir crappies that spend the summer in creek arms or the main lake are looking for environmental stability, as well. The classic fall destination is submerged, standing timber on the slope of a shoreline point (generally a primary or secondary point) where it tapers down to the edge of the main river channel.

Standing timber is the ingredient that turns a good point into a honey hole. Use sonar to find good trees in the proper depth range (40 to 50 feet is ideal). Move around the area at a slow idle and watch your electronics. In cold water, crappies suspend vertically and could appear anywhere within the timber, from the bottom to within 20 feet or so of the surface. In the best spots, sonar reveals tight schools within the branches of the trees. Surprisingly, one tree may hold hundreds of crappies, while a similar tree nearby seems devoid of life. The same trees can attract all the crappies year after year—until, of course, the trees rot away.

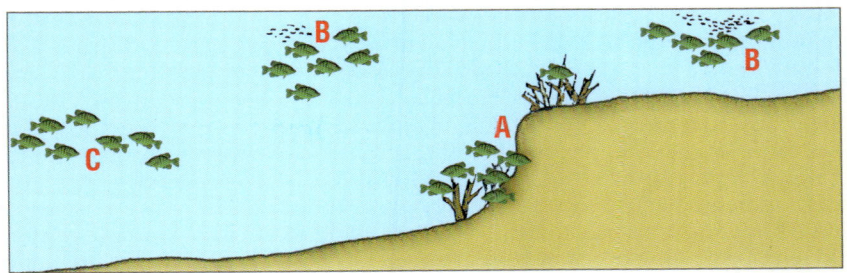

Position and Activity Relative to Cover

In shallow fertile reservoirs, crappies are most easily caught when they're in cover or near a drop-off **(A)**, or when they're drawn away from cover by passing prey **(B)**. Crappies become difficult to catch when weather or water conditions push them away from cover **(C)**.

Only a crappie knows for sure, but there must be subtle differences in the structural makeup of a tree, or in the water quality in the immediate vicinity of each type of wood, which acts to attract or repel baitfish, crappies, or both.

On many highland and deeper reservoirs, from Connecticut to Utah, crappies winter in coves or shoreline "cuts." Anywhere within these areas, a fallen tree with its roots on the bank and its top under 30 to 40 feet of water is a key spot for fall crappies. In less forested areas of deeper canyon reservoirs, a rockslide, where a segment of canyon wall has crumbled, often provides the only "shelf space" in those critical 35- to 50-foot depths crappies prefer to winter in.

Even in heavily forested New England, where many highland reservoirs exist, a land or rockslide can provide key habitat for fall crappies. From a layman's perspective, the geology of new England is simple. If it isn't rock, it's sand and gravel. A surface layer of topsoil and intertwined roots holds everything together. Along the shoreline of deep impoundments, this layer of topsoil quickly washes away. If the underlying layer is sand and gravel, it soon erodes. Eventually banks cave in, and in some instances the resulting landslides take large chunks of real estate into the steep-sided reservoir. Sometimes the landslide takes down entire, full-grown hardwoods. It's not uncommon to find such trees 45 feet down and 25 feet or more out from the new bank. And that's the purest definition of a prime-time crappie hot spot in a highland reservoir, when autumn rolls around.

Many reservoir crappies make a distinct shallow movement in fall. Ronnie Capps, a Crappiethon Classic and tournament champion many times over, spends a lot of time chasing hill-land crappies in Tennessee. "It's not just the patterns that are overlooked in fall," Capps says, "it's the entire fishery. I see very few boats in October, and that's the best time of year to find numbers of big crappies." In these reservoirs, gizzard shad provide the primary forage. "It's common for crappies to invade shallow 6-foot flats in October," Capps adds, "and I rarely see another boat working these shallow fish. As the water cools in September, gizzard shad move shallow, feeding right on top. Crappies follow, moving up the same migrational highways they used when leaving these same flats after spawning in spring. These routes leading fish from deep to shallow can be channels, cuts, weedlines, or depressions in the lake bottom. This is an active feeding migration during which crappies forage heavily."

After migrating, crappies move directly to flats and humps in the 5- to 15-foot range, about two-thirds of the way toward the back of a creek arm. "Look for areas with several thousand square yards of 6- to 7-foot depths," Capps advises. "Shad school in tight groups, and stumpfields or low brushpiles are good places to find crappies waiting in ambush. Crappies may remain in these areas until late November, and feeding activity stays intense throughout this period. As temperatures cool below 50°F, however, the fish disperse over larger areas and begin to suspend, becoming harder to locate," he says. "I use sonar, run farther, and troll more at this point, looking for any structure that might hold a concentration of fish. Creek arms, creek channels, and vertical structure attract most or all of the crappies in the lake, by the time temperatures dip into the mid-40°F range. On overcast days, crappies hug bottom right against the structure. On clear, calm, sunny days, they migrate vertically and suspend. Crappies may move right up to the surface when the water's cold, to bask in the sun."

LOWLAND AND FLATLAND RESERVOIRS

Many reservoirs are drawn down in fall, in preparation for winter precipitation and spring runoff. A radical Kansas drawdown is 3 feet over 2 weeks. In Connecticut, the water in some impoundments often fluctuates more than 3 feet within a day of fishing, and sometime during October the water may drop 10 to 20 feet in a matter of days. Drawdowns do not necessarily turn the crappies off in these impoundments, but they obviously affect their location.

When the water drops in some flatland reservoirs, it turns quite cloudy. Crappie may continue to bite, but angling success can be spotty. When the drawdown is completed and pool levels are once again maintained at consistent levels, the water clears and fishing can become spectacular.

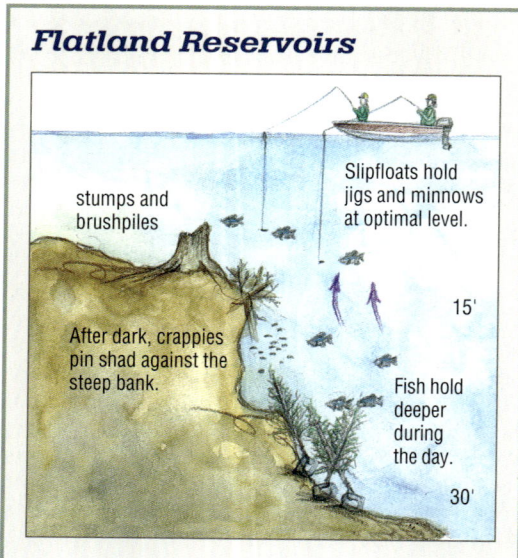

Flatland Reservoirs

stumps and brushpiles

Slipfloats hold jigs and minnows at optimal level.

After dark, crappies pin shad against the steep bank.

15'

Fish hold deeper during the day.

30'

By late October in Kansas, most river crappies near the head of a flatland reservoir move into brushpiles and submerged logs in 10 to 20 feet of water. These are shallower holes than crappies can find in the main body of the reservoir. Sometimes these crappies suspend within 5 feet of the surface during fall, loosely relating to woodcover. From this suspended vantage, they often drift horizontally right onto shallow flats. It becomes critical to check shallow shelves and flats surrounding deep bend pools, especially on the inside of a bend.

Crappies tend to relate to the more gradually sloping

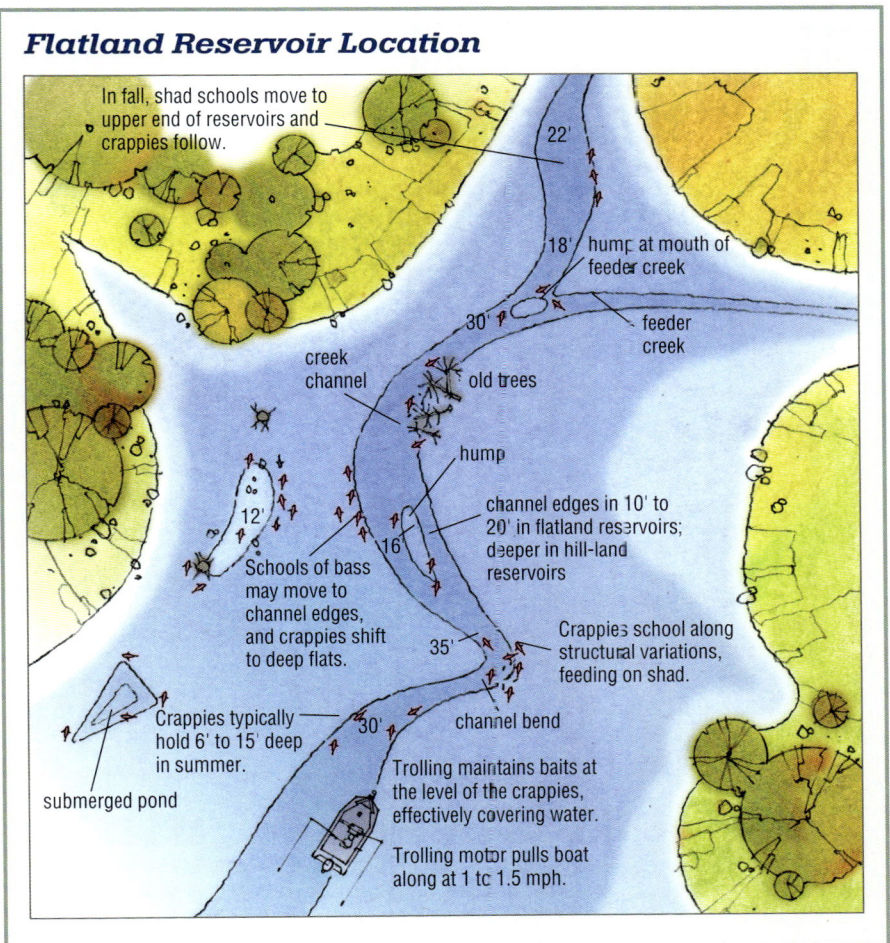

Flatland Reservoir Location

sides of the bank during early to mid-fall. Steep drops on outside bends, even with prime brushpiles staged along the lip, attract fewer crappies in these upriver areas. The fish may, however, wander onto shallower flats in 4 to 8 feet of water. Any woodcover in the form of laydowns, logjams, or submerged brush on shallow flats adjacent to inside bends can attract crappies during stable weather. With respect to scenery, solitude, and angling success, fishing the upriver areas of flatland reservoirs in fall can be rewarding.

When flatland reservoirs are drawn down in fall, crappies seem to hover near channel edges, perhaps becoming suspicious of shallow water. Often this channel edge is that of a secondary creek, though it could be the main river channel where secondary creeks don't exist or have silted in. Adjacent flats may be less than 3 feet deep after a drawdown, though depths ranging from 4 to 8 feet are common, as well. Cover in the form of brushpiles may be important to these fish during fall, though this depends on the clarity of the water and the availability of forage. Crappies need to stock up for winter, abandoning woodcover in favor of feeding almost constantly. Finding them 5 to 10 feet down in cover-free areas is not uncommon. But, fishing can be spotty during a drawdown: When pool levels stabilize, angling improves.

Another classic spot in flatland reservoirs is a submerged levee or small pond dam within the river channel of the main lake. Steep, rocky shorelines in the lower third of the lake draw crappies in fall, too. Larger specimens often suspend just below the lip of the drop in these areas, but more often are found in brushpiles associated with mudflats and other ledge areas not associated with the main river channel. These brushpiles are often in depths of 10 feet, or even shallower.

As fall progresses, crappies may gather into increasingly smaller spaces, as perfect habitat in terms of stability (ideal temperature, pH, forage, current, etc.)

Key Conditions

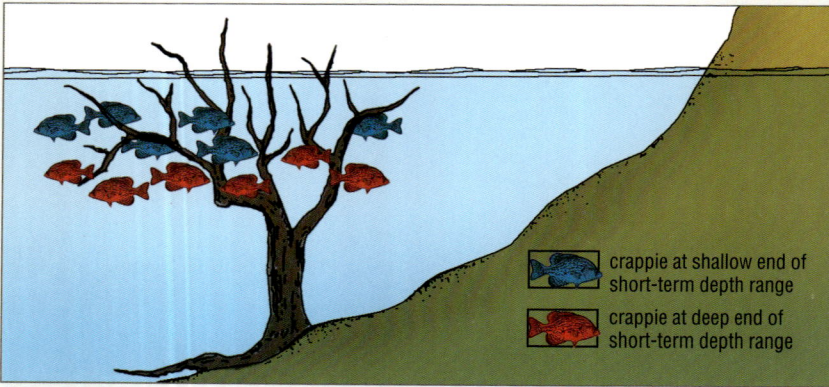

Spots that offer attractive conditions at a range of depths get long-term use by crappies. During early fall, crappies remain in summer depth ranges in this clear-water impoundment. The key depth is 10 to 12 feet, although fish could be anywhere from a few feet down to 20. Fish often remain active as long as they can change depth in response to changing weather conditions.

In contrast, when an area offers attractive conditions in one depth range, crappies leave or become inactive when conditions change.

gradually dwindles. This congregation continues after conditions stabilize in the North, but crappies may spread out a little more in southern waters. If water temperature steadily dips toward its lowest point of the year, crappies increasingly hold along steeper drops. During cold fronts, the bite doesn't slow as much in fall, but the fish shift deeper. It becomes increasingly common to find them in brushpiles 20 to 25 feet deep. Old stock dams and levees in the main river channel become key spots. Rocky ledges in the main river channel hold crappies during late fall, as well. But a week or so of mild temperatures can draw them back to shallower brushpiles and, in the North, to weedlines in areas 10 to 12 feet deep near mudflats and other edge areas not necessarily associated with the main river channel. By November, these shallow movements often cease in the North, but they continue on through Christmas in southern impoundments.

Even during late season (when the crappies hold in deep water), a spot with a variety of depth options holds fish.

Here a few stragglers remain shallow when water temperature drops into the low 40°F range. Most crappies move to areas where attractive conditions are in or adjacent to deeper water.

WHAT DOES IT ALL MEAN?

We collected and analyzed data on the catches of many thousands of crappies during the fall period in reservoirs. Looking for trends and tendencies, these were the most obvious:

• The best crappie fishing tends to occur when water temperatures at the surface read between 40°F and 50°F.

• The depth crappies use doesn't necessarily correspond to water color or light penetration, but they generally go to deeper water as the season progresses.

• They tend to be most catchable when relating to woodcover or steep drops during most of the fall season.

• Crappies are increasingly attracted to steep-breaking areas as water cools. Flats get some use, but movements there can be sporadic, related to stable weather, and short-lived.

• In water less than 44°F, crappies in clear water retain higher activity levels than those in dingy water.

The most telling pattern, however, may be the very unreliablilty of these general trends. Entries exist that contradict each of these tendencies, as day-by-day conditions often override trends. Fish are not automatons, nor creatures of strict habit driven entirely by instinct. In fact, the more we learn about crappies and other species, the more the word 'instinct' becomes obsolete. In other words, anglers who learn to expect the unexpected often rise above the rest, in terms of consistency.

Chapter 5
Understanding Seasonal Movements—III

Crappie Location in Rivers

RIVERS

Over the past third of a century, *In-Fisherman* has published enough information about crappies to fill an encyclopedia. Books, columns, and feature articles of the past form pieces of a huge mural. Combined, the pieces weave an intricate diagram of seasonal movements across the spectrum of crappie waters. From river backwaters to sprawling reservoirs, from ponds to huge natural lakes, the seasonal progression of crappie movements can be viewed in panorama across the pages of our back issues.

In-Fisherman has long maintained that some of the best and least pressured crappie fishing on the continent can be found in rivers, backwaters, and "river run" impoundments (flowages). Many of our Top 10 crappie selections over the years have been river sections, including the Rideau River in Ontario, the Mississippi River along the Minnesota-Wisconsin border, and oxbows in Mississippi.

River specs are an overlooked commodity, perhaps because river fish behave somewhat differently from their still-water cousins. Movements are more dramatic. Migrations of many miles are common among populations of river crappies, but uncommon among most populations in natural lakes. And river crappies

River Crappie Location Checklist

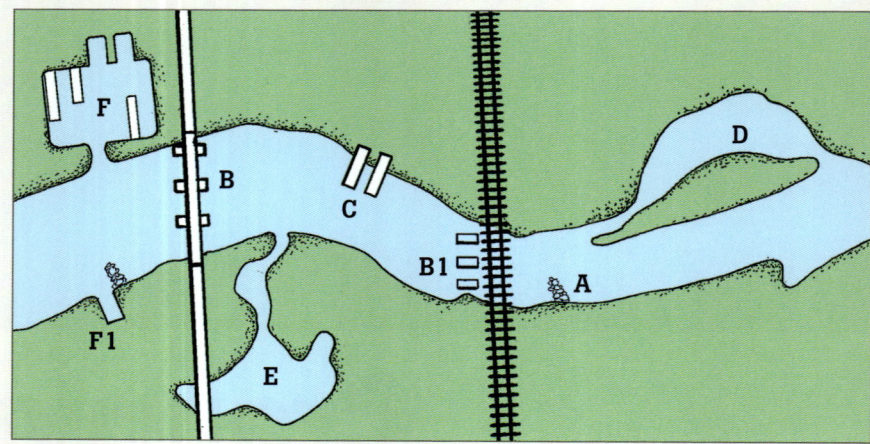

A. Wing Dam *(Summer/Early Fall)* — Key spots usually are riprap and wing dams if water is deep enough (ten feet or more) right against the bank in the most current-protected spot, where the wing dam meets the bank on the downriver side. Also check spots where spring floods lodge deadheads and brush against the upstream face of the structure.

B. Bridge Abutments *(Summer/Early Fall)* — In general, any bridge abutment or similar structure is worth investigating. The more irregular the surface, the better. Stone construction is better than concrete, and stone in conjunction with timber is better yet. Flat upstream faces are better than "V" shapes. Smooth concrete abutments, rounded at both ends, are the least likely to be productive. One of the most productive areas is where two bridges or a bridge and the abandoned pilings from a former bridge are within a few dozen yards of each other.

C. Piers/Docks *(Summer)* — A pier or dock set back from the force of the main river, but still with some depth, most likely holds fish. Timber in the water—pilings, cross members, and perhaps brush and deadheads lodged into the structure by floodwaters—almost serves as a wing dam, holding crappies even if exposed to the main river current. Avoid new docks, especially those constructed from pressure-treated wood which leaches arsenic into the water and resists the algae buildup that makes a dock attractive to baitfish and to crappies.

are quicker to adapt to adversity, since water-level and water-quality fluctuations are far more dynamic in rivers than in lakes. River crappies also tend to be more active after cold fronts, tend to fight harder, and often move more than lake dwellers.

If asked to describe the ideal shape for a river fish, no one would consider the crappie. A short, flat-sided creature that can be swept 30 feet downstream before it can twitch a fin should not make a good river resident. But crappies do quite well in rivers, thank you, because they're master adapters. They feed on what's most abundant, from crustaceans to insects to minnows. If it fits into that big paper

D. Oxbows *(Spring)*—Given their propensity to avoid current in the main river, crappies often gravitate to oxbows. In spring, treat oxbows as lakes, concentrating on shallow cover. If there's a causeway across the oxbow, the riprap bank of the causeway can be dynamite prespawn crappie territory.

D. Oxbows *(Summer)*—Look for the deepest water in the oxbow. Generally, that means the upstream end and along the outside bank, where the original river channel flowed when the oxbow was still part of the river proper.

D. Oxbows *(Fall/Winter)*—The area of heaviest cover in more than 10 feet or so of water almost invariably attracts most of the crappies that make fulltime use of the oxbow, as well as fish from the main river that winter there.

E. Backwaters *(Spring)*—Ponds and other backwaters connected to the river should all be checked in spring. Cover is more important than depth—unless the whole thing is little more than a swamp—in determining the potential of a backwater for holding crappies. Immediately after ice-out, concentrate on the remains of last year's weedgrowth.

E. Backwaters *(Summer)*—Concentrate on backwaters with some depth. Avoid weed-choked areas, as crappies seem to prefer some open water.

E. Backwaters *(Fall/Winter)*—The same backwaters that hold crappies during summer also hold them in fall, but expect fish to be more cover-oriented.

F. Marina Basins *(Spring)*—On big rivers, marinas usually offer what crappies need: Protection from current, either by a sea wall or a dredged-out basin off the river. Marinas built for larger boats invariably have adequate depth and lots of pilings. Concentrate on the pilings and docks along the bank.

F. Marina Basins *(Summer)*—Unless it's a huge marina that might function as a self-contained environment, summer isn't the best time to find crappies in a marina. Concentrate on mid-basin pilings and the entrance area that connects to the main river. Cut-back boat slips or boathouses along the main river are more productive, especially in conjunction with a small breakwall or wing dam, as in **F1**. These often serve as a holding area for groups of crappies during summer.

F. Marina Basins *(Fall/Winter)*—Large marina basins are among the best crappie spots in rivers once the water cools below 50°F. Early in the period, target pilings in the deepest water. As the water continues to cool, shift to areas with the most pilings, regardless of depth. Look for old sea walls and pier structures with downed timber, as opposed to newer pilings.

basket of a mouth, it's lunch. Location is often determined by finding the easiest forage crappies can utilize, and that tends to be the forage of greatest abundance in the right size during the season at hand.

While not perfectly suited to current, crappies adapt by avoiding the main flow most of the time, especially during cool- and cold-water periods. But current is where the food is, especially during summer, when water levels and current speeds drop. So from the late Prespawn Period or early Postspawn Period until fall, crappies typically favor current off the main channel. Where they have fewer choices or where current is relatively weak, they may hold near the main flow. The current breaks crappies choose vary in size and type from one river to the next, due to variations in current speed. In brawling waters like the Mississippi River, they don't fare well in the main river but flourish in backwaters and oxbow lakes. In the slow, ambling creeks of the flatlands, the fish thrive in the main stream behind minimal current breaks.

But, come winter, crappies in flowing water everywhere tend to seek backwaters, oxbows, pools, marinas, reservoirs, connected lakes, and other areas completely out of the main flow. In fact, the farther they can get from the main flow the better. So, current presents problems for crappies. Yet some populations shun the option to stay in reservoirs and lakes during the warmer months, preferring instead the feel of water sweeping across their broad sides and becoming true river fish.

Crappies maintain a unique relationship with current. Flowing water places more restrictions upon them than it does trout, smallmouths, walleyes, or catfish. Finding them in a river system involves understanding those restrictions. Though crappies may move more in rivers, summer habitat tends to be within 3 miles of spawning habitat. Understand the habitat they require during winter, the habitat they require for spawning, and the amount of flow they can tolerate at any given temperature, and finding them becomes much easier.

SMALL RIVERS AND STREAMS

Joe Monteleone is among the more highly regarded anglers in our *In-Fisherman* databanks under the classification *Riverine rodentia* (river rat). He lives in Tennessee, near rivers large and small. One of his favorites, the Stones River, is relatively small and slow. In such environs and at that latitude, crappies live mostly in or near the main river channel all year.

Stones River feeds Percy Priest Reservoir, yet crappies inhabit it year 'round. "These are true river crappies that rarely drop down into Percy Priest," Monteleone claims. "In some places, the river can be waded across, while other spots are 35 feet deep. Most years, heavy current occurs only in spring during the rainy season, which is when crappies burrow deep into cover near the bank to avoid current. Otherwise, current is rarely strong enough, or the temperature low enough, to sweep fish out of the downed trees in the main flow."

In spring, crappies move off ledges bordering the deep pools where they've spent the winter. In high water, they probe deep into shoreline cover. As the water warms above 60°F, they move to small backwaters to stage. "They won't spawn in current," Monteleone explains. "They use little backwaters. Stones River has no big embayments or sloughs or oxbows, just little cuts about the size of an average driveway. Crappies use these to avoid the increased current of spring and to get more sun, then stay to spawn." As in most river environments, peak spawning activity takes place in water temperatures of about 66°F to 70°F. Crappies find whatever cover they can to spawn within, which typically means woodcover, in river environments.

After the spawn, when water levels fall, crappies move directly to summer habitat. By August, the Stones River might reach the mid-80°F range. "Depending on current, wood becomes critical for crappies in these small flatland rivers," Monteleone says. "Stones is full of downed trees, stumps, and logs. Crappies prefer to have deep water nearby, but their main objective is to get out of the current and out of the sun. They favor the down-current side of woodcover—spots where weeds adjoin woodcover are perfect. Riverbends become key spots, too; they group on the inside of the bend where the current is reduced. Find woodcover on an inside bend, and you'll find slabs in summer.

"Crappies tend to hold at different depths according to water level, but generally hold in areas 5 to 8 feet deep on the down-current side of fallen trees. By midsummer, as the river drops and current slows, they move out to 10- and 12-foot depths in large pools. Yet when they seem to be suspended in open water, wood is usually nearby. In the Stones River, crappie location is almost always associated with wood. If bait is abundant in an area, a simple stump or two can hold a lot of crappies. But the cover generally has to be able to provide a current break for pretty good numbers, because crappies have a social side and tend to school."

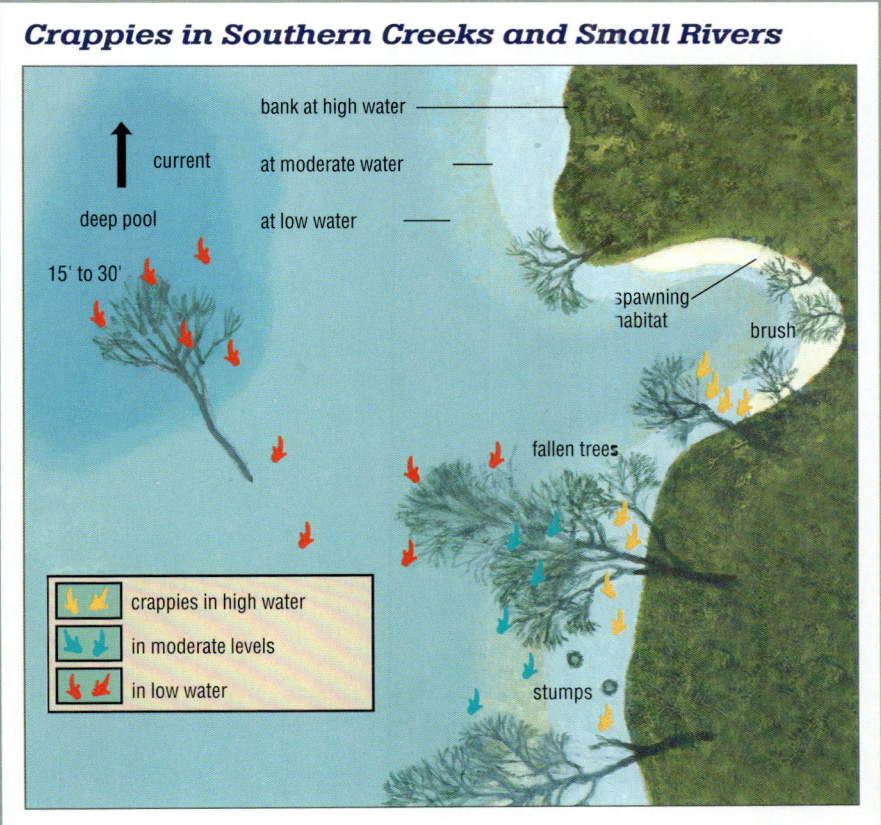

Crappies in Southern Creeks and Small Rivers

LARGER RIVERS

On larger rivers like the Mississippi in Minnesota and Wisconsin, crappies also spawn out of the current. The habitat of choice most of the time is within large, sprawling backwater areas. Crappies here occupy woodcover almost exclusively during the Spawn Period, when available. Some backwaters and embayments hold the fish all year. Current is too strong in the main-river areas of the Mississippi to hold crappies most of the time—until water levels drop quite low. But prior to spawning, crappies sometimes move 2 to 4 miles, farther in some cases, to reach spawning embayments.

In some instances, northern river crappies spend winter in natural lakes connected to the river by short canals or streams. In rivers with dams, crappies may drop down into a reservoir to spend the winter. In the northernmost latitudes of their natural range, river crappies tend to have two critical requirements: To get as far away from current as possible, and to find areas at least 20 feet deep. Crappies forced to winter in areas less than 15 feet deep in far northern climates generally suffer more stress and higher winter mortality rates—and it often happens, since the only available backwaters completely out of current often are less than 10 feet deep. However, ice-fishing for crappies is popular and productive in many northern Mississippi River backwaters.

As water temperatures climb into the 60°F range in spring, those crappies with options involving deeper winter habitat begin to migrate, usually downstream

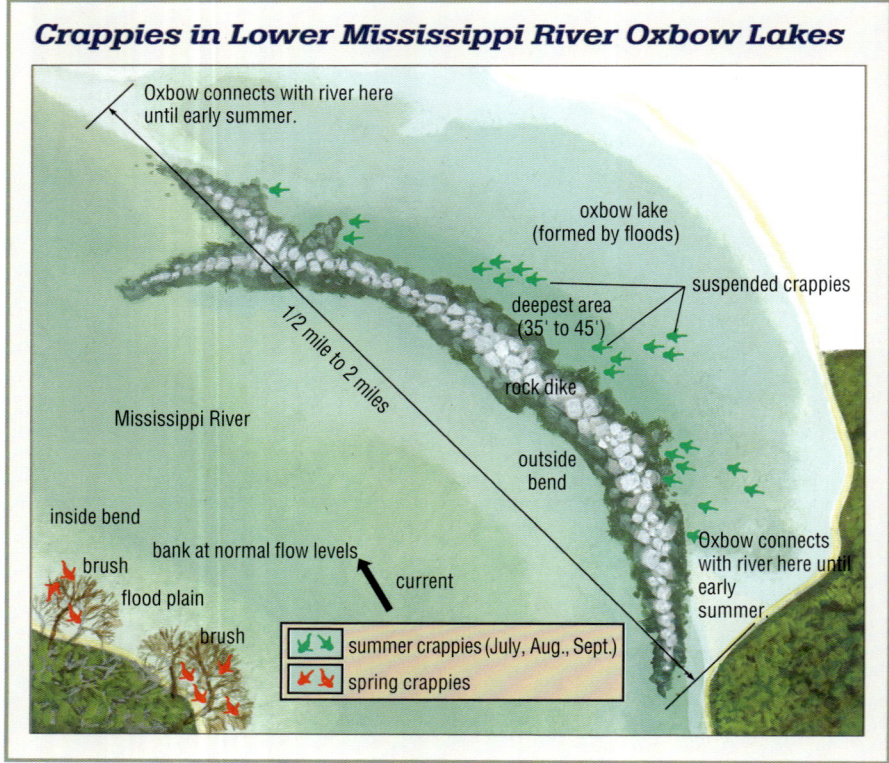

Crappies in Lower Mississippi River Oxbow Lakes

to bays and backwaters where they stage and eventually spawn. After spawning, they move directly to areas adjacent to the main current—or as close as they can get while still occupying woodcover. Big-river crappies often move throughout the summer, but continue to utilize backwaters, especially edge areas where still water borders the main flow of the river.

In these areas woodcover provides important habitat. A deadhead log may drift in, provide habitat for several weeks to several years, and harbor crappies during summer. When floods wash the deadhead away, crappies may not be found there again until the river deposits more woodcover. Those that stay in backwaters during summer become more difficult to approach, as many of these areas become choked with vegetation.

Ronnie Capps is a Tennessee Wildlife Resources Agency officer when he's not busy winning crappie tournaments. Between traveling to and from tournament sites, he chases oxbow crappies in the lower Mississippi River. Typically, in truly large rivers like this, crappies avoid the current of the main channel whenever possible, preferring sloughs, backwaters, and oxbow lakes.

"Oxbow lakes are created by exceptionally high flows that suddenly flood several hundred acres of land above an outside bend in the river," Capps explains. The Army Corps of Engineers piles up huge walls of rock where the banks of the Mississippi often blow out, but loss of wetlands, lock-and-dam mistakes, and other poor excuses for engineering over the years have caused floods to be much worse than in the past, so the water often rolls right over these rockwalls in a big flood. "The river then gouges deep holes in the tilled soil behind the dikes," Capps says. "Sometimes these holes are over 40 feet deep. These oxbows look more like rainbows. They're big, bow-shaped areas, long and narrow, from 1/2 to 2 miles long and up to 400 yards wide.

"Some oxbow lakes are connected to the river in times of high water," Capps notes. "But during summer, crappies are trapped there. The biggest crappie I've ever seen came out of an oxbow. If they had to live in the river proper, I don't think we'd see many of them in the Mississippi. Catching one out in the main river in that turbid, heavy flow is unusual. They would rather remain in the oxbows year 'round. And actually, oxbows create the finest crappie fishing in my home region of Tennessee."

In exceptional high-water events, crappies can be flushed out of oxbows. Rock dikes that follow the banks of the river are submerged in high water when spring floods wash out deep cuts behind the riprap. "Crappies often hold right there, behind that rock face," Capps says. "About 60 of these dikes have been placed near Dyersburg, Tennessee, to keep barge traffic moving through the resulting distinct channel.

"Crappies spawn in these oxbows and try to live there year 'round, if the river lets them. They spawn late in these environments. Males remain in spawning colors as late as August. In fact, the best fishing occurs during July and August, when the water drops to fishable levels. Much of the year, it's neither safe nor fun to be out there. I do better when the water drops and clears enough for fish to see lures.

"When the water's high, oxbow crappies move into secondary channels and sloughs, where they hug the bank. Most of them position behind points and bars and out of the current in 5 feet of water. But in times of high water, current is everywhere and crappies can't escape it. In April, May, and June, they're blown out of the oxbows and into the trees. The best time to concentrate on oxbow crappies in the southern portions of the Mississippi River is during the dog days of July and August, when the fish are concentrated, comfortable, and active."

FLOWAGES AND RIVER RUNS

John Kolbeck, guide and avid crappie angler from Wisconsin, likes to fish flowages, which are basically small hill-land or flatland reservoirs that usually have small dams and substantial current. Often dams are located at both ends, and flow is especially strong in spring, when snowmelt and rain send runoff through these narrow riverine environments.

Flowage crappies in northern habitats seek backwaters and large bays well away from the main flow of the river during winter. Crappies seem reluctant to leave these backwater areas until the surface is completely ice-free. When the ice is gone, with surface temperatures approaching 50°F, they begin moving out to current breaks in the main channel of a flowage.

"After ice-out, crappies move behind islands in the lower, downstream end of the flowage," Kolbeck says. "Around the end of April, as water temperatures climb into the mid-40°F range, they begin migrating upstream to the dam, where some stay into early summer. They move against the current by using a trail of classic breaks along the way, such as eddies, fallen trees, and stumpfields. They hold there for a short time in May, on their way to and from the dam. But the largest prespawn concentrations occur behind the dam, where they're full of eggs when we catch 'em."

Like all other species of fish that migrate into current, crappies always take the path of least resistance. Steelhead, salmon, smallmouth bass, walleyes—all fish faced with a major upstream migration—utilize inside bends, woodcover, concrete abutments, flood plains, undercut banks, deep holes, and the side of the river farthest from the main channel during upstream migrations. Where possible, they string these current breaks and reduced-current areas together to form a trail, one they use year after year when the time comes to move. Of all these species, however, crappies are positioned farthest from the main current. While a trout may use the outside edges of branches dangling in the main flow, and smallmouths the heavier branches in the midsection of a fallen tree, crappies often huddle right where the trunk intersects the bank. And it should be remembered when chasing migrating river fish that friction with the bank and stream bottom reduces flow. Current is often slowest near bottom, the reason river crappies are often found there.

"Most crappies hold below the dam until water temperatures reach almost 60°F," Kolbeck continues. "Several weeks later, some are still holding below the dam. Throughout May, the uneven bottom areas below dams hold the highest concentrations of crappies, which tend to lie right on bottom, out of the current behind structure. Once the water warms to about 60°F, the current is typically reduced from what it was a few weeks earlier, and crappies may no longer avoid the main flow, which is not that strong in most flowages to begin with. Some may position in front of a bar—on the upstream side—in 1 to 2 feet of water. In fact, we catch smallmouth bass in the same areas. This pattern holds into the low-60°F range. In years when crappies don't spawn due to extreme conditions or a series of severe cold fronts, they can be caught well into June, still stacked by the dam," Kolbeck says.

During early May, various species of minnows swarm into bays off the main river. In the afternoon as sunlight warms the water, some crappies leave the pool below the dam to take advantage of minnows concentrating in bays, shoreline cuts, and areas where the flowage widens. "Surface waters are warmer in those bays, attracting more baitfish," Kolbeck says. "Crappies tend to suspend high in areas out of the current, to take advantage of the warmer surface water.

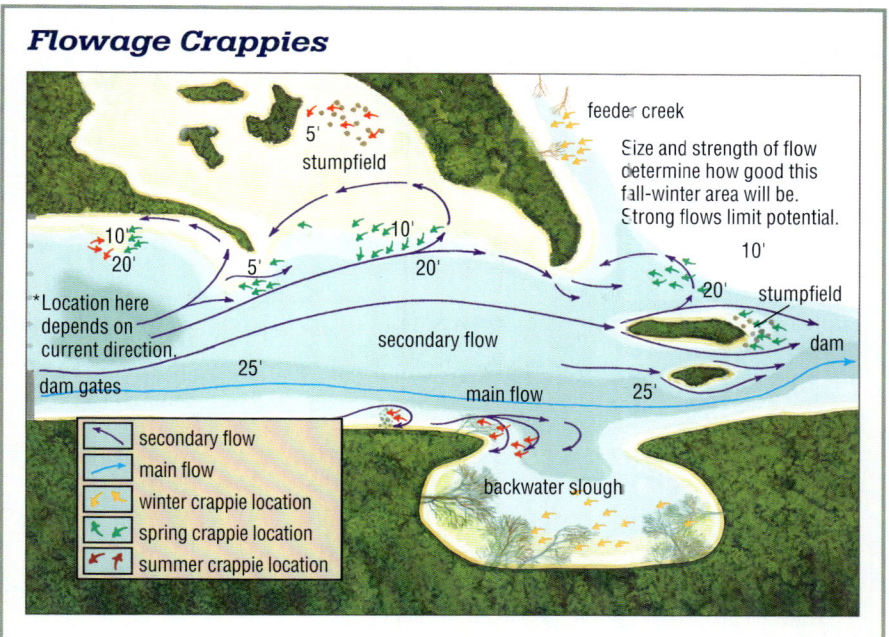

If the water in the main channel is 50°F, the surface of bays may be 65°F, and crappie activity increases proportionally. These bays may be 10 feet at the deepest point. Some crappies suspend in open water while others hole up in tall woodcover."

Bays might be inlet areas for feeder creeks, but one of the principle keys to finding the right bay is to seek spots without current. Bays with running creeks don't warm as fast and may have substantial current, which crappies try to avoid at this time. Prime bays tend to be off the main channel, according to Kolbeck. But he also likes areas where bays create wide, slow, current seams well offshore. "At some point, the still water of the bay meets the current of the main channel, and it could be a mile from shore," he adds. "Crappies scatter along that current edge throughout May.

"The exact location of a current seam varies from day to day, especially when water levels fluctuate. The best way to find it is with a bobber. A current edge can be 40 feet wide or very difficult to find. Just prospect with a jig and a bobber until the bobber begins to ride slowly downriver. The best spots are where the mouth of a bay narrows the channel against the far shore, while the land point of the bay blocks the flow over a large area behind it. The river wants to flow straight and the channel being created is narrow, focusing the current, with a big nothing pancake bay on the side of the flowage opposite the channel.

"Just fish toward the channel until you find current. It's like fishing by the dam, except that current seams by the dam are easier to find visually. In June, crappies move into side bays and hold around stumpfields in 7 feet of water. Apparently they spawn in there because it's completely out of the current, and the water is in that prime temperature range of 64°F to 70°F. I think they spawn at night and leave soon afterwards.

"In July and August," says Kolbeck, "crappies don't seem to bite as well, but I can find them in eddies on the edge of current seams off the main flow. Wood may improve a spot, but an eddy is a more important element of crappie location during summer. A current break off a shoreline point, a giant boulder, a bridge abutment, or anything that creates an eddy, becomes critical. And if you find one crappie in summer, you find a bunch. In fall, they return to their backwater wintering areas and stay until they move to islands in the main channel the following spring."

TIDAL RIVERS

Rich Zaleski, a longtime *In-Fisherman* contributor, has written widely about crappies and enjoys hunting slabs in large tidal rivers like the Connecticut. Tides influence the flow 12 miles or more inland all along the Atlantic seaboard, and when tides are incoming, the flow actually backs up and moves inland. When tides go out, the flow continues on its natural journey to the sea. These are unique environments and crappies must adapt.

"In these back-and-forth flows, crappies use one side of a current break as high tide approaches, switching to the other side as low tide advances," Zaleski says. "As flow increases, they become more active, positioning themselves to ambush baitfish that are funneled past big current breaks. At high tide or low tide as flow slows to a trickle, crappie activity declines.

"When the tide isn't moving, there's nothing to concentrate crappies or position them in a predictable location. It's best to move upstream or downstream 5 to 10 miles to moving water," Zaleski says. "On a tidal system, the water's always moving somewhere."

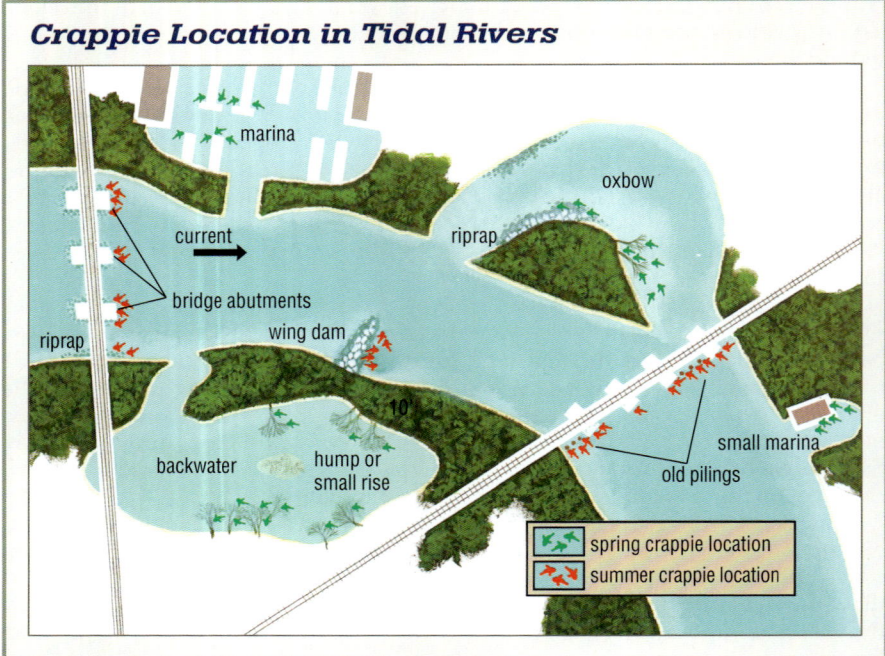

Moving well away from flowing water to spawn is a common trait among river crappies. "What I never find are early spring movements into shallow water in rivers," Zaleski notes. "I never find crappies shallow in March. They travel into bays and backwater areas behind blueback herring and alewives, which move behind any little current break they can find in 2 inches of water, where crappies can't follow. So, in spring, crappies move out into the middle of shallow bays, in 8 to 10 feet of water."

This movement takes place as water temperatures approach 58°F. "At 64°F, herring stack along the banks of those bays," he adds. "Crappies respond by holding near high spots or cover in the center of a bay. The best cover or structure reaches within a few feet of the surface, where crappies can get more sunlight on their bodies. This is similar to scenarios in lakes or reservoirs, where they use shallow cover in spring. But in tidal rivers, that cover is generally occupied by bass and blueback herring.

"Crappies in the Connecticut River spawn in May or sometimes the first week of June," Zaleski says. "Peak activity takes place when water temperatures are a bit under 70°F. The carp-like spawning activity of blueback herring and alewives that dominate the banks often pushes crappies into thick brush, where spawning activity is visible in fallen treetops over 5 to 6 feet of water. They don't spawn on the bottom but use the ends of trees, where all or most of the brush is submerged, spawning on conglomerations of branches between 1/2 inch and 1 inch in diameter. Even a sparse treetop with nothing more than a couple of sticks can hold 8 to 10 spawning crappies. They also spawn on banks, but there they often run afoul of spawning herring and alewives."

Treetops extending into 5-foot depths are prime. Tides apparently have little effect on spawning activity, as these backwaters are out of the current. "As soon as crappies finish spawning, they move into the main river, where they find sizeable current breaks," Zaleski says, "such as pilings and breakwalls next to the main current."

During early summer, crappies in some tidal rivers may concentrate in tight groups in spawning areas for a few days, before moving back into the river proper to hide behind those big current breaks. "The stronger the current, the more important big, stout, vertical current breaks become," Zaleski says. "Bridge abutments, seawalls, wing dams, or rockbars that extend above the surface and totally block the flow become key areas. The best vertical breaks extend above the surface and create large eddies on the downstream side of the structure. Bigger is better in most cases. A current break should be big enough to create enough slackwater to comfortably provide for 10 or more crappies at a time. These crappies are sociable, trying to maintain contact with the most abundant forage and with each other at the same time.

"Crappies move a lot in rivers during summer. One bridge might be productive for two or three days, but before your next visit, the fish have moved 1/2 mile to 2 miles upstream. Within a few days they might move a mile or so back downriver and finally locate on that original bridge again. Same school? Hard to say, but it's suspicious. For a short time when the water really warms up, crappies in rivers can be tough to catch. Or, perhaps I should say tough to find. If you can find them, you can generally catch good numbers," Zaleski says.

"Crappies seem to stay near the main channel in early fall, but the main river gets nasty in winter. Big concentrations of fish begin to form. Unlike river crappies in Canada and the far northern states, however, these tidal-river cousins don't go into the far ends of sloughs or backwaters to spend the winter. They usually stay in areas large enough for the entire school to congregate. That generally means bays adjacent to the main channel with minimal flow. And they don't seem to require extreme depths to winter in. Often an area with a maximum depth of 10 to 12 feet is adequate. A few hardy people get out on the water to chase them, as tidal-river crappies remain quite catchable all winter long."

OTHER FLOWING ENVIRONMENTS

Crappies live in and around current in a variety of other types of rivers and reservoirs. In the hill-land reservoirs of Maryland, they seasonally move into and back out of current areas. They move upstream in spring, out of 20- to 35-foot depths in the upper third of the reservoir to woodcover upstream in the main river. As mentioned in Chapter 4 on hill-land and highland impoundments, crappies living in the upper third of many reservoirs in North America move into and back out of the main flow of the river on a seasonal basis, dropping down into the reservoir during winter, but living in current areas from the Postspawn Period through mid-fall.

River crappies love current breaks, and current strength often determines how large a current break must be to attract fish. In rivers with minimal current, such as the Rideau River Chain in Ontario, they occupy the main river channel most or all of the year. Guide Jim McLaughlin, who works the Rideau, says crappies often position outside bridge abutments and pilings on the upstream side right in the main river channel during summer. But as Capps notes, only crazy crappies try to hold in the main flow of the lower Mississippi most of the year.

In some slow-moving rivers, crappies can use weedbeds as current breaks in the main channel. In large, powerful rivers, they're rarely found in the main channel, no matter how large the current breaks are. In northern rivers, the fish leave current areas entirely, moving as far from them as possible when the water dips below 50°F at the surface. In the South, they might stay in current areas all winter, depending on current strength and water temperature. In the North, crappies move miles to find 20 feet of water to hole up in for winter. In the South, 10-foot depths can be acceptable all winter long.

Different fish? No. Crappies everywhere are the same fish with the same needs, but different climates modify those needs. The natural range of crappies, from south Florida into Canada, covers a wide spectrum of climates, from subtropical to boreal. Crappies range through disparate river systems and topography, where varying conditions force different responses to different problems. Conditions change with latitude, climate, and terrain, but our flat-sided friends have built-in attitude adjustment capabilities that allow them to thrive in all kinds of rivers, lakes, and climates.

Keys to Finding River Crappies

- **Bays, Cuts, Backwaters**—North and South, crappies spawn out of current in areas that warm quicker than the main flow. Peak spawning typically occurs at water temperatures of 66°F to 70°F.
- **Eddies**—Heavy cover is secondary in rivers with heavy current. Crappies rarely use heavy cover without current breaks, but may use current breaks without cover. They rarely challenge the main flow of a river, preferring to use eddies where current is blunted and churns around an object or structural element, creating a large pool of slackwater in the center of the eddy.
- **Vertical cover**—Bridge abutments, sea walls, rock outcroppings, and other structures that extend from the river bottom to above the surface and block the flow of the river (especially secondary flows) are key areas in larger rivers with powerful current. The heavier the current, the larger (wider) the break must be to hold crappies.
- **Woodcover**—Trees, brush, and stumps become more important in smaller or slower rivers with less forceful current. The slower the current, the smaller a current break can be to draw crappies.
- **Current-temperature connection**—As water warms in spring, look progressively closer to and behind obstructions in the main current. As the water cools in fall, look progressively farther from the main current. In the coldest water, crappies in northern states retreat to slackwater sloughs and backwaters with good ground flow (springs or ground seepage from the water table). Crappies in the South may do the same or retreat to deep pools in slow, meandering rivers.
- **Downcurrent side**—Crappies almost always use the downcurrent side of cover, rarely positioning in open flow without a current break. Exceptions include the front face of shoals or gravel bars in slow current and large areas of reduced flow, such as a huge flat behind a land point or shoulder that diverts the main thrust of the stream.

Chapter 6
Weather and Location

The Weather Connection

HOW THE WATER WARMS AND FISH RESPOND

Does the sun warm lake water, or does the air warm it? What happens on cloudy days? Why do some backwater areas warm so much faster than others? Does the north side of a cove or lake always warm first?

Anglers want to know so they can locate where fish spawn and are active in spring, but most don't fully understand the dynamics of solar heating and water warming. The sun and warm air heat lakes and reservoirs, and cold air cools and slows the process, of course; but the details are important to understanding which waters warm first.

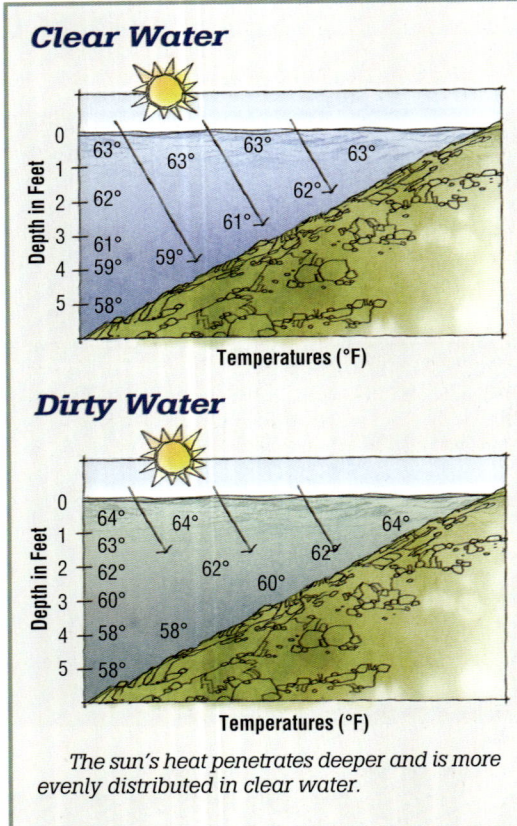

The sun's heat penetrates deeper and is more evenly distributed in clear water.

Warming waters often attract late-winter and pre-spawn crappies, while cooler areas remain fishless. Moreover, the metabolism of fish is accelerated in warming conditions. In these areas fish feed and anglers flourish.

Solar power—The sun is the dominant source of the world's heat. Sunlight heats water directly as light energy, mainly in the infrared (IR) wavelengths, and is converted into heat energy by absorption and dissipation. This heat is collected mainly near the surface as the infrared warming radiation is quickly absorbed by water molecules, silt, organic material, or plankton in the surface layer. IR radiation doesn't penetrate as deeply as other light wavelengths.

Demonstrate the rapidity of IR absorption for yourself the next time you go swimming. Your hand feels the sun's heat an inch or two under the surface, but move it deeper and the warming ends.

The air-water interface is a poor heat-exchanger. Air itself holds little heat—it's mainly the moisture in air that warms and cools. During seasons when sunlight is ample, the amount of heat exchanged between water and air usually is much less than that absorbed from sunlight. Water temperatures respond more slowly to changes in air temperature than to direct sunlight warming. Find a shallow pocket that's sheltered from wind on a warm early spring afternoon and you may be amazed by schools of sunfish, crappie, and bass seeming to bask in the sun's rays.

Weather fronts and wind effects—When cold fronts bring air colder than the water, heat is lost, and the amount of heat received from the sun usually is reduced while frontal clouds cover a lake.

Wind modifies how much heat is gained or lost. By stirring water and increasing its surface area in contact with air, winds increase the rate of heat exchange by radiation and evaporation. Heat is lost when water evaporates. But the most important effect of wind is mixing the upper layers of warmed water with the cooler water in sub-surface layers. Wind factors can be responsible for erratic fishing results—fish are here one day and gone the next, as wind shuffles the warming layers of water.

FACTORS INFLUENCING WARMING

The seasons—The angle of the sun and day length are determined by season and latitude. Higher sun angles and longer days increase the amount of heat the sun provides. From mid-December through mid-June, the sun's heat increases; from mid-June through mid-December, it decreases. Solar heating also increases during February and March, but arctic fronts repeatedly bring in air masses cold enough to slow or briefly reverse the solar heating process.

From April through August the sun's angle and day length are sufficient to steadily warm and maintain water temperatures. In many southeastern waters, the temperature can be in the high-80°F range. The dissipation of heat through evaporation and losses to cooler air put a flexible upper limit on maximum temperatures in most lakes and reservoirs that are not artificially heated by power plants. So, waters seldom exceed 95°F at the surface, even in direct desert sun.

Clouds—Water vapor of clouds absorbs some of the sun's heat. Clouds capture a portion of the warming radiation directly and reflect light, preventing some IR radiation from reaching the water. A thin cloud layer may allow solar heating to continue, while a thick overcast may block almost all solar input, allowing average air temperatures to become the dominant factor influencing daily heating or cooling of lakes. When the sun is blocked, and at night, winds and the exchange of heat between air and water become the major influences on lake surface temperatures.

Like the air-water interface, the substrate-water interface is a comparatively poor source for water warming. The sun's heat is reflected by light surfaces and absorbed by dark surfaces. Dark, shallow bottoms and rocks radiate heat rapidly into cooler air or water. This radiation can warm adjacent water slightly, but even small currents rapidly dissipate this heat, and overall water temperature isn't usually much affected in waters deeper than 2 to 3 feet during the day.

Bottom warming effects usually are significant only in clear backwaters less than 4 feet deep that have little wind current or inflowing water. Water clarity affects solar heating, too: The bottom releases significant heat only if the water is clear enough to let the

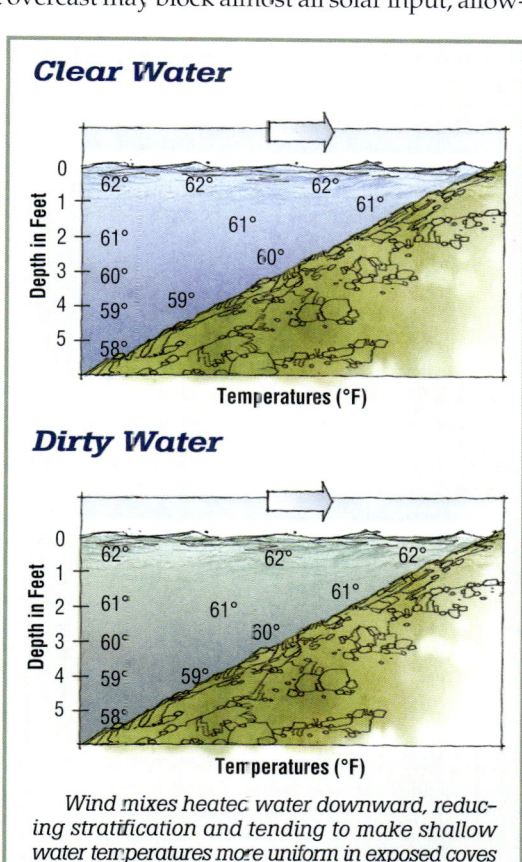

Wind mixes heated water downward, reducing stratification and tending to make shallow water temperatures more uniform in exposed coves and the mainlake, regardless of water clarity.

sun's rays reach it. Murky water traps solar heat, warming the shallow water more directly.

Lake size and shape—The size and shape of a lake greatly affect how solar heating and exchanges of heat with the air and the lake bottom influence water temperature. Large volumes of water warm and cool slowly. Ponds and shallow, isolated backwaters react much more rapidly to increases in air temperature and sunlight than main-lake areas or rivers. Main-lake waters warm more slowly and steadily as the sun's power gradually increases in spring, because winds keep stirring down the warmed surface layers and there's cold water below to absorb the warmth. Isolated coves may warm quickly, but may also cool substantially at night or during cooler weather.

Winds—Wind strength and direction are critical to whether or not temperatures of ponds and shallow coves warm or cool. When strong winds mix the surface layers of water, daily heat gains are rapidly dispersed and surface water appears to heat slowly. The overall amount of heating is the same as in wind-blocked areas, but the heat is more evenly distributed and the immediate surface layer seems cooler.

Calm days allow heat to collect in the top layer of water, so near-surface temperature measurements show much greater increases in temperature under calm conditions. But water 3 or more feet below the surface remains much cooler. If winds eventually stir down these warm surface layers, surface temperatures drop noticeably, even if air temperatures are increasing.

Strong winds often are associated with clouds and fronts. Wind effects can make it appear that cloudy frontal days are allowing no heat input, but there still can be a net heat gain if the average air temperature isn't much cooler than the surface.

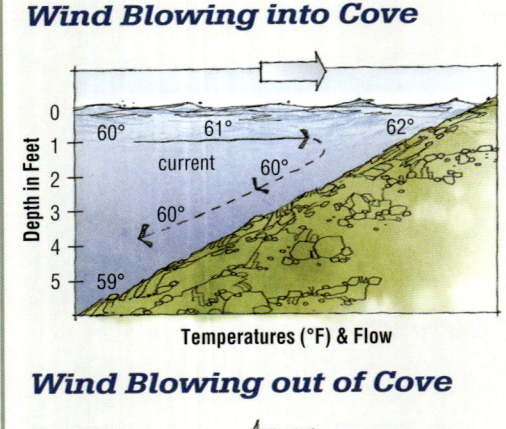

Wind can build up warm areas or flush out warmth.

HOW WARMING TRENDS AFFECT THE CRAPPIE SPAWN

To get a significant and steady warming of water to a depth of 3 to 5 feet, it usually takes a steady increase in air temperature, some sunny days, and moderate winds. To heat shallow areas as deep as 3 to 5 feet under totally calm conditions, it takes longer and sunnier days than in similar areas with wind exposure under cloudy skies. As a result, wind-blocked but deep coves may be suitable for spawning later than those exposed to some wind, even though the latter have higher surface temperatures.

The 3- to 5-foot zone is important because it takes stable conditions at these depths, rather than at the surface, to trigger crappies to spawn. They spawn when the temperature at nest depth and slightly deeper is stable and increasing, near 68°F. Males may move to nesting areas at temperatures between 62°F and 67°F and build nests at 58°F to 62°F degrees, but stable increasing conditions at nest depth are usually necessary. Very shallow nests are the first to be lost if a cold front hits after eggs are laid.

An anglers' axiom claims that the north sides of coves and lakes tend to get the most sun and warm fastest in early spring. This is partially true if trees or bluffs shade the southern shores for a significant portion of a spring day. But without shade, both sides receive equal amounts of sun, and the average and recent wind directions determine which side is warmest. Wind blows the warmer surface layer to the downwind side. If the wind has been from the north, southern shores may be warmer. Coves stretching north and south and blocked from strong winds may have one side warmer than the other, depending on prevailing wind direction. When planning a spring trip, plot recent wind trends to predict warmer locations.

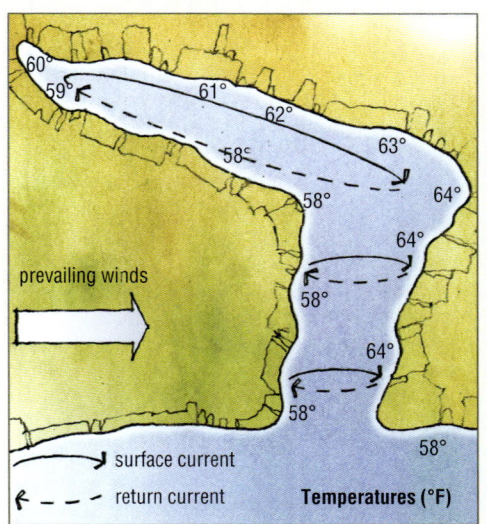

Effect of Cove Shape

The shapes and orientations of coves relative to prevailing winds modify places that warm most rapidly, and thus where bass, crappie, and sunfish spawn earliest in the season.

Air temperatures don't solely control water temperatures. But steadily increasing average air temperatures are often the most available predictor of a steady and adequate water-temperature rise sufficient to promote a spawn.

Inflows influence the process as well, and can cause mixing at different levels. Warm inflows can actually become the surface layer, while cold inflows may sink and move under warm surface layers. If they run deep enough, cold inflows may not slow a spawn at all. This is where a "down-temp" gauge pays dividends.

RAIN AND OTHER FACTORS

In spring, gentle warm-front rains often bring warmer water that floats on top of lakes and ponds, accelerating the warming process. But rain from taller clouds may come down cold, chill the surface, mix away warm surface layers, and sink to make nesting areas inhospitable to crappies for several days.

Local conditions influence warming: Light-colored vertical surfaces like an adjacent bluff or even a building can reflect additional sunlight into local areas, hastening the warming and creating earlier local spawning conditions. Outflow from a deep aquifer can supply warm water all year. In the Austin, Texas area, springs flow at 68°F to 72°F.

Anglers should monitor average air temperatures and measure surface temperatures in likely spawning coves. A continuous and steady increase in the average day and night air temperature, combined with several days of clear skies, is a good sign. Also consider the wind and rain history of the area, and look for gradually increasing surface temperatures in the coves you plan to fish. At the lake, use a temperature meter with a cable to the probe, like the Cline Finder from Catalina Technologies, to check how deep the warming effect has reached in areas protected from wind.

The past may be a good but not a sure guide to the next season. Crappies that hatched a few years earlier are the ones spawning this season. Their experience of day length and temperature stability as fry at the place they were spawned is their clue to where and when to spawn. If you caught and released their parents four years ago at a particular time and place, surviving offspring are likely to repeat the process. And individual crappies often select the same spawning location as in previous years, if habitat and water level remain suitable.

Anglers should seek areas that warm early in the spawn and those that warm more slowly later in the spring. Spawning areas exposed to wind and adjacent to deep water likely host the last spawns.

The layout of creek arms and coves can reveal places where shoreline bends trap warm water by preventing winds from blowing the warmer surface water back into the main lake. Coves with 90- to 180-degree bends often warm much earlier than straighter, wind-exposed waters.

Be sure to consider previous prevailing winds and weather patterns when studying your lake maps. Monitor surface water temps with sonar units and drop a probe to investigate key spots.

PRESPAWN PREDICAMENTS FOR CRAPPIES

If fishing were always easy, would we love it so much? Part of its fascination is facing the challenges that each day on the water brings—where to find fish and how to get them to bite.

Some days, all goes as planned. And that's fun—to a point. You can tire of catching dozens and dozens of crappies, especially if they're running the same middling size. Eight or 10 for dinner, and it becomes more fun to experiment and see what they won't bite, or whether color or lure shape makes much difference.

Without more challenging fishing trips, more of us might take up golf, a headbanger sport if there ever was one. When Tiger double-bogies, is there hope for any of us? Let's examine conditions that conspire to make spring fishing difficult, and consider ways to continue catching fish when others give up.

COPING WITH COLD FRONTS

There's no greater enemy to a hot spring crappie bite than a sudden rise in barometric pressure, coupled with chill northwesterly winds that accompany the passing of a cold front. The term brings nervousness to seasoned crappie pros and weekend anglers alike.

From our readers, TV viewers, and website browsers, *In-Fisherman* staff frequently receive the question, "What is it about a cold front that causes fish to stop biting?" There's no sure answer, though we know of several effects that alter fishing as weather patterns progress from prefrontal to postfrontal conditions. How these environmental variables physically affect fish remains a mystery. Decades of chasing crappies has revealed solutions beyond putting away the boat for a few days or driving halfway across the country.

Location solutions—Crappies aren't magic and don't disappear like creatures in David Copperfield's magic shows. Just because your hotspot has failed doesn't mean fishing as a whole has turned sour. Both black and white crappies typically make one of two position shifts under adverse conditions.

The first option is to bury deeper into cover. On a fine bright day under stable and warming conditions, you can sight-fish crappies holding in the upper reaches of brushpiles or under the floating pads of a lily patch. Pick a fish, pitch your jig-and-float, wait 6 seconds, and set the hook. Following a frontal passage, previously productive spots typically fail to produce much because crappies have shifted position and moved into thicker cover.

Instead of holding on the outskirts of brushpiles, for example, postfrontal crappies often bury within the protective branches. They seem to reduce activity and have a smaller strike window, but still bite baits placed near their faces. In natural lakes where weedgrowth, not timber or brush, offers most cover, crappies shift their position in like manner.

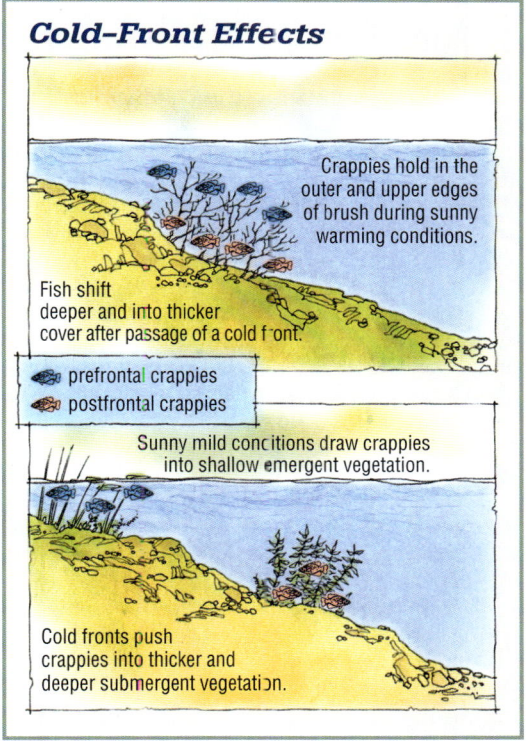

Cold-Front Effects

Crappies hold in the outer and upper edges of brush during sunny warming conditions.

Fish shift deeper and into thicker cover after passage of a cold front.

- prefrontal crappies
- postfrontal crappies

Sunny mild conditions draw crappies into shallow emergent vegetation.

Cold fronts push crappies into thicker and deeper submergent vegetation.

During mild conditions, they hover amid the upper stalks of cabbage and other grasses that grow early in spring. When the sun angle is right, you can spot fish as you drift along. Cloudy colder weather drives crappies toward the base of the vegetation, where they bury among the stalks. They're no longer visible and harder to present baits to, but they still can be caught.

Crappies that have been holding extremely shallow shift deeper after cold fronts. Fish that were holding in reeds or lily pads, for example, move out to the first breakline off the flat or toward the edge of a feeder-creek channel and suspend. These edges could be 6 to 20 feet deep in clear lakes, or just 3 to 4 feet in murkier impoundments or river backwaters.

During sunny warming conditions, crappies spread out on shallow flats, and individual fish relate to isolated cover. Once they shift deeper in response to a frontal change, however, crappies school in tighter groups. To relocate them, move the boat deeper and cast along the outside of the break, moving until you get bites. Trolling this deeper edge also works. Scouting with an underwater camera reveals groups of fish that have bailed from the banks.

Presentation solutions—Once you relocate crappies that have shifted deeper off a flat, fishing can be good, despite frontal effects. Though crappies tend to be less aggressive, their greater density means you're fishing a group of fish, not loners or stragglers. Tighter grouping also tends to heighten their competitive urge. These groups take the shape of Christmas trees on sonar. Fish the top of the "tree" first.

Relocating lost crappies is accomplished with searchbaits like mini-cranks, crappie-sized spinnerbaits, and jig-spinner combos. Run a horizontal bait through the top of the school, and a few fish will take a whack at it.

Once you start to get bites, you've probably found a concentration of fish. If action slows quickly, switch to smaller lures and fish more vertically. A small slipfloat is ideal when crappies have moved into the 6- to 15-foot zone and are holding closer to bottom in the water column.

When crappies bury deeper into cover, you have to hunker down and tease them out. Anchor by fallen trees, brushpiles, or weedbeds, and rig with small weedless jigs on delicate floats that signal the lightest bites. Delicate plastics like the Puddle Jumper, Cubby Mite, and Little Atom Nuggies Tail usually tempt some bites. Fish the baits as deep as you can without hanging up too much. Pole fishing also works well in this situation, as you can softly lower a bait into a small pocket, with or without a float.

WATER-LEVEL FLUCTUATIONS

Another confounding factor that particularly plagues anglers on rivers and reservoirs is the frequent rise and fall of water levels. Fronts generally bring heavy rains, and rising water covers shallow bays with extra feet of water, often curbing a hot bite.

Rising water location solutions—Rising water provides special challenges for spring crappies, since the fish tend to follow the rising water and move into newly flooded habitat, as long as the shallows remain warm. The murkier the water, the shallower they go.

Spring fishing on major rivers like the Mississippi means coping with variable flows and water levels. Rains upstream in the watershed or in the local pools mean rising water. The rate of the rise is difficult to predict, as these waters are under control of the Corps of Engineers and other water management authorities. Heavier rains may not mean faster-rising water, if the gates on the downstream dam are opened to allow water to move down the system.

A gradual rise in water level often stimulates a good bite, particularly if the rains haven't been chilly. Water that encroaches into backwaters and feeder creeks often covers shallow brush, grass, and logs that provide cover as fish push shallower. Waters that flood trees along main river channels or feeder creeks also provide thick, shallow cover.

Problems arise when rising water makes interminable stretches of shallows available to the fish. Crappies keep pushing shallower and scatter, making them hard to find. Rising water often floods forests along the bank, rendering it impossible to navigate through the trunks or brushy tangles. Where cover is thinner, all flooded objects look like they should hold fish, but the fish are usually too scattered to catch.

In this situation, look for flooded areas that abut a steep bank that stops any fish migration. Dikes, levees, and railroad grades often provide this sort of barrier along navigational waterways. In more natural systems, rising water may push inland until it reaches a hillside or bluff. To find fish, move to the barrier structure and fish whatever cover is available there.

Presentation solutions—Once found, crappies in flooded waters often bite well, as inflows of nutrients attract shad and minnows. These shallow areas also warm quickly and stir active feeding by bass, bluegills, and crappies.

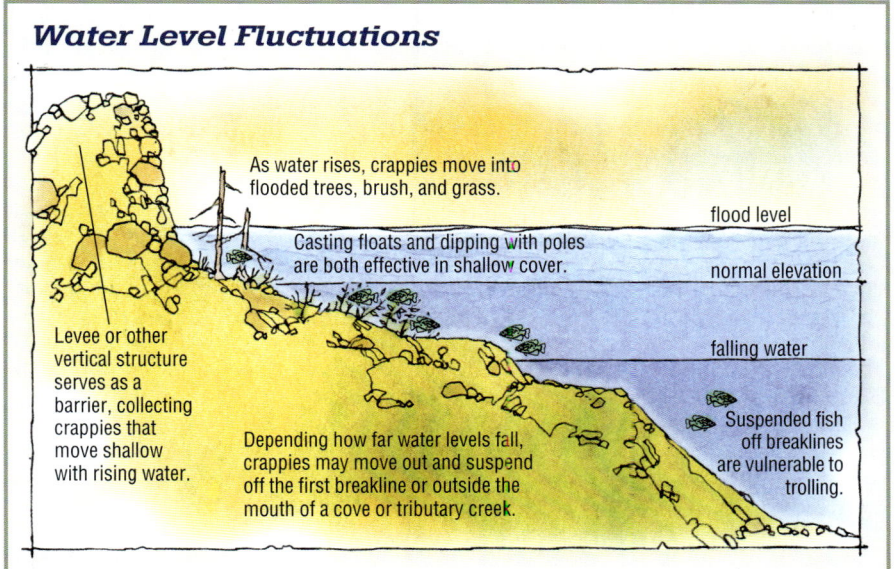

Water Level Fluctuations

As water rises, crappies move into flooded trees, brush, and grass.

flood level

Casting floats and dipping with poles are both effective in shallow cover.

normal elevation

Levee or other vertical structure serves as a barrier, collecting crappies that move shallow with rising water.

falling water

Depending how far water levels fall, crappies may move out and suspend off the first breakline or outside the mouth of a cove or tributary creek.

Suspended fish off breaklines are vulnerable to trolling.

At the other extreme is the dreaded drawdown, which can occur with seemingly little climactic impetus and more at the whim of power company authorities. One day you find your productive stumpfields baking in the sun or inaccessible to boats, as waters drop. It's a sad sight to see your previously productive lilypad or lotus beds slumped onto a mud bottom.

Falling water location solutions—As water levels fall, crappies evacuate the shallowest areas, perhaps feeling vulnerable to predators or instinctively moving to avoid being trapped in stagnant pools. Where dense cover remains, they may persist in water less than 2 feet deep, as long as it doesn't get any shallower, and may spawn among that cover.

More often, however, crappies undertake a major shift as water levels drop. Groups of fish abruptly evacuate previously flooded areas and suspend off the mouths of bays or feeder creeks.

Presentation solutions—Trolling jigs is effective once fish move to the edges of creek channels or the mouths of bays. By varying the depths of baits, you can start to pattern their position on various spots. Slipfloats also help define preferred depth ranges, once you've found the fish again.

To be successful consistently, be ready to shift location, depth, and presentation approach. Prespawn crappies might seem like easy game, but changing conditions often bring a greater challenge than we expect.

CRAPPIE PATTERNS AND WATER TEMPERATURE

Air temperature can be a guide to human behavior. As temperatures fall in autumn and early winter, outdoor activity slows dramatically. If outdoor activity ceased altogether, one might say air temperature was a controlling factor in behavior.

It's not. It's simply a guideline that points out how most people respond to conditions. Some, for instance, spend more time outdoors in winter than in summer, highlighting individual differences and preferences.

The same is true with fish. Water temperature is a guide that helps us understand how most fish react most of the time, but it's not an absolute controlling factor. Take panfish in spring. When the ice breaks up in northern states, the water temperature can be as high as 50°F in shallow, dark-bottomed bays with lots of sun exposure. Many of the panfish in any given body of water will be there, feeding—but not all of them. Some stay deeper longer in spring. Those fish tend to spawn later on main-lake spots.

Using temperature as a guide is wise, but thinking of it as a determining factor in fish behavior can be misleading, even when it always seems to work. Fish may move out of so-called comfort zones and stay out. One bluegill may react differently than another to the same temperatures. But we can predict what most panfish do most of the time by using temperature as a guide. So consider the following as general guidelines, not a list of edicts.

DIFFERENCES NORTH & SOUTH

Temperature profile is one of the main differences between northern and southern panfish location in spring. In Minnesota, a shallow bay with good sun exposure generally freezes in November and won't reach 50°F again until late April or early May. In Florida, a shallow bay on a good panfish lake might never get cooler than 50°F all winter. In Minnesota, when the water hits 50°F in spring, the panfish throw a big party and eat themselves sick. When the temperature drops to 50°F on a Florida lake, the panfish might shut their mouths and refuse to eat again for days.

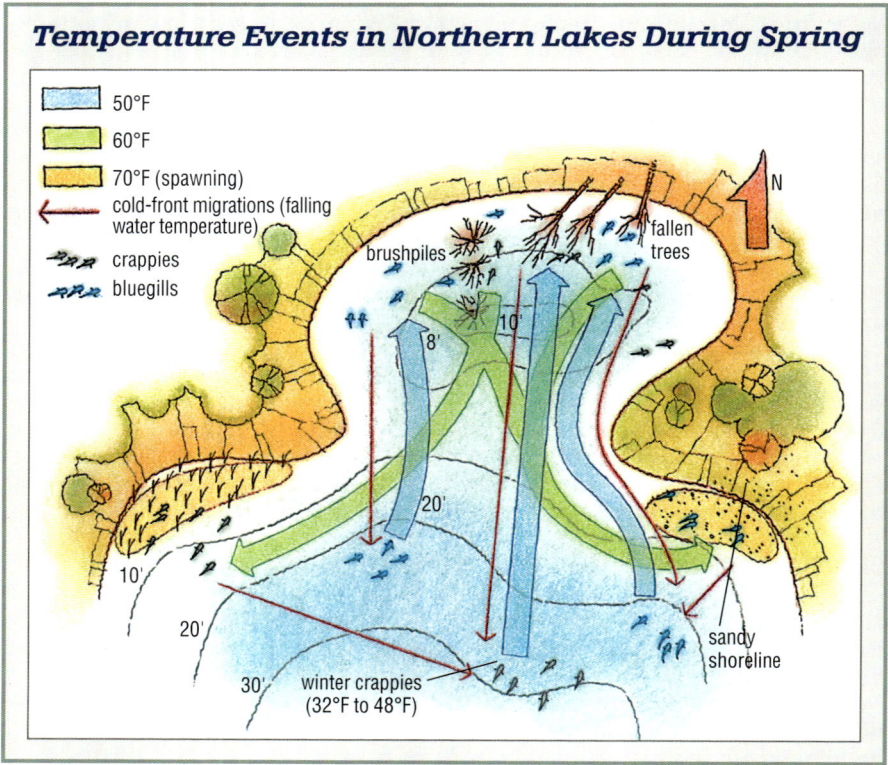

Temperature Events in Northern Lakes During Spring

That's a drastic contrast, but consider this: Traveling 50 miles north or south usually crosses a substantial climate line anywhere between Canada and Alabama. The panfish in lakes just north of you might shut down during a cold front that hardly affects the lakes near you. The fish of every lake carry with them the genetic reactions to the weather of their own micro environments over tens of thousands of years. That lake 50 miles north? The panfish in it might look the same as those outside your door, but they might react differently to similar conditions. A lake is like a library, each with its own unique genetic lineage.

Micro climates exist that consistently make certain areas on a lake colder than other areas of the same lake—springs, shade, depth, current, and water clarity. Panfish living in an area that's colder don't necessarily leave to find warmer water. Forage can become an overriding factor. The fish that do leave deep water to find warmer, shallower water probably aren't triggered by temperature at all. Panfish sometimes move from water that has been a consistent 39°F for months. The trigger could be length of daylight. Increased sunlight penetration through the degrading ice? Ennui? We don't always know precisely what triggers panfish to move from winter to spring habitats.

If water temperatures have been under 50°F for a time, that particular point on the thermometer becomes important. As waters broach that temperature, panfish turn on. It's a good time to be on the water. In Tennessee, where water temperatures typically hover in the low-40°F range all winter, 50°F water temperatures might first occur in early or mid-March. But even shallow bays in Wisconsin or New York might not reach 50°F until May.

EARLY SPRING MOVEMENTS

When the ice goes off northern lakes, some panfish may have been shallow for weeks or months. Water temperature in the main lake typically is around 40°F the day after the ice breaks up. During winter, panfish in northern natural lakes tend to spend most of the winter deep, on 20- to 40-foot flats. In many lakes, panfish arrive in shallow spots during last-ice (late March, early April). Ice fishing late in the season can produce big crappies and bluegills in reedbeds no deeper than 5 feet in some lakes. But in others, panfish won't arrive until ice leaves the shallows altogether.

If the main lake is 41°F at ice-out, shallow bays can sometimes register as high as 48°F to 52°F, especially after a few days of sunlight. Dave Genz, long-time contributor to *In-Fisherman* on panfish subjects, follows the sun in spring. "The biggest panfish move shallow first, usually during the first calm, sunny days after ice-out," he says. "It's always a big-fish pattern. Sunny days warm the shallow bays, and the lake's biggest panfish tend to be the first to arrive. Even when ice still covers the main lake, the biggest fish arrive first in bays that have thawed. I'm not a big temperature-gauge guy, but calm, sunny days in early spring are my cues to hit the water. Several days like that always precipitate hot panfish bites in early spring. The first places to check for bluegills, crappies, and perch are bays with wood like stumps, fallen trees, and brush, which seem to absorb additional solar energy. A creek flowing in, bringing warmer water, is another good sign."

Thermal zones that warm quickest in spring are prime attractions at most latitudes. In states where lakes never ice up, 50°F is still a key temperature. Bob Holmes, an accomplished bluegill guide in Tennessee, says, "...50°F is like an awakening. The water's been colder than that for months, and it triggers a major feeding spell."

Predicting Water Temperature

It's possible to predict within a few degrees what temperature the water will be. Water temperature is influenced by surrounding air temperatures. Take a reading of the water late in the day (usually its highest point). During the following days and weeks, the average daily air temperatures control what the water temperature will be. If the water reads 55°F, then nights with a low of 45°F and days with a high of 65°F won't change the water temperature much. At that point, to warm the water, look for highs of 68°F or more, with nighttime lows over 50°F.

One way to predict water temperature during spring is to keep track of daytime highs every day and add them. Divide that by the number of days to get an average daily high. Then add the nighttime lows and divide that by the number of nights, to arrive at an average low. Add the two averages together, divide by two, and the result should be pretty close to the prevailing water temperature in the main lake.

Solar influences can raise the temperature higher in shallow water, though; so to predict water temperatures in shallow bays, add about 2°F to 4°F to that total during cloudy, windy weather, and up to 10°F during sunny, calm weather.

A sample calculation: Over a three-day period, the high temperature reaches 50°F the first day, 54°F the second, and 56°F on the third. Add those together (160) and divide by 3 to arrive at an average daily high of 53.3°F. If the low temperatures those three days were 38°F, 42°F, and 44°F, the three-day total would be 84. Divide that by 3 to arrive at an average low for the three days of 28°F. Add the high average to the low average (53.3 + 28 = 81.3), dividing the total by 2 to arrive at an approximate water temperature of 40.65°F. So, in shallow bays, the water temperature could be 42°F to 50°F, depending on prevailing weather. Use simple calculations like these to keep track of water temperature and to key panfish events when you can't get on the water.

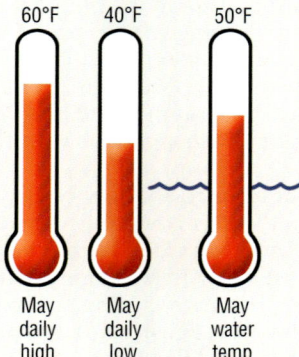

60°F   40°F   50°F

May daily high   May daily low   May water temp

Holmes spends most of his guiding days on Reelfoot, a natural lake formed by an ancient earthquake. It's a large but relatively shallow lake, with some holes approaching 20 feet. "Some crappies use those deep areas in winter, but others use shallow, dark-bottom bays, and flats thick with timber. Maximum depth is about 3.5 feet. The dark bottom and wood absorb solar energy, and we can sometimes catch crappies all day, every day, in areas like this during January and February."

Northern crappies rarely occupy such shallow areas during winter, except in flowages, backwaters, and other riverine environments.

When surface temperatures hit 50°F in shallow bays and coves, especially when temperatures have been colder than that for some time, magic happens in the panfish world. The fish bite like they've been starved for weeks, which, in fact, they have been, in some cases. Some panfish remain deep or suspended in the main lake or in the back third of major creek arms in reservoirs in the South, but they tend to bite well. In the North, the most active panfish are shallow at 50°F, using coves and shallow south-facing bays with brushy shorelines.

Since at this point, bluegills and crappies won't spawn for a month or six weeks, the main attraction could be forage density, as opposed to warmer water. Several species of panfish might occupy the same bays or spots, because small minnows concentrate in these shallow bays, too, and the warming water encourages insect hatches in shallow, soft-bottom areas. It doesn't have to be a cove or bay; big shallow flats draw them, too, when water temperatures broach 50°F.

When conditions dip back below 50°F during the day due to a cold front, the bite changes dramatically. Bluegills may move out to the base of drop-offs outside these bays, while crappies move back over open water and suspend, in a complete reversal of the shallow migration.

In states like Arkansas, Tennessee, and North Carolina, reservoir crappies in winter tend to congregate near the intersection of the main river channel and a creek channel. They occupy the front third of major creek arms, suspending over 30- to 50-foot depths or holding on breaklines in that range from November through early March. Fishing can be good at this time. "Crappies start moving out of those wintering holes at about 50°F," according to *In-Fisherman* co-founder, Al Lindner. "The first thing they do is rise. Straight up. They suspend for a short time, then begin moving toward the creek arm. Not all of them go at once. Little pods of crappies rise and slowly begin to migrate, 10 to 20 feet under the surface. Later another pod follows, so fish are spread out over a large area.

"Crappies stay or stop where they're at during bad weather," he says. "They gather for a time and stage at the creek mouth at the head of the creek arm. Huge concentrations sometimes occur, suspended over the area around the intersection of the creek arm and the main river channel. Then they spread out and migrate to the back third of creek arms, as water temperatures approach 60°F. At 60°F, most crappies begin making the transition to shallow brushpiles and wood along shorelines where they later spawn, when water temperatures reach the high 60°F to 70°F range." Of course, some crappies spawn later on main-reservoir shorelines, because it takes longer for that bigger, deeper body of water to warm.

In northern lakes, much the same happens at all key temperature points Lindner mentions. At about 50°F, large groups of bluegills and crappies gather in shallow bays, though some stay deep in the main lake (Mother Nature putting eggs in various baskets). This is not a spawning movement or "staging" in the classic sense. It's a foraging movement. Somewhere above 60°F, actual staging begins, and often, many panfish leave the areas they inhabit at ice-out, moving toward traditional spawning areas. Bluegills seek out sandy shorelines and old lily-pad beds, while crappies head for reedbeds or emerging weeds. Both species begin spawning in water temperatures approaching 70°F.

At any given juncture during these spring migrations at any given latitude, cold fronts and falling water temperatures slow the progression or even reverse the migration pattern. In Canada or Arkansas, or any point in between, panfish often retreat from shallow spots into deeper water after a severe cold front.

CRAPPIE COMPASS

Springtime slabs milling all over the place. Right here. Yesterday afternoon. But not any more. Happens to anybody who fishes crappies long enough, but where did they go? The answer is on the screen of the nearest depthfinder. Not the depth or the structure or the absence of fish showing on the screen, but the temperature readout.

Warmwater fish, like crappies and bluegills, tend to be most sensitive to temperature changes at the cold end of the spectrum. In spring, when water temperatures range from 40°F to about 60°F, crappies are more likely to relocate after a 2°F drop in temperature than they are in the balmy 80°F waters of midsummer.

The water in lakes, rivers, and reservoirs cools almost every night in early spring. The overall effect is a gain in temperature as days continue to grow longer than nights, but every night the water chills and radiates away some of the heat it gained during the day. Severe cold fronts can cause water temperatures to drop during the day. Snow, cold rain, and heavy cloud cover hold the temperature steady or allow it to slide downward, too. But these are all examples of overall cooling. In these scenarios, the water temperature drops everywhere in all local bodies of water (except in the presence of a thermal discharge, warm spring, or inflow that's warmer than the lake).

Other Temperature-Related Considerations

In perfectly calm weather, the areas that warm fastest in spring are shallow, south-facing enclosures or protected bays with dark bottoms. These areas are solar collectors, and the water that has the most sunlight striking it through the course of the day collects the most energy. Dark substrates like silt and muck absorb and radiate more heat than light-colored substrates like sand and gravel. Plankton and insect life are most active and prolific early on in these shallow, dark, south-facing areas, drawing lots of minnows. If a breeze or wind is blowing into such an area, all the better.

Shallow solar collectors are the areas we've always advised people to focus on for crappies in early spring. But just because these areas create warm water faster than other areas, it doesn't mean the warm water stays there. Check these classic spots, note the water temperature, and if crappies seem inactive or not present, move around and look for warmer water that might have been redistributed by wind or convection currents over the past few days.

In reservoirs, at least some crappies roam shallow during late afternoon and evening. Prime brushpiles and deadfalls in the warmest water collect the most active fish. Some of these areas are quite large, and it takes some hunting to find the warmest spots.

Consider the wind history of the past few days and note the current wind direction before determining which shoreline to cover first. Again, finding an area that's 2°F warmer than the rest of the creek arm tends to be more important than making the rounds of all the brushpiles that produced hot bites in the past, especially when the average water temperature is less than 60°F.

Crappies don't like any of that. In every case of overall cooling, they tend to shut off or at least become neutral during early spring. Before the dogwoods bloom, the best times to pursue crappies tend to be afternoons after the sun warms the water, during stable weather on sunny days. It's sometimes possible to finesse a bunch of crappies early in the morning or after a spate of poor weather, but it's not likely to produce lifelong memories unless somebody falls out of the boat.

But water can cool in other ways. Some of the finest crappie spots in early spring are semi-enclosed or entirely enclosed, with only a channel leading in. River backwaters, small connected basins, and partially enclosed bays are the most stable environments crappies can find early in the year. If such habitats are not available, crappies may use channels or boat canals that connect marinas or housing developments to the main body of water. Crappies find rooks, crannies, and cuts along the lakeshore, or anything they can find that reduces the effect of the wind. The fewer directions the wind can take to reach them, the better, because wind can cool off an area even when the lake is warming overall during a sunny day.

Finding enclosed or semi-enclosed areas can be less than half the battle. Some river backwaters are vast and convoluted. Some connected basins and semi-enclosed bays are huge. Where to look now?

The wind pattern has predictable problems. The shoreline where the wind blows directly in to shore only warms on sunny days or under light cloud cover. During a cold rain or snow squall, areas taking a direct wind can actually cool down. In those situations, enclosed or completely protected areas become the odds-on call. If the water temperature is dropping, even by 1/10th of a degree an hour, the bite probably is about to fade away, if it hasn't already. Look for warming water. And, in overall cooling situations, it might be a better idea to chase steelhead or trout and wait for the weather to turn.

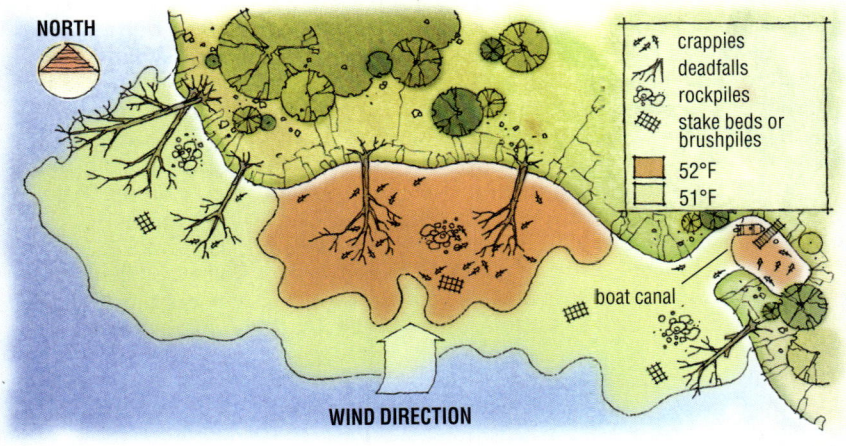

Whether crappies must endure the vagaries of large, open bays or enjoy the cozy comfort of a small isolated backwater is not the point. The point is, crappies are temperature-sensitive, more so right now than later in the season. On a warm, sunny day, crappies are biting somewhere. But you say the crappies were here yesterday? No bites today? Winston Churchill said, "If you are going through hell, keep going." Don't anchor. Don't stop. Keep one foot on the trolling motor, one eye on the temperature gauge, and keep going until you find the warmest water around.

The temperature gauge becomes the most important locational tool on the boat in spring.

It's possible to predict where that warm water is, to some extent. Even in backwaters and semi-enclosed bays—and even in well-protected canals—wind can affect localized water temperature. On a sunny day, the surface water of the lake or bay warms fastest. The warmest areas tend to be where the wind is blowing directly into shore, because warm surface waters are carried along by wind-driven currents. Where wind strikes the shore at an angle, the water tends to be cooler than where the wind hits the shore dead on. This can be an important distinction in spring, when a temperature differential of 1°F can mean the difference between a hot bite and a tepid one.

In spring, the temperature gauge becomes the most important locational tool on the boat. The key is to find the warmest water available in whatever micro environment you're in, whether it's a bay, a creek arm, or a series of canals. Say the water is 49°F in the middle of the bay. Where the wind is blowing offshore, the temperature might be 47°F. Even if the hottest bite ever known in the crappie fishing universe occurred on that spot yesterday, it probably won't be happening there today (unless the wind shifts again). Head over to the opposite side, where the wind is blowing in to shore.

Over there the first reading could be 50°F, but no biters right away. Start moving along the shoreline where the wind is blowing in, keeping an eye on the water temperature. It hits 51°F, and almost immediately you get a bite. But keep moving. I like to toss a 2-inch grub on a 1/32- to 1/16-ounce head using ultralight tackle (a 7-foot ultralight rod with 4-pound line). I slowly swim the lure back in if I'm moving fairly quickly along the shoreline. Or I could throw a Rainbow Plastics A-Just-A-Bubble and suspend a jig-minnow combo, marabou jig, or a tube as the boat progresses slowly along a break from shallow to slightly deeper water. I pull the clear plastic bubble along a foot or two at a time, then let it sit long enough for the bait to settle before moving it again.

Where the water temperature hits 52°F, crappies are everywhere, with one coming in on every cast. Keep moving down the shoreline. "What?" some might bellow in protest. "Don't leave fish to find fish." True enough. But you're not leaving, just measuring the parameters of this bite, and perhaps proving to yourself that this harebrained temperature scheme works. So, keep moving. If the warmest water in the area is 52°F, the bite should begin to taper off as soon as the temperature reading drops back to 51°F again. That's how sensitive crappies can be to temperature this time of year. If the bite doesn't taper off drastically, you may have found a massive school of fish that can't all forage together in the comfort zone.

Tomorrow this temperature band could be back on the opposite side of the bay or enclosure. It depends on the wind. In a series of canals, the way the wind affects temperature could be far trickier to predict. But the crappies are almost as easy to find. Keep fishing right through the entire area until you find the warmest water.

A pattern will develop. Each east-facing corner or turn might hold fish, or every south-facing bend, and so on.

In the scenario above, when the bite finally cools off and it's time to check other areas, you know what to look for. Wherever the water temperature reaches at least 50°F in that body of water, you should be able to find active, biting fish.

It's possible to have water temperatures over 55°F in one bay or area, while the next area you check has no water warmer than 50°F. Crappies that have committed to a bay or area won't leave and cross the lake to find water that's 5°F warmer. Find the warmest water in the area (in this case, 50°F), and the bite could be just as hot as it is in that 55°F water a mile or two away.

Check the places where crappies bit furiously last year and the year before, yes. But if crappies seem to be absent, start hunting for warmer water. Even spots devoid of proper cover can draw more crappies if the water is a couple of degrees warmer than the surrounding area. Use the "crappie compass" (your temperature gauge) to find more and bigger fish this spring.

WHEN CRAPPIES MOVE SHALLOW IN WINTER

Standing a few feet over the head of your targeted species, drilling holes in ice with 4 feet of water underneath seems ridiculous. Everybody knows that the warmest water in a frozen lake is down near bottom in deep to mid-depth basins, because water is most dense at about 39°F. Water warmer or colder than that rises. Panfish, as a rule, leave the shallows to trout and pike in winter. Even in reservoirs with open water, in states like Arkansas and Tennessee, most of the panfish move deep—usually somewhere between 20 and 40 feet. But not all of them, and not all the time.

Exceptions to the winter-equals-deep-panfish equation abound, even in the ice-bound states. *In-Fisherman* Editor In Chief Doug Stange: "In several Iowa lakes I once fished, several series of canals are dredged for homeowners. These canals are no deeper than 5 or 6 feet, yet sometimes draw panfish during winter," he says. "A typical canal might go straight for 100 yards, then elbow or branch off in another direction for another 100 yards or more.

"Panfish sometimes push all the way to the back end of these features during fall and throughout the ice season. Eventually, they settle into some little pocket of slightly deeper water, or a spot with slightly better environmental stability, or something of that nature, until anglers or pike find them.

"Fishermen find a pocket of panfish on these canals and catch them until they thin them out—or pike move in. Then they catch pike for a few days, and eventually the panfish set up in that spot again. Or not. It really isn't a stable pattern. But, for those who find it, it's theirs and theirs alone for several days to a week."

Dave Genz, professional ice-fisherman extraordinaire, says marginal-ice states like Iowa have more green weeds throughout winter. "The weeds stay green and oxygen counts are higher in states where the ice doesn't get as thick and snowfall measures less," he says. "In places like Michigan's lower peninsula, Illinois, New York, and Nebraska, I've found lots of panfish biting in water less than 8 feet deep during January.

"You're looking for 39°F water," Genz continues. "When the sun is up, the water under the ice will actually warm up, warmer than the ice itself, late in the season. At times it can reach temperatures up to 44°F a few feet under the ice. That's why panfish locate right under the ice sometimes. I always thought it was because of food—which is probably a factor—but since I started taking temperature readings with Aqua-Vu underwater cameras, I've noticed surprising variations in temperature 2 to 6 feet down. That phenomenon only happens late in the year up in Minnesota or Canada when the sun gets up high in the sky and melts the snow, and water runs through holes in the ice. The rays of the sun penetrate at that point, and the angle of the sun is high enough to actually warm the water just under the ice."

In more southerly latitudes, that warming under the ice or on the surface of lakes that cooled over the previous months is possible at any point during winter. "In lakes that support vehicle traffic in winter, you won't find as many shallow patterns in midwinter," Genz says. "In southern Michigan or northern Indiana, weeds tend to stay green all winter because more ultraviolet light gets through."

Yet, even in northern Minnesota, shallow panfish bites can occur in shallow water. Stange says: "We have a few large lakes near the office (in Brainerd, Minnesota) that have little bays or basins connected to the main lake by small channels. These often hold panfish all winter. In one case, panfish have to squeeze through a little channel that's only 4 to 5 feet deep. They might have only a foot of water under the ice to travel through.

"Nobody was fishing these bays through the ice until about 12 years ago," he says, "and now it's a popular spot. One small bay beyond the channel has a 20-foot hole, but no inlet. Somebody has to investigate before most of these shallow patterns are found throughout the country, because factors that can't be registered with the naked eye play a role in determining where panfish might hold in winter."

Genz directs the Trap Attack circuit of ice-fishing tournaments each winter. "In southern Michigan, during the first weekend in January, fish are caught in 6 to 15 feet of water, inside the weeds. In Illinois, during the Trap Attack in mid-January last year, participants were catching Chain of Lakes panfish inside the weedline in 5 to 7 feet of water, because the oxygen content was high in the shallows. Some of the weeds were green, but a lot were brown, too. The oxygen counts remained high, possibly because of plankton counts. What we can't tell by looking at the water is the plankton count."

Zooplankton requires oxygen, too, and it's provided not only by green weeds, but also by phytoplankton—plants of the microscopic world. Biologists studying plankton counts throughout the year have noted that populations can crash during winter, especially in the Far North, and especially during harsh winters with thick ice and heavy snowfall. The more snow and ice a lake has over its surface, the harder it becomes for sunlight to penetrate. Sunlight is, of course, the key to photosynthesis—the process by which green plants create food, giving off oxygen as a by-product.

Dying weeds not only stop producing oxygen but also create an oxygen deficit. The bacteria and other organisms that aid in the process of decay increasingly consume oxygen as death rates and decay increase. Normally, larger fish can't be found around brown, decayed weeds. But in the presence of unusually high counts of phytoplankton, panfish sometimes remain. The only way to find out is to look. Traditional thought patterns are hard to break—something any fisherman can turn into an advantage over the locust-like swarms of winter panfishermen we find out on the ice.

"On the Finger Lakes, in New York, we caught nice bluegills in the weeds during late January last year," Genz says. "We don't catch panfish deep in those lakes during winter. The water is exceptionally clear, and the weeds stay green all winter. And it doesn't freeze until Christmas, giving wave action an extra month or so to mix oxygen into the water, compared to lakes in Minnesota, Canada, or northern Wisconsin. In cloudier lakes near the Finger Lakes, however, deep panfish patterns exist. The thing to keep in mind isn't what panfish generally do, but what they generally do in your area. In all the mid-latitude areas we've mentioned—southern Michigan, Illinois, and Iowa—deep patterns for panfish persist all winter. It's just a matter of knowing the environment where you're fishing."

And even that can change. "When heavy snow comes early, look deep. When snow cover is light, look shallow," Genz advises. "Mild winters tend to promote shallow patterns, while harsh winters tend to drive panfish deep in many of these systems. The key is knowing your lake."

PATTERN IDENTIFICATION SYSTEMS

The keys to winter patterns for panfish are oxygen, food, and environmental stability, which includes water temperature, sunlight penetration, and mixing effects caused by convection. Certain systems and their characteristics tend to promote shallow panfish patterns in winter. River backwaters probably comprise the best-known shallow patterns for bluegills and crappies during the cold months. Some of the finest ice and shallow open-water fishing for big crappies from Minnesota to Louisiana occurs in 6 feet of water or less on backwaters of the Mississippi River.

Panfish really don't want to deal with current during winter. When the water is cold, current becomes for fish what wind chill is for humans. In long stretches of river between dams, where panfish have no lakes or reservoirs to retreat to, they push back into oxbows and backwaters off the main river, as far from current as possible. In many cases, these backwaters are no deeper than 5 or 6 feet throughout.

A 10- to 12-foot hole can stack panfish dramatically in these environments. If no deeper holes exist, panfish tend to find areas (1) protected from north winds, (2) with islands, reeds, or cane between them and the current, and (3) with a mix of substrates. Different bottom types hold different kinds of invertebrates, so a mix of hard and soft bottom is good to find when hunting backwater panfish in winter.

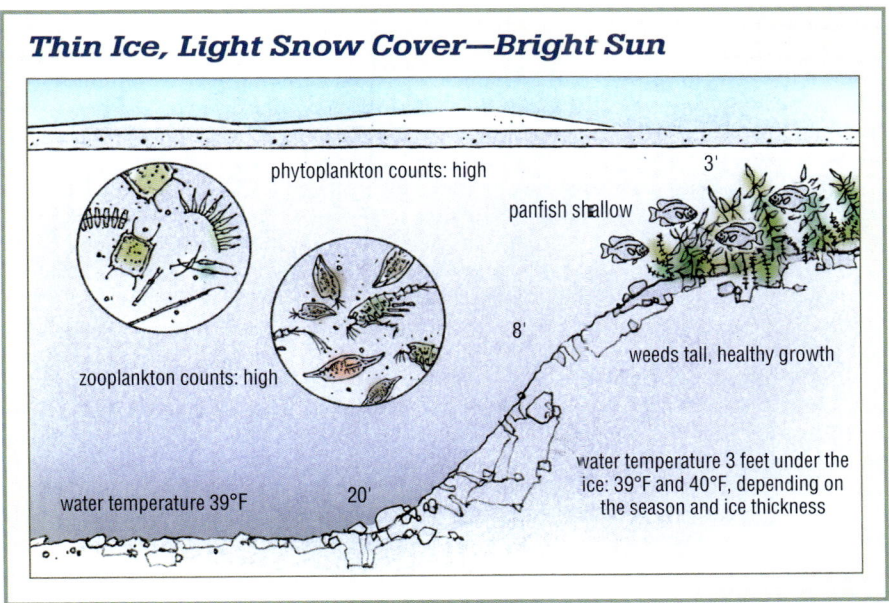

Thin Ice, Light Snow Cover—Bright Sun

The Weather Connection

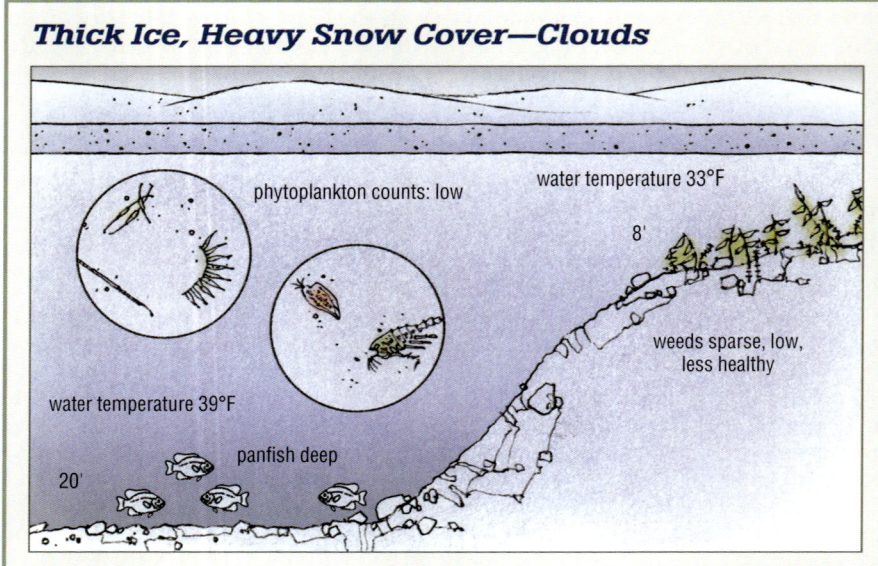

Thick Ice, Heavy Snow Cover—Clouds

phytoplankton counts: low
water temperature 33°F
8'
weeds sparse, low, less healthy
water temperature 39°F
panfish deep
20'

Even though river backwaters become encased in ice in Minnesota, North Dakota, and northern Wisconsin, panfish populations can flourish in 6 feet of water because the main river delivers oxygen and plankton to the periphery of these environments, and it mixes in through the process of convection. If oxygen content drops in backwater areas, panfish are forced to relocate in areas closer to (but never in) the main current.

In southern reservoirs that never ice up, crappies still tend to locate deep. Here, vertically jigging for crappies in 50 feet of water is not uncommon during January and early February. These fish tend to congregate near primary and secondary points, near the confluence of creek channels with the main river channel. But creeks entering secondary arms within these major creek arms can sometimes collect large numbers of crappies in water 10 feet deep or less. Flowing creeks become solar collectors, pushing warm or highly oxygenated water into the reservoir.

As Genz mentions, clear lakes permit more sunlight to reach weeds even with a layer of ice on the surface. And in latitudes where ice cover lasts only two months or so, panfish can survive in much shallower environments. In Canada and Minnesota, it's rare to find panfish in lakes with main basins shallower than 20 feet—shallow lakes "freeze out." Oxygen content becomes too low during winter to support anything bigger than a minnow. As you move south, panfish can persist in increasingly shallow environs.

In the Valentine National Wildlife Refuge in Nebraska, for instance, lakes with basins no deeper than 8 feet support trophy bluegills—some weighing more than 2 pounds. Genz, who has fished the Valentine lakes, says the key is just to keep drilling holes and looking for the thickest patches of green weeds, then concentrate all your effort there. Most trophy bluegills are caught in 5 feet of water.

Even in southern Michigan, bass and panfish populations eventually establish themselves in ponds created by highway construction. Many of these ponds are only 12 feet deep or even less, yet support bass over 4 pounds and crappies over a pound, which would be unheard of in North Dakota or Minnesota.

By late winter, even the harshest panfish environments of the Far North begin to develop shallow patterns. The first places where the ice thins are near shore and throughout shallow bays. The thinner the ice, the higher the plankton count. More sunlight hits bottom, and water warms fastest under the ice in shallow bays. With ice pulling away from shore, air and water once again mix, providing another source of oxygen. Up North, reedbeds surrounding these shallow bays, even out on the main lake, can provide hot fishing for bass and panfish under the ice. As holes develop through the ice around the stalks of old reeds (also thermal collectors), allowing both sunlight penetration and a slight mixing of air and water.

In river backwater areas, in extremely clear lakes that freeze over, and throughout the mid-latitudes of the United States, shallow patterns for panfish persist all winter long, and some interesting techniques have developed for approaching fish swimming around just a rod length under our feet.

SHALLOW WINTER TACTICS

In southern reservoirs, where open water permits casting, checking for big midwinter slabs in shallow water can be relatively quick and easy. Find an inlet protected from the wind, anchor, and ply two or three methods at once. Cast one line rigged with a minnow on a light jig under a slipfloat, while casting light jigs and 2-inch plastic grubs on 4-pound line. A 2-inch actiontail grub can be retrieved slowly and sometimes draws following fish toward the bobber rig.

Use a 7-foot ultralight rod to propel these little packages out there, and cover a lot of water from one spot. In deep hill-land reservoirs, cover the top 5 feet of the water column over nearby openwater areas, too. Sometimes crappies suspend just off the first or second break from inlet streams. In shallow reservoirs, check the surrounding flat. My favorite plastic colors when searching for slabs in reservoirs are white, salt-and-pepper, and natural shad patterns, since crappies are hunting shallow shad and shiners in most (if not all) of these environments.

Up North, look for reedbeds near openings to shallow bays. If panfish have evacuated these areas, they might return during the late-ice period sometime in March or, farther north, in April. Check shallow bays with inlet streams that have enough current to prevent the creek from freezing up altogether. And find shallow areas where green weeds persist well into winter. The easiest way to find the densest patches of healthy weeds is in a boat, just before ice-up.

To investigate new areas, drill a few holes, look around with an underwater camera, and quickly move on if fish aren't present. If fish are visible, give them a quick try. No action? Move on. Genz says drilling holes attracts fish (I believe it sometimes attracts fish, and sometimes not). Come back to those holes and check them again, especially if you're pulling up green weeds with the jig. Leave the weeds next to the best holes for a quick visual reference, and toss decaying weeds off to the side.

Genz generally prefers to fish for shallow panfish the same way he fishes for deep panfish—using the same jigs, line, and rods. Most of the time, he uses Berkley ice rods that he designed, with 2-pound line and small Lindy ice jigs (most of which he also designed). He baits the jigs almost invariably with live maggots (Eurolarvae, in various colors). The Trap Attack tournament trail, however, opened his eyes to the effectiveness of certain shallow tactics.

"Some of the anglers from southern Michigan, northern Indiana, and Illinois are effective in shallow water, but they're kind of lost in deep water," Genz says. "They're learning fast, but some of them thought they could adapt their shallow-water methods to deep basin fishing and discovered it really wouldn't work. But deep-water fishermen can't beat these guys around shallow weedbeds."

Midwesterners with lots of shallow panfish under the ice have developed some interesting techniques. Ice fishermen from Indiana showed us over a quarter century ago how effective they can be in shallow water. The weapon of choice is an old-style rod with a set of wooden pegs just above the handle. Line is looped around the pegs, which serve in place of a reel. The line of choice is original golden Stren, which is tough, coily in cold weather, and highly visible.

The pegs and the memory in the line are integral to the technique. The lure is an unbaited ice fly—basically a weighted nymph, much the same as might be found in any fly-fishing vest. Bright green or chartreuse threads are favorite colors among the materials used to make these flies, due to the darker waters these men fish. The hook is wrapped with just enough copper wire to ensure a slow, vertical drop. Nymph hooks used to tie these flies vary from a #10 to a #6, and the size of the body varies accordingly. The fly can't be extremely small, because visibility is poor. The fish being caught were only 3 to 6 feet under the hole most of the time, yet they couldn't be seen.

As the fly is lowered into the hole, the line is slowly uncoiled from the pegs. It retains kinks, and that's the key to the technique. The kinks become, in essence, the bobber. A lightly weighted fly is slow to drop. When drop speed increases or kinks in the line straighten, it's time to set the hook.

Setting the hook into a bull bluegill or rogue largemouth with 3 feet of line out can prompt a real fire drill. Pegs don't have drag. Veterans quickly turn the rod and hold it over the hole, letting line run off the pegs while pressing a finger against it to keep it from all uncoiling at once. These boys use some pretty stout line—6-pound test or so, and original Stren is pretty tough. If they choose a good nymph hook for the fly, landing big fish isn't that much of a problem.

Many of the shallow winter bites encountered, however, involve clear water. Black crappies and bluegills are the most likely species found shallow in extremely clear water, where weeds have the best shot at staying healthy under the ice. Stealth becomes critical. Don't move around much, drill holes early, leave the area, and quietly creep back later.

Use 2- to 3-pound-test fluorocarbon line and tiny 1/100- to 1/200-ounce jigs tipped with a single maggot, or use a #12 treble with a small crappie minnow. Forget the split shot. It takes only 10 to 20 seconds for a tiny jig or unweighted treble to fall 5 feet or so on fluorocarbon line. Use a shelter to keep sunlight from flooding down the hole, and use your eyes as opposed to a camera.

Shallow winter bites for panfish are one of the last frontiers under the ice in the North and in many southern reservoirs. Most anglers apparently refuse to aggressively pursue some of these possibilities until classic patterns thin out. They'll find intrepid anglers with a flair for exploration waiting for them.

Crappies and Cover _____ **Chapter 7**

How Crappies Relate to Cover

WEEDCOVER

The crappie is a swimming contradiction, a common household fish enshrouded by myths. Many of the generalities about crappies don't hold true much of the time.

A small panfish? Maybe, if anglers have cropped too many big ones. Everywhere they exist, crappies of the black and white persuasion can reach three pounds or more. The world record is a 6-pounder.

Skittish biters requiring small baits, bobbers, and the like? Not when they've cornered a shoal of minnows and viciously slash the surface to engorge several fish at a time.

How Crappies Relate to Cover 135

An open-water fish demanding skilled sonar use and tackle to suspend baits at their chosen depth range? Not in spring, when they camouflage themselves and sulk among the densest cover.

This last aspect of the capricious crappie is the topic of this tale. During spring, anglers have or soon will have a shot at some of the best, yet some of the most challenging crappie fishing of the year.

The crappie's preference for cover makes spring crappie fishing easy while simultaneously challenging, yet another contradiction. A recount of recent early-season crappie trips shows how choice of cover can be critical to fishing success.

The first outing involved the exploration of a large, mesotrophic natural lake just as the ice was breaking. We found access to most bays off the main lake impassable, as great sheets of ice pressed against the northern shore, propelled by a mild southerly wind.

Relaunching in a small bay, we began to check patterns, experimenting with livebaits and lures, depths, and cover options. The dense brush gathered by beavers seemed likely, in depths from 1 to 5 feet. Nobody home—a verdict arrived at after 5 minutes of watching floats bob in the afternoon breeze. Tattered remains of lily pads similarly failed to yield crappies, though some bass made things interesting on our light rigs.

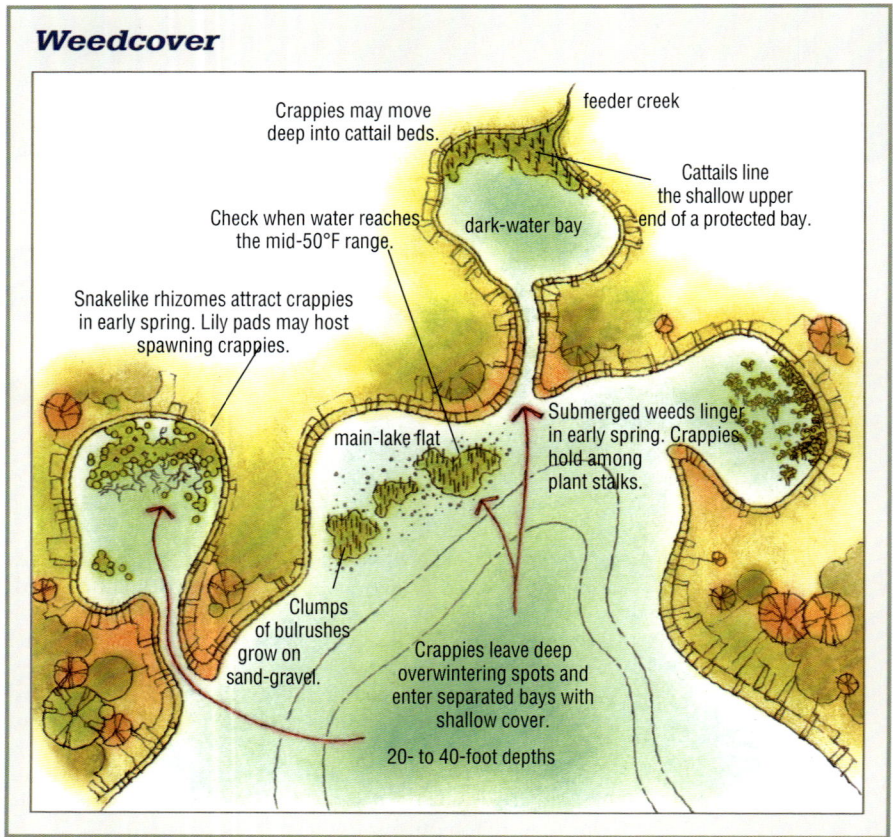

Finally, drifting within hailing distance of a local crappie guide and his client, we discussed the bite. Seems the pair had begun picking up a few fish by letting their Puddle Jumpers barely tick the tops of eelgrass and decaying cabbage that carpeted the bottom in 3 to 5 feet of water. Though they tried to minimize the splashing at boatside, they clearly were onto something

We, too, were ready with Puddle Jumpers, a staple year-round soft plastic bait, and we soon joined the action. We rigged our 1½-inch lures on minute jigheads and suspended them on Thill Shy Bite floats. Toward dusk, the crappies ventured more confidently from the thick bottom-hugging weeds, offering a torrid bite in the 42°F water.

A week of mild temperatures opened the lake completely and raised water temperatures in protected bays well into the 50°F range. In shirt-sleeve weather, we fished another bay, one that warms fast due to dark bottom sediments and shallow depths. Here, lily pads provide cover throughout, but the ravages of winter ice left only the sturdy rhizomes from which the plants grow.

Some of these root systems were as big around as baseball bats and twisted like boa constrictors. Eliminating several other cover options, we investigated the rhizomes closely. We could see big black crappies hanging under the stems, their ebony snouts tight to the musty stalks.

They were black as coal with hardly a gold fleck to their flanks. Crappies turn dark to absorb maximum sunlight. The heating process then keys their metabolism for greater feeding and quicker egg maturation.

Some anglers suppose that only spawning males turn coal black. That transformation does occur, but these early prespawn fish were of both sexes. Though we had found the fish, they weren't so easily caught. An hour or two of altering rigs indicated that either pitching a small float and bait or dabbling with a long rod would entice bites.

The long-pole presentation was precise but spooked some fish as the boat approached, maneuvered by the trolling motor. An underhand pitch with a 7-foot spinning rig was nearly as accurate, and less alarming to the fish when rigged with a clear-plastic casting bubble set just a foot above a tiny Cubby Jig. But both methods took good numbers of beautiful crappies, many too big to keep.

COVER CATEGORIES

In those early-spring excursions, crappies favored two types of vegetation in two bays. But plenty of other options exist.

Cattails—In a tracking study on two South Dakota waters, crappies favored cattails for spawning sites in one of the waters, a narrow reservoir.* But they didn't just move into the edge of the emergent grasses; they burrowed into them. Ultrasonic telemetry equipment allowed the researchers to locate a fish to within a square yard, but murky water and dense plants prevented them from visually detecting the fish. In that study, several crappies couldn't be found, and the biologists felt they might have ventured into grassbeds so thick that they couldn't be heard on the hydrophone or approached via boat.

Cattails are prime crappie cover in darker waters where submerged vegetation is limited. The stalks stand year-round, though in winter they turn yellowish-brown. In early spring, crappies swim among the grouped stalks, feeding on minnows and invertebrates. Later they spawn on nests swept on harder spots within the stands of plants.

Like lily pads, cattails tend to grow in shallow bays and creek arms protected from prevailing winds and warming early in spring. In the South Dakota tracking study, another key factor emerged. The study reservoir contained two major arms, but only one had a deeper channel running through it. The crappies strongly favored that arm over the shallower one, which also offered abundant cattail beds.

Maidencane—Maidencane is an emergent grass that grows in water from 2 to 6 feet deep. This plant provides more corridors among its stalks than cattails, offering excellent spring habitat for crappies, as well as largemouth bass and sunfish. As a rule, maidencane grows on harder bottoms than cattails and more often thrives on offshore humps and bars.

Bulrushes—Several species of rushes or reeds offer prime cover for crappies in spring. Bulrushes grow in stands that vary greatly in density. At times, clumps of stalks grow several feet apart, providing access lanes and pockets in every direction. At other times, the plants form an almost impenetrable wall. In any case, they grow best on a combination of sand and fine gravel.

Not coincidentally, crappies often select this type of bottom for nest building. Occasionally smallmouths also spawn here, while bluegills and largemouth bass typically find slightly softer bottoms, and rock bass favor areas without much cover.

Once water temperatures rise into the mid- to upper-50°F range, crappies begin exploring stands of bulrushes, first holding in the deepest outside fringes of the grass and later pushing toward shore in the shallowest reeds. In clear lakes, crappies can be spotted by perching high in the bow and slowly meandering through the area with a trolling motor.

Submerged vegetation—On lakes or reservoirs without shallow bays, crappies hold much deeper until water warms into the mid- to upper-50°F range. Submerged plants offer prime cover in water from 8 to 12 feet deep. Often the bright sprigs of cabbage can be seen glistening in the depths on a sunny day. Suspending a minnow, grub, or small jig can produce steady action, as fish tend to be grouped in particular spots.

Pondweeds offer rather elegant cover, but crappies aren't aesthetically inclined. They also rest under the slimy remains of dead coontail and algae in early spring, which hides them and also seems to absorb heat as the dark mats float under the surface. This type of vegetation is difficult to fish, particularly as it's often ultra-shallow, and the crappies in it are spooky.

After crappies spawn, they sometimes hide in thick vegetation like cabomba and milfoil that often carpet bays in depths of 4 to 8 feet deep. Casting a Roadrunner or Beetle Spin over these beds, like slow-rolling for bass, can work incredibly well, as the warming water boosts the fish's metabolism to chase slow-moving lures.

Fallen trees—In undeveloped natural lakes and reservoirs, fallen trees also create prime spring cover for crappies. The horizontal spread of branches provides protection from above and allows crappies to suspend just inches below the surface, absorbing the sun's strongest rays. Tree branches may, of course, hold crappies year-round, depending on depth. Shoreline fallen trees are prime cover in late spring.

Crappies tend to favor branchy trees such as pines and willows, contrary to largemouth bass who like broad branches and massive trunks. In early spring, trees that stretch from the bank over water 4 or 5 feet deep, or even more, hold fish first. As the water warms, shallow trees also attract them.

Stumps—One of the top spring crappie patterns in older hill-land reservoirs is stumpfields. Prior to flooding, reservoir managers trim trees in most shallow

Woodcover

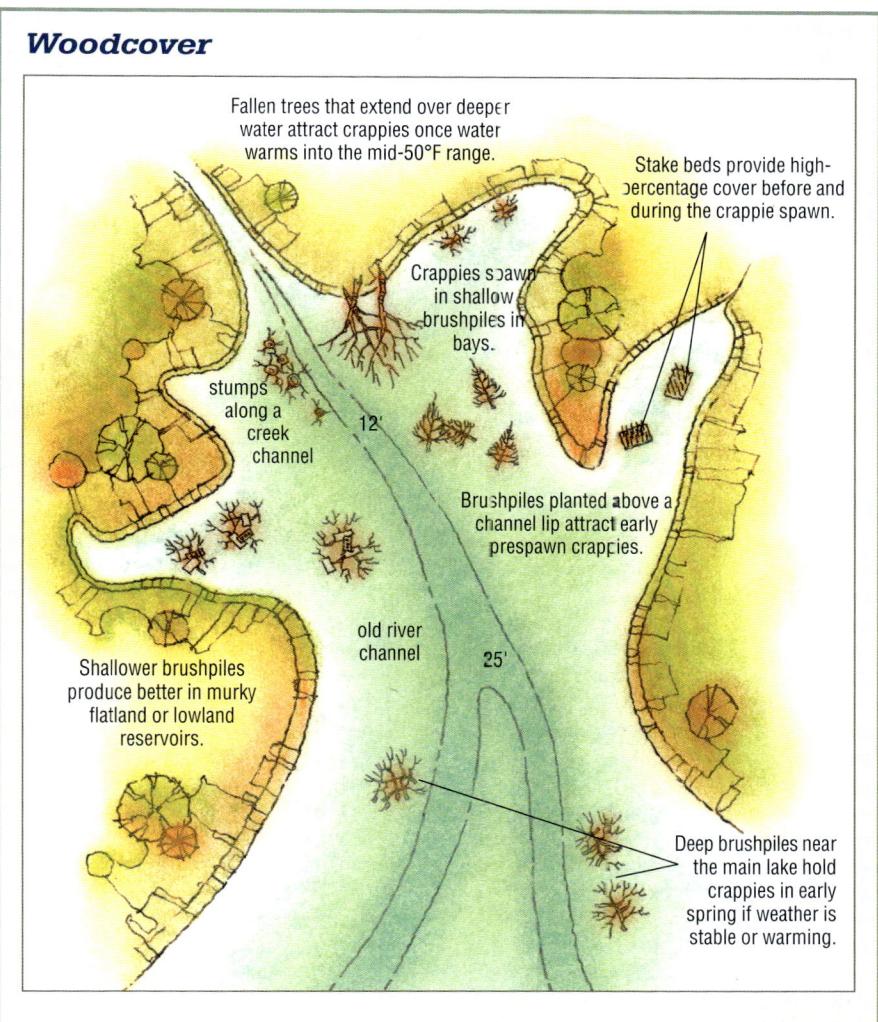

Fallen trees that extend over deeper water attract crappies once water warms into the mid-50°F range.

Stake beds provide high-percentage cover before and during the crappie spawn.

Crappies spawn in shallow brushpiles in bays.

stumps along a creek channel

12'

Brushpiles planted above a channel lip attract early prespawn crappies.

old river channel

25'

Shallower brushpiles produce better in murky flatland or lowland reservoirs.

Deep brushpiles near the main lake hold crappies in early spring if weather is stable or warming.

coves but leave the stumps. Over the years, wave action unearths the root system of many stumps and tips some on their sides. This expansive cover draws fish as they move from deep wintering areas toward the shallows.

Stake beds—In reservoirs where crappies are king, like Kentucky Lake, anglers and management agencies plant stake beds to attract crappies in spring. These artificial structures, formed from a plywood base with 1' x 2' planks nailed to it, are powerful springtime crappie attractors. Groups of stake beds are placed in creek arms, where flats off the channel provide level bottom in 1 to 6 feet of water.

After the stakes have been planted, algae forms on the wood, attracting small shad that in turn attract crappies. Crappies sometimes spawn alongside the slats, as well. Anchoring within reach of several productive beds can yield hours of fine fishing.

When biologists electrofish these structures to test their effectiveness, the water turns black and silver with floating fish. At times, anglers give up too easily, abandoning a structure after a few minutes. In early spring the bite can be slow, particularly if cool winds and cloudy skies chill the water. An ultra-slow presentation and lots of experimentation with color pays off.

Brushpiles—These constructed tangles of Christmas trees, brush, and small hardwoods are another important category of cover wherever anglers or fishery agencies have planted them. As crappies move from wintering areas on deep flats toward shallow bays, they often linger in piles placed at structural transitions at the mouths of feeder creeks.

Look for piles placed on the shallow side of the break, in water from about 8 to 15 feet deep. In murkier flatland impoundments, crappies push shallower and use shallower brushpiles than in clear hill-land or highland impoundments.

The first shifts into brush are tentative, however, and cold fronts push the fish back out until water temperatures stabilize in the mid-50°F range. As the water continues to warm, crappies push shallower, occupying shoreline cover or shallow brushpiles in the back of creek arms.

PRESENTATION OPTIONS

Each form of cover demands modifications in lure and bait presentation; sometimes rod and reel combinations must be switched, too. As crappie anglers become more versatile, they need more than one "crappie rod." Bass anglers, of course, have taken this to the limit, with tournament competitors often toting more than a dozen sticks with different blank actions and spooled with various lines, each for a particular situation.

In the toughest cover situations, say in dense cattails, crappies are almost unreachable. In the tracking study, the researchers couldn't push their jon boat far enough into the marsh to hear the tiny tags beeping. You probably can do no better with your fishing boat.

And trying to wade these soft-bottom sloughs is messy, perilous, and prone to spook fish even if you reach them. In most cases, you're best off testing the edges of the thick grassbeds, for their pockets and proximity to deeper water usually make them high-percentage spots in early spring.

Rod choice—Casting with a 7-foot light-action spinning rod equipped with a sizable reel and 4-pound abrasion-resistant mono or 6-pound flexible line is a great starting point. If fish are spooky, as when they hover just below rhizome stalks, you can stay back but make long casts past the thicket, then gently pull a float and bait close to the fish. For closer action, use the same rig to make an underhand pitch. Accuracy is superb and the entry splash minimal.

Try that approach when you find spawners scattered among bulrush beds or lily-pad fields in late spring. The pitch also works well for moving down a bank with fallen trees, picking fish from pockets among the branches. In dense trees, increase your rod power and line strength so you can bend hooks that snag. Crappies in trees tend to be less line-shy than those holding in vegetation in clear, shallow water.

For casting small spinners, choose a 6- to 6½-foot medium-action spinning rod spooled with abrasion-resistant 6-pound-test mono. When retrieving over dense vegetation, try SpiderWire 4/20 or other thin-diameter braid. These lines cut through vegetation and maintain contact with fish in the thickest mats.

Long poles are traditional for probing stumps and stake beds in crappie hot spots like Kentucky Lake and Lake Eufaula in Alabama-Georgia. They work well anywhere crappies hold in shallow cover. Rigging with a small balsa or Styrofoam float pegged a foot or two above a tubebait is hard to beat.

With a pole, you can impart the slightest wiggle to the float, causing tentacles on the tube to barely breathe. When the float disappears, hoist the fish out of its woody abode without spooking the rest of the nearby clan.

Most commercial telescoping crappie poles run from 8 to 15 feet long. European-style poles—up to 41 feet long, yet telescoping down to just 4 feet—are available from Aurora Rods. Cane poles work too, a lower-cost and functional option.

Baits—Crappies are in a positive feeding mood in spring, first as they hunt and fatten up for the spawn, then as they go into their annual growth spurt. In early spring, small minnows draw them into narrow channels and shallow bays. These inch-long fish are a staple, hence the popularity of "crappie minnows."

Some aficionados who use only artificials for crappies claim greater success with marabou jigs, tubes, plastic tails, and other lures. The debate won't be settled, as an almost equal number of anglers believes in livebait above all.

From earliest ice-out into the Postspawn Period, we always hedge our bets by bringing a selection of artificials, a bucket of minnows, and a box of waxworms. We've frequently watched several boats within casting distance of each other all pulling in fish with completely different baits—minnows on bare hooks, plastic tails on a jighead, and feathered jigs. At other times, crappies define the term finicky.

Then, minnows seem too active to entice crappies. Stillfishing a tiny hair jig or plastic tail under a float, or impaling a grub on a 1/64-ounce jighead, is the ticket. When crappies are more active, a lively minnow with lead shot set 4 or 5 inches above the bait allows it freedom of movement that turns crappies on. But in timber, including stake beds, stumps, and trees, active minnows can get into trouble fast. Go with plastics or hair, or at least restrict the minnow with a large shot just above the hook. Weedless jigheads like Lindy-Little Joe's Timber Jig are another good choice.

Rigging Up

In general, smaller baits and lures combined with a stationary presentation or slow retrieve work best in the colder water of early spring. As water warms, larger baits moving a bit faster take more and larger fish. Finally, in early summer, casting and slowly retrieving a 1/8-ounce lure often works best.

Boat control—In some waters, wading is an option in emergent grasses in shallow hard-bottom areas. Slinking along with a pole under your arm lets you approach crappies in shallow cover more subtly than with a boat, unless you paddle a canoe or scull a small aluminum craft.

An electric trolling motor allows for slowly moving through shallow cover, looking for fish and casting or dabbling. It's important to stay back from the fish, as shadows from rods, boat noise, or the hum of the motor can alarm them. They may not swim off, but they'll be much harder to tempt.

When breezes make positioning tough, either blowing you onto the spot you're trying to fish or pulling you away and making casts into the wind a hassle, drop the hook. Anchoring with one or two anchors holds the boat on the spot without the noise and turbulence of a motor or paddle.

In shallow bays, a pair of large coffee cans filled with cement can pin a small boat nicely. Among thick brush or large fallen trees, a brush anchor or two may work better, since anchors often foul in timber and create disturbing vibrations when dropped in deeper water.

A final spring tactic is trolling, extremely effective for covering mid-depth areas with stumps and brush and when crappies hold in thick vegetation after the spawn. In southeastern reservoirs, spider-rigging is common—jon boats bristling with 8, 10, even 12 or more poles jutting across the bow and gunnels.

Set tube baits of several colors at various depths, held vertical with a large split shot. Ease along the edge of flats or over sunken brushpiles. A pattern should soon emerge, and you may find yourself hooking more crappies than you can handle. With a pole, though, fish usually remain hooked against the steady pressure of the pole, and you can pull in one fish after another when action gets hot.

When fishing an old favorite crappie lake in spring, you already know what type of cover to expect, based on years of trying various patterns. But don't take the fish for granted. In some years, crappies don't enter certain bays with cabbage, for instance—or they may enter briefly and then leave, not to return. The length and severity of winter, water temperature regimes, water color, or other factors may play a role in movement patterns.

Keep trying likely spots, even if they haven't produced lately. A spot may finally yield the mother lode of slab crappies, often so elusive this time of year. In unfamiliar waters, local anglers can provide pointers on what's worked for them—cover type, depth, popular bays, and so on. But again, don't take that as the final story. The encyclopedia on spring crappie behavior is still being written. Add your own chapter next spring.

THE KANSAS FILE

Ned Kehde, longtime *In-Fisherman* contributor and former archivist for the University of Kansas, loves to fish for crappies in his home state. Kehde, a flatland-reservoir crappie expert, has long depended on brushpiles to draw crappies to the many featureless flats found in his home waters. He always carries a counter, clicking away madly through a hot bite, so he can tell everyone exactly how many crappies came into the boat. But sometimes the clicking isn't so madly. Especially in fall.

"We have a situation that's different from other segments of the country," Kehde says. "Gizzard shad, the crappies' main forage, enter the creeks in late September or early October. The shad settle in the upper half to upper third of secondary feeder creeks, focusing on 8- to 12-foot depths. Because the shad suspend and roam, and crappies follow, October is an extremely difficult time to fish."

One thing that can keep and hold a few of these nomadic, high-riding crappies for short periods, Kehde explains, is a well-placed brushpile. "The brushpiles we make are osage orange mixed with willow. I cut off four major branches of an osage orange or hedge tree. These have big plumes of green leaves, branches, and thorns.

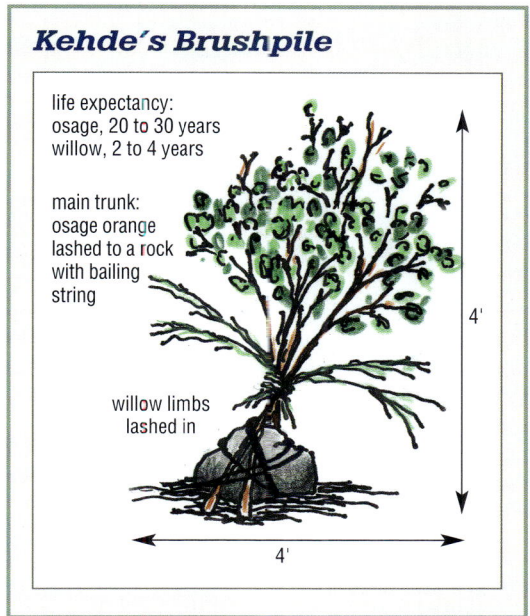

Kehde's Brushpile

life expectancy:
osage, 20 to 30 years
willow, 2 to 4 years

main trunk:
osage orange
lashed to a rock
with bailing
string

willow limbs
lashed in

4'

4'

Osage has mean thorns, and tough wood that lasts 30 years underwater. And for whatever reason, crappies are attracted to willows. We interlace four to five green willow branches with each segment of hedge and use bailing string to wrap them together, in a shape that looks like a small tree. The finished product is about 4 feet high and four feet across. We bundle it at the base to a big rock, take it out with several others in a couple of boats, and drop them in a line that's at least 20 feet long and 10 feet wide. We try to place them several feet apart so there's a spot to fish between. By stringing more piles together, we get more crappies to stop, especially when they're roaming around suspended, chasing shad. More of an opportunity—better odds—for them to make contact with a bigger area of brush.

"Height and thickness are fairly important," he says. "These brushpiles are about 4 feet high with spaces created or cut out. Some anglers make the piles too thick. A little space is a good deal. It's nice to be able to penetrate it, because when crappies feed on insects, they go right to the bottom, and I like to leave space for my jig to get through the branches."

As Kehde relates, crappies in Kansas reservoirs tend to be in secondary creek arms by October. Placement of a line of brushpiles, as always, is a critical consideration. "Sometimes we want the string to run parallel to the contour, sometimes we want it perpendicular," he notes. "Key depths are 8 to 12 feet at this time of year, and water fluctuations make some piles too deep or too shallow. Placing brushpiles at a variety of depths is critical, so you know at least some are at the right depth, no matter the water level.

"The secret," he says, "is to have at least 40 good piles to hit in a day, because you'll get only 5 or so fish off each one in October or November. The crappies are constantly moving and almost pelagic, but they do seem to stop on well-placed brushpiles for a while. So I don't fish each pile for long. Five to ten minutes and I move on."

Brushpile Placement for Big Crappies

Tennessee crappie guru Bobby Holmes has some definitive ideas about bigger crappies relating to brushpiles. "For general fishing, brushpiles are like shotgun pellets," Holmes says. "The mo' brushpiles the mo' better. But to attract giant crappies, scarce piles are better. The biggest fish will concentrate better in brushpiles where cover is scarce.

"First, giant crappies in clear water use brush at least 12 feet deep in fall. And in clear water, big crappies tend to suspend over the brush more of the time. So if I place a brushpile in 12 feet of water, I want at least 8 feet of open water above for them to hover in.

"In clear water on deeper flats, situate brush in 12 to 20 feet on a flat with no other form of structure, cover, or sharp contours around it—no other attraction to draw crappies. With fewer options to choose from, the biggest fish take command of the best cover available.

"Also in hill-land reservoirs, place brush in 12 to 30 feet of water on the outside bend of any creek or river channel somewhere in the general vicinity of the confluence where the creek channel meets the river. Place one on top of the break, another about midway down, and

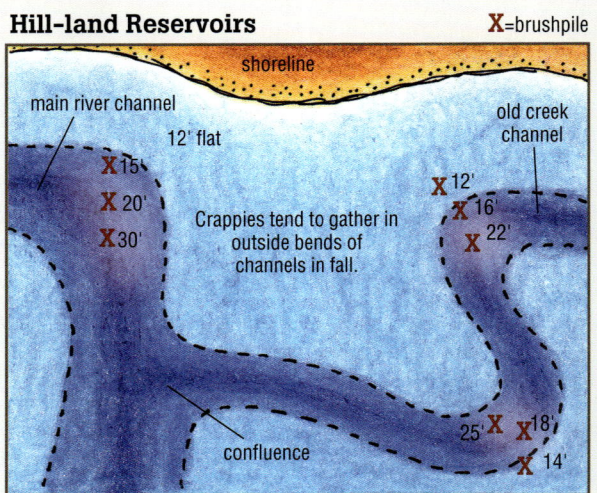

Hill-land Reservoirs   X=brushpile

Crappies tend to gather in outside bends of channels in fall.

When shad counts are low because of a poor hatch in spring, Kehde's crappies switch to insect forage and tend to stay on brushpiles longer. "Brushpiles provide a terrific source of aquatic insects, but crappies go right to the center of the piles. You have to pitch jigs and finesse your way through the brush or get right on top and vertically fish down through the branches and sticks. I use 8-pound test, usually a 1/16-ounce or sometimes a 1/32-ounce jig tied with marabou or chenille or tipped with a plastic body. Nobody ever tips with bait here, except the Kentucky spider-rig fishermen. They do quite well when crappies are in open water, but not so well in brushpiles."

Kehde's first choice most days is a Bailey's Magnet, a solid tube. "It's a tough piece of plastic," he says. "It doesn't tear up in the brush. Another great bait is the Bait Rigs Grub Master in a tube, a grub, or one of the new micro spider grubs in the Grub Master kit. It has a slow, horizontal drop, great for crappies hanging high in the brush, when we pitch and swim jigs through the tops of the piles. But we mostly work jigs vertically, in fall. The only way to penetrate the brush is vertically. When crappies hold in the interior or around the base of the piles, we want to be directly above them, finessing light marabou or chenille jigs."

another flat on the bottom at the base of the break on steeper outside bends. You don't want a lot of brushpiles. If you're looking for the biggest slabs in the lake come October-November, too many piles spread them too thin.

"In lowland reservoirs, place brushpiles in 4 to 8 feet of water on shallow flats near small creeks or lateral ditches. The biggest crappies cruise these areas. Again, less is more: Situate no more than three brushpiles at least 50 feet apart across the flat. Another thing about big crappies in lowland reservoirs—in a silted-in bay where contours are no longer sharp, the biggest crappies are right in that old creek bed, if they can find it. That's the place to drop brush for fall slabs."

Lowland Reservoirs

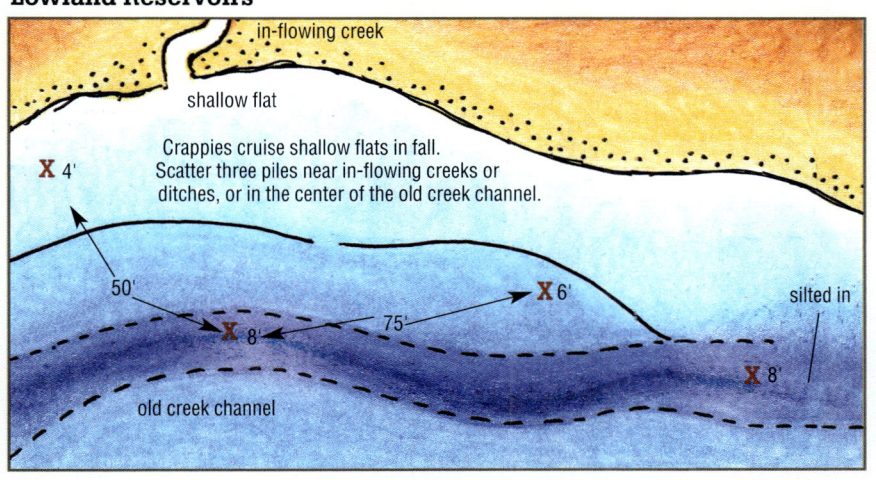

THE SANTEE-COOPER FILE

Pete Pritchard, longtime guide for crappies, stripers, cats, shell crackers and, well, just about anything that swims in Santee-Cooper, recently demonstrated on In-Fisherman television how he constructs and fishes brushpiles.

"Placement is the main thing for big crappies," Pritchard says. "The lake averages about 25 feet—so Santee-Cooper isn't really all that deep. I try to place brushpiles in a zone that crappies use to travel back and forth from shallow to deep. If you can find a creek channel heading into a cove and place a pile right on the point of that, you've got it made. That's not to say other places won't work but, in my experience, that's the place to be for truly big crappies."

Pritchard constructs his crappie condos out of hardwood. "We use major limbs of oak, cherry, or dogwood, because hardwood lasts 4 or 5 years. Start with 16-inch concrete blocks, the ones with just two holes," he says. "Lay one on its side with holes parallel to the ground. Stick the butt of the brush right in the block and wire it so it stays. One in each hole. Then wire another block to that block and create a second tree. When you drop one of these brushpiles in

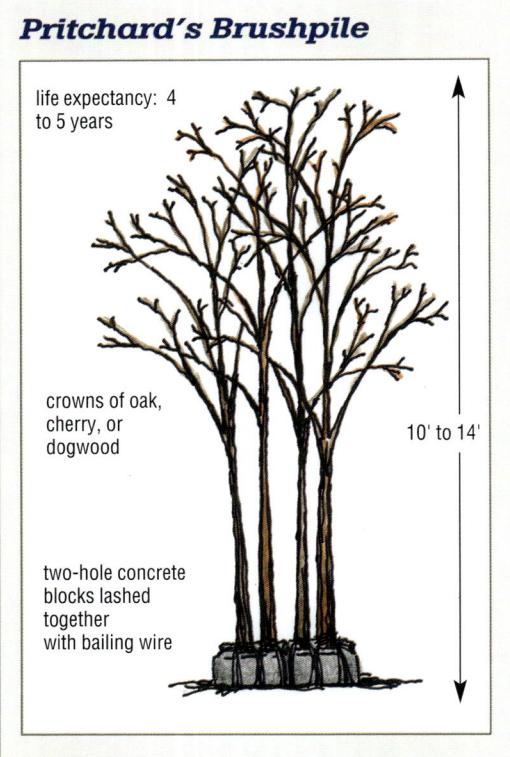

Pritchard's Brushpile

life expectancy: 4 to 5 years

crowns of oak, cherry, or dogwood

10' to 14'

two-hole concrete blocks lashed together with bailing wire

the lake, it will stand up like a tree. We try to make our trees at least 10 feet tall, sometimes 14 feet unless the water's only 8 or 9 feet deep—then we shorten it up. It's good to have some open water above the brush so crappies can suspend where they're easy to catch. More importantly, don't make it easy for other anglers to find your brushpiles.

"Crappies like the long, skinny limbs. I like to get the top of the brush to spread out, so I prefer to use whole tops from trees the right size. If somebody's taking down a hardwood around here, I take a close look at the crown. I place piles no closer than 100 yards apart. Fungi grows and minnows feed there. A good brushpile produces both shelter and food.

"I have brushpiles on featureless flats that work pretty well, but they have to be situated in an area that crappies use. In Santee-Cooper, crappies go back to the same areas they use in spring as the water cools a little in October and November. I use the same brushpiles I use in March, April, and May, in water 10 to 22 feet deep. Actually, in a shallow reservoir like this, a brushpile in 13 to 16 feet of water is productive all year. But cool water can push the fish a little deeper than normal.

"In October, the biggest crappies generally inhabit 12- to 13-foot brushpiles in coves and backwater ponds, but they may move as shallow as 8 or 9 feet. With brushpiles at every conceivable depth, I might check those from 8 down to 20 feet every day in fall. It's good to have a lot of brushpiles to check, but spread them out. If you saturate one area with brush, you're just spreading the fish. In a really good cove, I might put out only 8 or 9 brushpiles. Any more than that and the fish just scatter."

Pritchard uses small shiner minnows on Aberdeen hooks with a split shot. He and his clients present this rig with 8- to 10-foot flyrods matched with small spinning reels. From a pontoon boat rigged with a trolling motor, he lines up, using permanent objects on shore to triangulate. Then he edges the boat right over the top of the pile, where everyone can reach out and dap jigs down through the branches. "Measure line by using the rod length and stripping line off in measured amounts," he advises. "Being exact about depth is critical. If you know how deep a crappie was when it bit, you can duplicate that depth the next time.

"Santee-Cooper doesn't drastically change overnight, but it fluctuates quite a bit from year to year. A change of 5 feet would be a drastic change from one year to the next, so placing brush ahead of time is easier. It's critical to have brush situated throughout the key depths crappies use, which in fall ranges from 8 to 20 feet. And I think this is crucial: Put brush where it's protected no matter which way the wind blows."

THE TENNESSEE FILE

Fishing guide and radio-show host Bobby Holmes has been guiding for crappies and bluegills since 1983 in West Tennessee on shallow waters like Kentucky Lake and Reelfoot, and in deeper hill-land reservoirs like Percy Priest. When it comes to brushpiles, his degree in botany certainly doesn't hurt.

"I mostly use willow and river birch, which tend to create an infusion earliest, meaning living things begin to invade or infest the wood more quickly," he says. "Peach or apple branches infuse quickly, too. Willow is best but it's also the most delicate. With a willow brushpile, you tend to leave one third on the bank, one third in the boat, and you might get one third in the water by the time you plant it. If you handle it with care, you might get two thirds. I set two cinder blocks in the boat and lap, head to toe, two large willow limbs or whole saplings and wire them in place with electric fence wire.

"My brushpiles are 20 feet long, 4 feet wide, and average 4 feet tall. I use major limbs and tree trunks. Big brushpiles are easier for both crappies and anglers to find. As far as height goes, my rule of thumb is: In 20 feet of water, 6 feet wouldn't be too tall. In 6 feet of water, a height of 3 feet would be plenty. No sense letting everyone know where your pile is by having it show above the water. If it rises above the surface, give it a haircut.

"Willow lasts 2 to 3 years and has holes you can get a jig through," he adds. "With river birch, you have to cut strips through the middle of the pile so you can get your jig down through. Apple or peach-tree trimmings can sweeten a brushpile. Find out when the local orchard owners prune. They're usually anxious to get rid of the brush.

"Add five or six nice brushpiles to a flat with no cover and, presto, you'll have crappies there. Around here, brushpiles should be in 12 feet of water in October and November. You need some idea about the fluctuations of the reservoir, and you need to know where the water level will be in fall. So if you drop it in spring, drop it deeper. Around here I drop brush in 16 feet of water in spring, knowing that most years the water will drop 4 feet by October."

Holmes rarely puts brushpiles down in the same pattern twice. "Place a distinct pattern in each area you use, so when you make contact with one brushpile, bingo—you know how it's laid out. Hexagon, straight line, circle—doesn't matter; just know your own pattern so you know how to follow it. I like to space my brushpiles at least 40 to 50 feet apart," he says. "That way, if someone comes by and gets a fix on you with GPS, he gets only one fixed point. You're the only one who knows the pattern. Make the other ones hard to find. Use a notebook. Triangulate and make notes on your topo map, or just use GPS. Or put buoy makers on each pile, back away and take photos with a Polaroid camera, then staple them into your log book.

"No matter what type of water I fish in western Tennessee during fall, I want brushpiles on big flats next to river channels, on steep rough banks or long-tapering points, or on outside bends in the main river channel or main creek channel. In cut stumps you only have to add brush in the backs of the creeks where natural cover has silted over. In lowland reservoirs like Ross Barnett or highland reservoirs like

Percy Priest, find cover and you find fish. Where water is clear [water clarity has as much to do with it as anything], placement should be deeper. I want brush at 15 to 20 feet minimum on Percy Priest in October. The best action could be in 30 to 40 feet. In shallower, cloudier lowland reservoirs, brush should be 4 to 12 feet deep.

"If the water is discolored or we have cloud cover, I reach all around the brushpile with a long, 12-foot jigging pole. With a 1/32- or 1/16-ounce jig fished vertically on 4- to 6-pound line, I touch-lift and finesse that jig all around the brushpile. I use B&M poles and little Mitchell Spider Mite reels.

"For vertically fishing in deep water, I don't use a long pole," says Holmes. "I don't tip with bait, either. I use dyed kip tails [calf tails], which have a lustrous effect in the water, or I tip with plastic tubes. Lacking wind and if the water's clear, I pitch jigs because the crappies will be spooky. I suggest little fiberguard jigs, and I trim the fibers. I use an 8-foot Classic, a spinning rod especially designed by B&M for vertical fishing. Best way to figure out depth is to use rod length for the first 8 feet, so you can always strip line off the reel in 2- or 3-foot lengths to figure out precisely how deep you're fishing. You want to know exactly where you are in terms of depth around a brushpile, because biting crappies tend to be at the same level most of the time.

"I go over the top of the brushpile first and read it, so I know what depth to start. If I don't have to penetrate it, I don't. When crappies suspend over the brush, I note their depth and measure my line accordingly.

"Scatter brushpiles in slightly different depths," Holmes suggests. "That way you're covered when water levels fluctuate. And place brushpiles so you always have somewhere to fish out of the wind. Make sure a few are protected from the west, some from the north, and so on; so that no matter which direction the wind blows, you'll have protected brushpiles." (Not that crappies won't be out there when the wind blows, but it's difficult to maintain position and vertically finesse jigs through brush in wind and waves.)

"Dropping brushpiles will teach you more about a lake or reservoir than you otherwise could learn," he says. "While using good electronics in the search for existing brush or new drop sites, you're going to find old roadbeds, ditches with fence rows, stumps, channels, and other key elements that aren't on the map. Diligence never hurts."

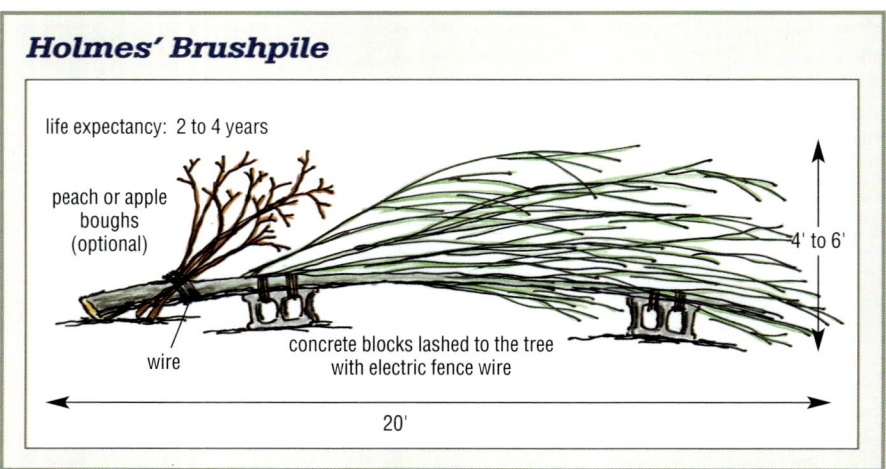

Holmes' Brushpile

WELCOME TO THE JUNGLE

Submerged vegetation fuels bluegill and crappie patterns like an elixir, even during seemingly sterile winters. Although plant biomass decreases significantly as ice builds, in many lakes—particularly the clearer ones—certain evergreen plants continue to photosynthesize oxygen throughout the cold months.

Although we're talking mainly from an ice-fishing perspective here, aquatic plants undergo similar winter cycles in climates where lakes experience cold winters but don't necessarily freeze up. So these patterns often apply to anglers fishing open waters during the colder periods.

Science tells us that at early- and late-ice, all through winter if snow cover is negligible, sunlight feeds rooted plants, at least intermittently. Despite this, dissolved oxygen (DO) levels in shallow zones continue to erode throughout winter because of decomposition. In milder winters, however, DO replacement via plant photosynthesis can be enough to sustain life. Panfish, in these cases, potentially feed and hold in these littoral zones all winter.

Opposite conditions, on the other hand—turbid water, deep ice, and snow—reduce sunlight penetration and oxygen production by plants, and decomposition depletes DO at an accelerated rate. Eventually, bluegills and crappies fade from flats and reassemble in deep basin holes, where large groups band together. Anoxic conditions can prohibit longterm fish survival, yet we can't say for certain that all littoral flats lack bearable oxygen levels, as anglers have no simple way to measure oxygen.

We know that panfish, like other species, venture into low-tolerance zones if these areas harbor abundant forage. Some invertebrates eaten by panfish, particularly chironomid midge larvae, thrive in low-oxygen environments outside fish comfort levels, yet these "bloodworms" frequently pack panfish stomachs tight. The same for shallow, decaying weeds that provide food for backswimmers, water boatmen, and certain microcrustaceans. Bluegills love foraging on these critters, even though in winter they often cling to decomposing plants.

Some shallow, weedy flats offer sufficient DO (roughly 6 parts per million and greater) all winter. This is true more often than anglers suspect, even during late-ice. Certain key species of winter-hardy plants continue adding oxygen throughout winter. Groundwater streams percolate through the substrate, creating oxygen-rich microhabitats. Such microhabitats consist of a bubble of highly oxygenated water—a capsule of life in hostile surroundings, an oasis of vegetation with invertebrates and fish packed into a finite area.

Clearly, the well-worn line about green weeds luring flocks of hungry panfish isn't as simple as it seems. Still, given a little plant knowledge, the process begins to make sense. Some plants wither in fall, some crumple in summer; others, given the right water conditions, remain evergreen throughout winter, continuously producing oxygen. Some of these evergreens actually appear more brown than green.

Finding stands of live plants is a tricky business until you get comfortable with plant identification and corresponding habitat. It requires inspecting the terrain in search of certain species of plants, rather than trying to arbitrarily determine which ones on a weedflat remain alive. Lots of the searching today involves an underwater camera, such as an Aqua-Vu.

Plant vitality can't always be determined without pulling a strand through a hole, and even then, it can still take a botanist to make the call. Even a seemingly upright stalk of something like pondweed isn't necessarily photosynthesizing. Until anglers regularly employ and interpret DO meters, camera work remains the best way to help us make judgments about where to fish.

The DO Mystery

Dissolved oxygen (DO) levels within a body of water remain the great unknown to anglers, perhaps the last major mystery relative to fish location, winter panfish notwithstanding. Oxygen, of course, is as basic to life in water as on land. It's an important indicator of a lake's ability to support aquatic life. Levels above 5 parts per million are considered suitable to good for most fish, while few species survive for long at levels below 3 parts per million.

As important as DO is to aquatic life, we still know little about its persistence from lake to lake, or even between varying lake zones. Eventually, DO meters may become more widely available to serious fishermen. Today, most accurate DO meters remain too costly, as well as technically difficult to operate.

Some anglers have long questioned the theory of panfish and green weeds, as we've often observed and caught panfish mingling within forests of decaying plants. One point rarely addressed is that adequate oxygen levels often permeate vegetated littoral zones even throughout the last vestiges of prolonged North country winters. Data collected over a multiyear period by the University of Minnesota continue to demonstrate this. Consider a few facts:

• Mid-ice: January 20, 2000—Halsteds Bay, a hypereutrophic (highly fertile) basin of Lake Minnetonka, MN: 13 to 10 parts per million (ppm) DO from ice level to nearly 16 feet.

• Mid-to-late ice: February 25, 2000—Halsteds Bay: 7 ppm DO from ice level to 13 feet.

• Last-ice (just days before ice out): March 24, 1999—Ice Lake, MN (mesotrophic): 8 ppm DO from ice level to 23 feet.

• Mid-ice: January 16, 2002—Ice Lake, MN: 14 to 10 ppm DO from ice level to 24 feet.

• Late-ice: February 25, 2000—Lake Independence, MN (urban late mesotrophic): 6 to 8 ppm DO from ice level to 19 feet.

"Water on the Web" is an educational program instituted by the University of Minnesota-Duluth. The program teaches about lake and stream water quality through real-time data obtained from the project's Remote Underwater Sampling Stations (RUSS units). The website (*wateronthewhweb.org*) provides water quality information, much of which helps anglers better understand the waters they fish.

MACROPHYTE MASTERY

When biologists study aquatic plants, they find a diversity of native species that creates a patchy underwater landscape. Minnesota Department of Natural Resources Senior Research Scientist Paul Radomski is among them. "A patchy field composed of many different plants creates lots of the edges, nooks, and tunnels panfish need to both hide from and pursue prey," he says. "Multiple fish species and age-classes depend on a diversity of plant habitats for feeding, spawning, and refuge."

Radomski's "patchy" concept is key, for a diversity of plants suggests a balanced environment in which each species of plant offers something unique that certain invertebrates or fish require—food, habitat, or both. "We could talk a lot about native versus invasive plants," he says, "yet of primary importance is that native plants coexist best, while invasives such as Eurasian milfoil tend to overgrow native plants, reducing the patchiness of littoral zones."

Taking the concept a step further, he adds: "Plant diversity is highest in heterogeneous lakes. These are generally larger or deeper waters with various types of bottom substrate and more convoluted depth variations. Conversely, homogeneous lakes, which are often more turbid, host greater phytoplankton (algae) densities relative to rooted macrophytes. Ideally, you like to see an abundance of submersed plant species, because they increase the probability that at least one is winter-hardy." But which macrophytes overwinter? Where do they grow? And when do they attract panfish?

THE JUNGLE

Coontail (Ceratophyllum demersum)—This common macrophyte tolerates cold water and low light levels, allowing it to frequently overwinter as an evergreen. "Live winter coontail appears green and bushy, while dying stalks easily fall apart in your hand," Radomski says. "Unlike most plants, coontail isn't always rooted to the bottom. Instead, plant masses can drift between different depths—10 to 20 feet—on spacious flats."

Providing nearly optimal winter habitat for bluegills and occasionally crappies, coontail creates homes for a host of invertebrates, including certain species of mayfly, caddisfly, and midge larvae—critters that make up that gelatinous goo you find in panfish stomachs.

Sometimes you get especially lucky and find swarms of scuds, little crustaceans that crave coontail salads. Likewise, bluegills pop scuds like candy, bulking up rapidly. It's a sweet weed-prey-panfish link worth the extra detective time. While traveling the winter panfish trail, we've found a number of lakes housing this pattern, one that appears strongly tied to clear ponds or small lakes cut into treeless valleys and windswept prairies. The presence of scuds becomes immediately obvious, as they swarm entire plant beds.

Elodea (Elodea canadensis)—Canadian waterweed is another name for a plant anglers encounter often, though rarely identify. Its stems sprout small waxy-green leaves

Coontail
Ceratophyllum demersum

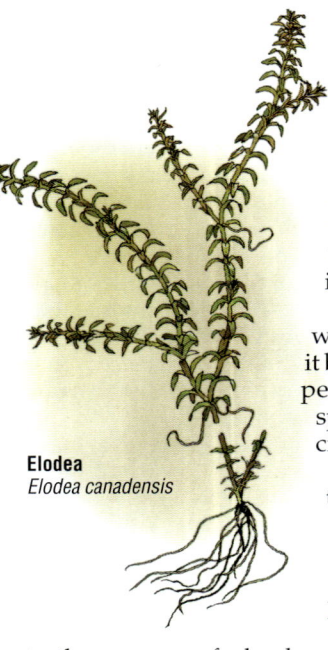

Elodea
Elodea canadensis

that crowd together toward plant tips. Typically, waterweed grows in softer sediments enriched with organic matter. Some of these areas lie in shallow water, although this plant often grows to depths beyond 25 feet. Like coontail, elodea tolerates lower light conditions and murkier water, which often allows it to remain evergreen, continuing photosynthesis through winter.

"Waterweed is probably the most common overwintering plant," Radomski says. "Larger panfish seek it because it produces considerable infusions of oxygen, perhaps in greater abundance than other submersed species. And you usually find lots of midge larvae associated with it, which is a key winter food item."

Searching for overwintering elodea takes time, as the live plants typically grow in isolated patches. Still, even though it can be more elusive than other species, finding a few live patches can seem like finding treasure, often attracting visits from small pods of real palm-stretchers.

Patches cover areas from the size of a typical kitchen to the expanse of a hockey rink. Shallow bays fed by creeks, river backwaters, and oxbow lakes offer top shots at finding wintergreen elodea fields. Marina bays kept partially open by aerators can host elodea and bluegills all winter. Otherwise, late-ice represents a peak phase for finding 'gills in waterweed, as stems sprout new growth early in the calendar year, inviting fresh infusions of life.

Large-leaf Pondweed (Potamogeton amplifolias)—What fishermen call cabbage remains widely familiar, if slightly misunderstood. Big broad leaves furl away from lanky stems that remind you of giant beanstalks. Pondweed holds fish like few other submersed plants. Under ice, though, it only occasionally remains active. Stems of decaying pondweed break underwater, leaves shriveling like dried tobacco. A live pondweed remains erect and intact, brownish leaves absorbing sunrays that generate oxygen. Turbid water, thick ice, or snow cover cut the probability of encountering living plants.

Large-leaf Pondweed
Potamogeton amplifolias

"Large-leaf and fern pondweed [another occasional overwinterer] often intermix with coontail," Radomski says. "Finding live winter pondweed, which is a relatively frail submergent, indicates a high probability of other persistent macrophyte life and also a good chance of finding panfish."

Revisiting the "patchy" concept, multiple living plant types in a given area, such as pondweed in conjunction with coontail, accentuate invertebrate and panfish appeal. Further, the presence of bass and pike in these live weed zones nearly assures that panfish swim somewhere in the neighborhood. Keep popping holes until you find those tight-knit schools of thick-bodied bluegills or crappies clustered around small forests of giant beanstalks. These fish feed a bit like birds—pecking baits aggressively then flitting away to avoid predators.

Curlyleaf Pondweed (Potamogeton crispus)—Even though this overtly abundant aquatic plant is a Eurasian exotic—one capable of overgrowing native species—a couple of elements bear mentioning. "Curlyleaf pondweed is a coolwater specialist," Radomski says. "It dies back around mid-July, lies dormant during late summer, then produces winter foliage starting in September. When water temps drop into the low-70°F range, plants produce winter foliage, remaining active under snow and ice, often even in murky waters."

Found primarily in softer bottom sediments, this pondweed sprouts slender, rippled leaves that are easy to identify. Again, even live pondweeds often appear more brown than green.

Beyond the obvious wintertime appeal of live curlyleaf to many aquatic animals, this plant is positively related to populations of large bluegills. "When curlyleaf pondweed dies back in summer, previously hidden juvenile bluegills are exposed to predation, reducing their numbers," Radomski reports in a study of submersed plants.** "The high lake fertility levels associated with curlyleaf indicate abundant crappie food. Meanwhile the plant's early spring propensity to overgrow spawning sites potentially limits crappie propagation."

Curlyleaf Pondweed
Potamogeton crispus

As you become familiar with those certain submersed plants so attractive to winter panfish, each new lake greets you like your home waters. You soon know right where to look, even if you can't exactly explain how you know. You'll find panfish glory sooner rather than later.

CRITTERS & CRAPPIE PATTERNS

A hot bite, going gangbusters a few minutes ago, is now seemingly dead. Crappies were hitting minnows on Aberdeen hooks before the float could even settle and stand up. One on every cast. It happens every year: At some point, a torrid bite dies as if somebody turned it off with a switch. More often than not, a brief examination of what's going on around the boat solves the mystery.

Panfish can switch from one forage type to the next in an instant, a change caused by things we often can't see, such as a sudden migration of crustaceans, plankton, leeches, or insects; or a sudden "bloom" of minnows. Panfish may not be as selective as trout, but they're not stupid. If the water they're swimming in suddenly comes alive with little brown wormy things, minnows are off the menu for a while.

Sometimes nature gives us clues. When the air is clear of insects and suddenly gnats or midges are crawling on your sunglasses, expect the panfish bite to change. This is most pronounced in spring, and every spring when we begin to see bunches of flying insects for the first time (usually in the afternoon), switching baits can make all the difference. If fishing with minnows, especially, a switch to maggots, waxworms, or softbaits that imitate larval stages of insects almost always precipitates a faster bite when insects begin to hatch. A hatch can last only a few minutes or all day. When it dies, switching back to minnows, other softbaits, or leeches tends to increase the regularity of bites again.

In summer, with insects all around us all the time, a new hatch can pass unnoticed. In fall, hatches start to become rare, and most insect migrations take place near bottom. From June through November, the whys and wherefores of sudden changes in the panfish bite can remain entirely hidden from view. But it's possible to make informed guesses. When a hot bite suddenly dies, the question begging to be asked is: "What's the bottom of the lake composed of around here?"

SUBSTRATE WISDOM

Most anglers know that rock, gravel, and clay-bottomed areas can have a substantial crayfish population that should, at many points during a season, attract the undivided attention of crappies, bluegills, and perch. But what lives in the muck? How about in marl, silt, sand, or in combinations of these substrates? Rest assured, when panfish concentrate in any area it probably has a lot to do with bottom composition and what thrives on or in it.

For instance, some of the most common forage items for panfish during the cold months are bottom-dwelling worms called annelids (segmented aquatic earthworms). Another huge food source for panfish during the warmer months—leeches—are related forms of these annelids. Both can be found in greatest number wherever particle size in the substrate is relatively small, suggesting mucky areas. Some species of annelid do quite well in silt (0.6 millimeter particles and smaller), which includes the smallest particle sizes of all possible substrates. Rich, organic sediments (with finer particles in the .07 to .09 millimeter range) tend to harbor the densest populations of annelids.

Such sediments also tend to harbor weeds. Which plant species grow best depends to some extent on the combination of bottom types that exist. Marl, calcite, sand, muck, clay, gravel,

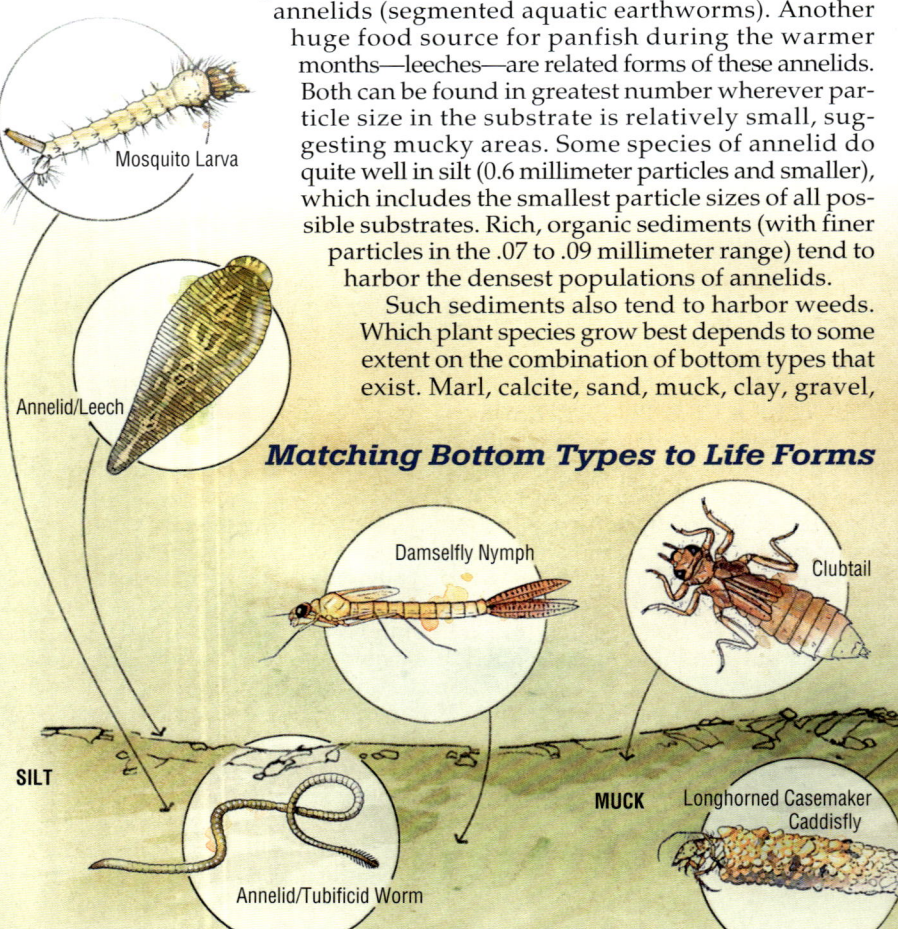

Matching Bottom Types to Life Forms

and other substrates each favor specific weed types. Reeds, for instance, grow well in sand mixed with gravel. Cabbage, milfoil, hydrilla, coontail, crispus, hyacinths, lily pads, and others thrive in substrates of varying composition, and each harbors its own particular crop of weed-clinging invertebrates, like grass shrimp.

One can tell what the bottom type is by the weed type growing in it, what comes up on the anchor, and by viewing with underwater cameras. Several clues point to what's living in that substrate. Samples can be scooped from the bottom and sieved. Flying insects that appear during a prolific annual hatch can be captured and identified, so that the larval form of that creature can be found in books on aquatic biology. Examining stomach contents of caught fish, however, might be the most proficient means of determining what's down there in the greatest abundance.

Many of the macroscopic (visible) invertebrates living in hard-bottomed areas have a well-camouflaged carapace, or case. Stonefly nymphs, mayfly nymphs, crayfish, and mysis shrimp, for example, all have some version of protective armor, possibly because they're exposed to predation a higher percentage of the time than creatures that burrow or hide in softer substrates. Many critters living in soft substrates tend to have a soft outer layer (epidermis), in shades that vary from dull green to bright red. Caddisfly larvae appear in a wide variety of shades. Many species of caddisfly live in rocky areas, creating their own camouflage and armor by building a case or shell made of tiny bits of wood, gravel, or both.

Some invertebrates that panfish prey upon spend most of the summer clinging to weedstalks and the bottoms of lily pads. Moth larvae, scuds, and darners are examples of epiphytes, weed-clinging critters from various families of invertebrates. These tend to be brown, green, off-white, or black. Some appear like little black beads with a tiny shell, some look like maggots, and some have legs and a carapace.

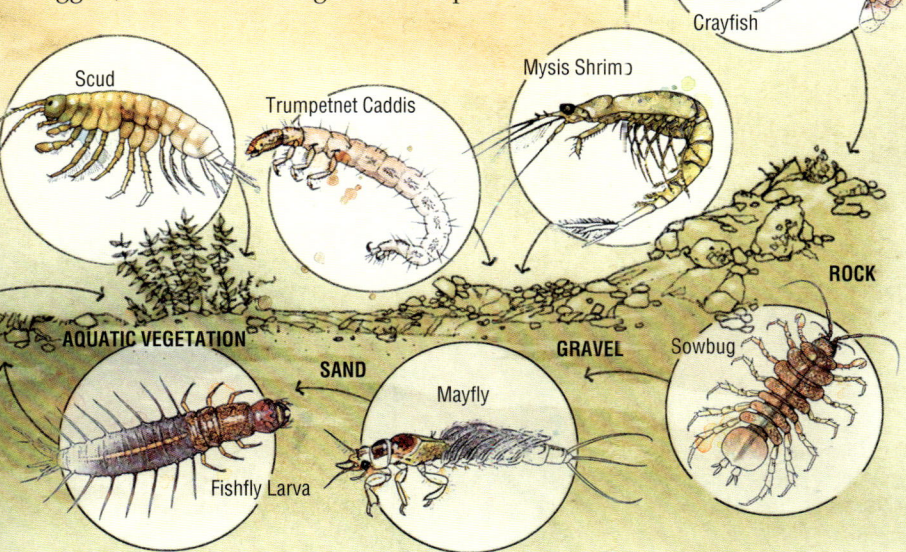

How Crappies Relate to Cover

BOTTOM PATTERNS

The basis of every angling pattern is the approximation of something the targeted fish eats. Whether presenting an actual livebait, lure, or soft plastic, the idea is to imitate the size, profile, and color of things actually being eaten underwater just a few feet away. If you're fishing with a good approximation of what fish are eating most, you're onto a primary pattern.

Primary patterns for crappies in many southern reservoirs are relatively easy to deduce. Imitate a shad or present a live one, and you're halfway home. Crappies of a size anglers pursue eat small shad all year in many of these environments. If you can see or net the clouds of young shad that crappies are targeting, you can easily imitate the size of the primary forage.

Uprooting patterns in natural lakes, backwaters, northern reservoirs, and ponds tends to be more complicated. We can't always see what the fish are feeding on and have to rely on noting what they spit up, examine their stomachs, or fish blind—the reason it pays to experiment with a variety of baits. Anglers often believe the only requirement for catching panfish is a container of the same type of fresh bait that worked last time. And, with few exceptions, it does produce. But something else always works better for at least a portion of the day.

Finding a panfish bite is one thing. Staying on the hottest bite is tricky. When a hot bite dies entirely, it rarely means all the nearby panfish became inactive or vacated the area. With two hands on deck, or—where the law allows use of more than one rod—somebody on a second (or third) rod should always be experimenting with something different. That goes for southern reservoirs too, where panfish are not entirely immune to a sudden hatch or migration of billions of tiny critters that offer an easy meal. During a mayfly hatch, even shad fingerlings take a back seat on the food-chain train.

FINE-TUNING PATTERNS

Maggots—A logical progression: Start with the most prolific, universal form of all insect larvae worldwide, the maggot. Berkley, FoodSource, Custom Jigs & Spins, Lindy Legendary Fishing Tackle, and I.S.G. are just some of the companies making a plastic or softbait version of a maggot. A small, cylindrical, off-white or butter-yellow piece of plastic imitates the larvae of mosquitoes, caddisflies, shoreflies, dance flies, watersnipe flies, soldier flies, marsh flies, crane flies, and literally thousands of other flying insects that "hatch" (really, metamorphose) from aquatic eggs and larvae. Most, if not all of these critters spend their underwater years in silty areas around the softest substrates, so start searching areas like lily-pad fields and weedbeds with maggots or some version thereof.

Worms—Following the "maggot form" is the basic worm. Basic, perhaps, but not garden variety. Aquatic worms live in a variety of substrates from silt to sand and gravel and appear in most shades of the rainbow. Some are pink or red, so a red 3-inch Berkley Power Micro Crawler isn't just another pretty colored plastic designed to catch the fisherman's eye. It's a natural color, down there. Natural can also mean lime, pale blue, metallic green, and a rainbow of nail-polish shades you've never heard of. The real deal is stranger than fiction, and real colors exceed our wildest Technicolor dreams in the world of aquatic invertebrates. Many species of aquatic worm are mere millimeters in length—thus, the success of very small artificial varieties from Custom Jigs & Spins, I.S.G., Lindy, and other companies.

Those two patterns skip lightly through the many possibilities for fishing the softest substrates. Predictably, imitations of mayfly, dragonfly, and damselfly nymphs perform well on sandflats. Examples include the Berkley 1-inch Micro Power Nymph and Case's Little Hellgrammites. And who says a fly has to be fished on a flyrod? Local fly shops have imitations of nymphs and larvae that match the naturals in your area.

On rockpiles and other hard-bottomed structure, a tiny craw imitation is a good starting point. Spike-It, Berkley, Bass Pro Shops, and many other companies market plastic craws in the 1/2- to 2-inch range. Without other indications to go by, simple logic can direct us to the most likely inhabitants of the substrates we're fishing. Over time, other clues fall into place—things found in the livewell, insects that land on the boat, or critters you see with an underwater camera—that allow you to better match the colors, sizes, and shapes of the primary inhabitants of the lifescape below.

The logical syllogism to extract from all this would run something like this: A) All aquatic invertebrates have specific habitat requirements, and most require specific substrates to thrive; B) invertebrates in areas of homogeneous substrates are limited not in number but in type; C) invertebrates in areas where a variety of substrates mix together might not be limited in either number or type. If A, B, and C are true, the areas that harbor the greatest variety of substrate types harbor the greatest variety of invertebrates. Areas where diverse types of weeds and substrates all come together tend to provide the fastest fishing for panfish.

Livebait—It pays to be ready for sudden changes in the bite. We seldom go fishing for anything without at least one livebait option but rarely have more than two. When panfishing, we go with at least three varieties. Redworms, waxworms, maggots, crickets, grasshoppers, crappie minnows, panfish leeches, live nymphs—we'll take them all, and more, if possible. Worms, maggots, leeches, and waxworms are particularly well suited to imitating aquatic invertebrates that can be found in any waterway on the planet. And if we can't find the live version, our trusty panfish boxes have a reasonable facsimile of almost anything that swims, scoots, or crawls along the bottom, no matter where we go.

While panfish may never be as picky as trout, a lot of evidence and experience suggests that slow bites can be prompted to speed up considerably: Just imitate critters that panfish are finding in abundance and feeding on to the near exclusion of all else. You should be ready to imitate any naturally occurring invertebrates that are abundant in the environments you fish. Consistent panfish action is a direct result of being in touch with their environment. But take note. The more you know about it, the more you'll want to protect it.

*Guy, C. S., R. M Neumann, and D. W. Willis. 1992. Movement patterns of adult black crappie, *pomoxis nigromaculatis,* in Brandt Lake, South Dakota. J. of Freshwater Ecol. 7(2): 137-147.

**Radomski, R., and T.J. Goeman. 2001. Consequences of human lakeshore development on emergent and floating-leaf vegetation abundance. N. Amer. J. Fish. Mgmt. 21(1):46-61.

Modern Electronics Made Easy _____ *Chapter 8*

Tools for Fine-Tuning Crappie Location

TOWARD
UNDERWATER
UNDERSTANDING

In this chapter, we examine techniques and technology for learning more about how crappies operate in their world. Included are continually expanding electronic capabilities that were beyond the realm of NASA just 20 years ago. Others are no more complex than using our eyes and centuries-old weather measuring devices.

Tools for Fine-Tuning Crappie Location   159

FISH-WATCHING

The human eye and brain are as sensitive, in their way, as crappies' are in their world. If you want to learn more about crappie location, start with the two "fish finders" on the front of your head. Crappie often cooperate in this regard, since they spend much of the early part of the season in shallow water and often remain visible at other times, at least in clear waterways.

As we've discussed in the section of this book on seasonal movements, crappies often move to shallow weedy habitats weeks or months before ice leaves northern lakes. This pattern strengthens as March progresses on northern waters and snow melts from lake surfaces, bringing higher light levels and more oxygen to the lake below. Savvy ice anglers make great catches by sight-fishing, stealthily moving from hole to hole to spot slabs slowly moving among submerged plants, and tempting them with small baits.

As in any other sight-fishing, shading the eyes with a hat, coat, or being in a portable fish house (shutter the windows for best viewing) helps greatly. A good pair of polarized sunglasses is essential as well. Finally, keeping a low profile and moving quietly on the ice can help you sneak up on a real monster. Crappies quickly recognize when they're being pursued, and all their instincts put them on the defensive, not what you want when you're looking for a bite.

After ice-out, crappies remain shallow in some systems, particularly where pelagic forage isn't important in the diet. In lakes with abundant minnows, crappies move shallow to feed on them along with invertebrates, while beginning the warming process in sun-baked bays. They're spooky in this situation too, but stealthful exploration can often reveal big fish among dead vegetation or even telltale sail fins carving across narrow channels.

While sight-fishing under the ice is limited to vertical presentations, long casts often are needed during early spring to tempt bites without scaring fish off. Standing high on the deck or even gaining vantage with a platform or simple wooden crate can help find fish before they find you. As waters warm further, shallow patterns continue to strengthen as more fish push into shallow backwaters, bays, and canals. Spot a couple of crappies, and there may be 100 in an area the size of a dock. They lurk in clumps of lily-pad rhizomes, fallen trees, beaver lodges, and other shallow cover. Approach these spots and areas with stealth, always scanning ahead to spot fish before they detect a disturbance and disappear.

Trolling motors are great inventions and we couldn't fish without them; but in spring, push-poling gives a quieter approach if the wind doesn't nag. While a motor tends to churn up silt and slice and dice lily pads, a pole pushes with far less disturbance. When you spot a target, drive the handle into the bottom and hold in place by tying off with a dock rope.

When you find a major concentration, it's best to anchor securely. They settle down once quiet resumes and fish will start to move from the thickest cover to edges where you'll spot and catch them without alarming others.

The Aqua-Vu DVR (Digital Video Recorder) allows viewers to record and store underwater discoveries and replay them for entertainment and learning purposes.

UNDERWATER CAMERAS

Of course, crappies spend most of the year at depths beyond what even the keenest-eyed angler can detect. The development of underwater cameras extends our ability to peer into the world of our quarry. Underwater cameras have proven extremely popular with anglers who fish clear lakes and reservoirs, which we might define as those where a crankbait can be seen two feet below the surface, directly down from the side of the boat.

In-Fisherman co-founder Al Lindner has been a fan of underwater cameras since field-testing them in the late 1990s. "After scouting with an Aqua-Vu, my mind is alive with new places to take it," he states. "I thought I had a pretty good idea of what structures looked like, so I was shocked to see how wrong I'd been about some spots."

Minnesota fishing pro Ted Capra echoes Lindner's enthusiasm. "Underwater cameras are one of the most important new tools for anglers since sonar. I've wondered why I've caught fish on only one side of a bar, and now I know. Does the camera give anglers an unfair advantage? Typically, if I view a spot and see 10 or 20 fish, I may catch a few of them. But at times, schools seem uncatchable. There's no way to make fish bite. When I first started scouting I caught lots fewer fish, because I spent more time looking and less time fishing."

Today, underwater viewing systems are available with features like lights for night viewing and enhanced camera positioning systems. Many can be bought for less than the cost of a good sonar or trolling motor, or about the same as a top-of-the line reel.

We've found that a camera doesn't usually spook panfish or bass. Rather, fish often seem curious, swimming up to investigate the apparatus. Closely examining specific cover objects on favorite spots demonstrates that subtle characteristics attract groups of crappie, while other nearly identical areas remain fishless. We've discovered that it isn't odd to spot crappies roaming far above the bottom, sometimes removed from cover objects. We've also learned that crappies sometimes do swim downward to chase prey.

Beyond solving mysteries, underwater viewing during fishing trips brings an immediate boost of confidence, whether you're exploring a new lake or preparing for tournament competition. Accurate visualization spawns this confidence, a mindset that inevitably yields more fish.

While clear water might seem a prerequisite for underwater viewing, many reservoirs and rivers often called "stained" offer potential, too. In rivers, current often washes particles through the upper or mid-sections of the water column. Water near the bottom is much clearer, quite suitable for viewing. Similarly, plankton blooms may cloud surface waters of lakes and reservoirs, while deeper water is clearer. Cameras often prove useful in such waterways, as well as in obviously clear systems.

Underwater cameras also have been great tools to introduce kids and novice anglers to the world of the fishes, which inevitably proves fascinating. Even experienced anglers often find themselves spending more time gazing at the screen than making casts to targets below. Until recently, underwater viewing pretty much precluded angling, so it worked well to have one angler fish while a partner scanned the scene below, pointing out all the slabs the angler running the boat had fished right through. Since staring at a screen for prolonged periods can cause mild seasickness in some people, trading off after a half hour or so works well.

Nature Vision, a pioneer in the industry, has broken through this barrier with the MAV (Motorized Aqua-Vu), a camera secured to the hull and featuring a foot-operated motor that deploys the lens, raising or lowering it to follow bottom contours and scan structure for fish. A large LCD screen mounted at the bow or console displays what lies below, while the angler is free to watch the camera as well as sonar, while casting.

Several manufacturers offer underwater cameras in a variety of configurations suitable for either open-water or ice fishing. Most offer black & white images. While anglers accustomed to color TVs may seek color versions, present technology and requirements for viewing in sunlight mean that black-white units typically provide better detail, particularly in low-light conditions. Larger monitors have advantages for viewing, especially when shaded with a sunscreen.

Some models offer readouts of water temperature, depth, and give the direction the camera is pointing. Monitor size and quality vary, along with cable lengths and storage systems. For most freshwater viewing, a 50-foot cable is sufficient. Many models come with longer cables, since these units often are used by biologists and law enforcement personnel. Some units feature infrared or colored LED lights to provide better viewing in dim light or at night. Rechargeable battery packs and chargers are typically included, although you can run cameras off your boat's 12-volt system as well. Video recorder jacks allow you to plug in and record what you see, then replay on a TV.

WHAT'S AVAILABLE

Nature Vision—The Aqua-Vu series of cameras is the most diverse, with models from the Scout II, retailing for $229.99, to the MAV, priced at $1,999.99. Their screens range from 4 to 10.4 inches. Several units have a blend of red and blue lights to create optimum light transmission and enhance viewing, especially at night. Their fish-shaped lenses (7 species) have been popular for their natural and streamlined shape. Many accessories are available (866/777-0733, *naturevisioninc.com/aquavu*). Prices are for 2007 and vary check google.com.

Atlantis—A SportsCam and Panning Camera are offered, with black-white and color versions. Priced at $199.99, the SportsCam II has a high-resolution, 5½-inch black-white monitor with infrared night vision. The Panning Camera rotates 320 degrees with directional indicator, depth and temperature readouts, and 100 feet of cable, priced at $599.99 (*atlantis-camera.com*). Prices are for 2007 and vary.

MarCum Technologies—MarCum offers two units with Darkwater Technology, blue LED lights that minimize reflection off suspended particles. The VS 560 includes depth, direction, and temperature displays. It can be set to pan 360 degrees for ice-fishing applications ($599.99, *marcumtech.com*). Prices are for 2007 and vary.

SONAR

In 1957, using technology developed for the military, Carl Lowrance began marketing his original Red Box and Green Box. Sonar has since taught generations of anglers how to locate fish and interpret bottom features.

Does sonar technology help anglers find more fish? That depends on how well it's understood and used. Without factoring in all the other elements covered in this book, you won't get very far with a sonar display—you'll be too busy checking out unproductive parts of the lake and then puzzling over display results. But used as an adjunct to what your eyes tell you about lake or river structure, weather, water temperature, and where fish are in relation to the Calendar Period, sonar units can fine-tune the task of locating crappie.

Original sonars used a lighted wheel, called a flasher. Paper graphs soon followed, drawing intricate pictures of the bottom and fish. Many anglers found them difficult to operate and maintain, but avid structure-fishermen recognized them as being far more accurate than other methods.

The market for sonar is driven not by the few professionals but by the large market of amateurs. As a result, sonar manufacturers have abandoned paper graphs entirely, and only a few continue to build true flashers. Even after two decades of refining liquid crystal displays (LCDs), manufacturers know that flashers penetrate matted vegetation better than LCDs. They're also easier to tune, and most provide reliable depth-readings, even at speeds of more than 60 mph.

Traditional flashers still have certain advantages over next-generation liquid crystal technology, particularly in ice applications. Flashers are also quite effective in weedbeds, where they're able to decipher the bottom and define weed clumps without blanking out the screen—a common problem with LCD units, unless you manually turn down the sensitivity. Flashers also are able to read bottom in extremely shallow water. Cruising a shallow river in a jon boat, for instance, you can see a subtle change from 24 to 20 inches in depth, suggesting you'd better slow down or risk restyling your prop.

LCD threatened to eradicate flasher technology when it first appeared and, in fact, nearly did. LCD screens make use of tiny pixels, the more the merrier: The greater number of pixels, the more precise their portrayal of fish, vegetation, and bottom features. Pixel displays are generally considered easier to interpret than flasher signals—although, as with all electronics, sometimes what you think you see is not what's actually there. What appears to be fish may in fact be weeds, wood, rocks, or suspended matter, just as with flashers. LCD units are great for open-water applications but often experience difficulty at the cold temperatures associated with ice fishing.

LCD units have come a long way, with greatly improved picture definition, thanks to new screen technologies. New electronic circuitry has improved the speed of readings,

Lowrance's original "Green Box" is a collector's item but some remain in use today.

approaching "real time." The latest generation includes new colored displays featuring TFT technologies (thin film transistors) that enhance screen clarity in bright sunlight. Each pixel has its own transistor, allowing the unit to provide a full scale of 256 color variations, the same technology as in a flat-screen TV.

In the following sections, we'll examine key aspects of sonar units, how to tune them, and how best to interpret them to get the most relevant fishing information.

TRANSDUCERS

For many anglers, transducers are those black things mounted on the back of boats or placed somewhere in their hulls. They get blamed for poor images, poor high-speed performance, and unit failure. But if you know how these small but important objects work and how to make them work better, they'll become the objects of interest they deserve to be.

All transducers have one thing in common: They contain a crystal that vibrates in response to electrical current. The crystal converts that current to sound energy, which is emitted at a particular frequency and in a direction. In the case of fishing sonar, the operating frequency from 50 kHz to 400 kHz is aimed at the lake bottom. When the sound energy bounces back—whether from fish, from bottom, or other objects—it's reconverted (transduced) to electrical energy. This travels to the locator head, where it's displayed as an image. Screen images are displayed as cross-sections of depth, and objects that have impeded the sonar unit's sound waves are displayed at their respective depths.

Discussions of transducers usually center on their frequency and cone angle (beam width). Most freshwater sonar units operate in the 50- to 200-kHz range. Every frequency within this spectrum offers advantages and disadvantages; manufacturers choose frequencies to optimize particular performances and functions. It's important to know what these are before choosing a unit.

Cone angle or beam width refers to the diameter of the three-dimensional cone of water covered by the unit's sonar at a particular depth, which is usually referred

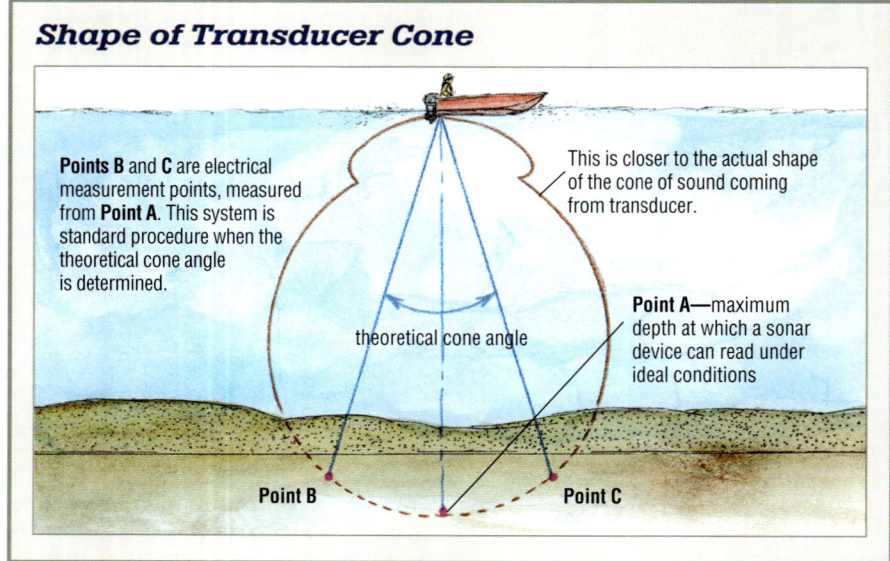

Shape of Transducer Cone

Points **B** and **C** are electrical measurement points, measured from **Point A**. This system is standard procedure when the theoretical cone angle is determined.

This is closer to the actual shape of the cone of sound coming from transducer.

theoretical cone angle

Point A—maximum depth at which a sonar device can read under ideal conditions

Point B   Point C

164 Critical Concepts . . . All About Finding Crappies

to as the "half-power point," or –3 dB. Though sonar coverage is not always symmetrical, it's helpful to think of the cone angle as an inverted sugar cone, with the point as the transducer. A narrow cone angle looks like a narrow ice cream cone, while a wide cone angle looks like a broad one. Depending on frequency, cone angles typically range from about 8 to 50 degrees. Usually the cone angle is narrower at high operating frequency and broader at low frequency. These are physical limits that design can't overcome.

A narrow cone angle—say, one of fewer than 20 degrees—provides more accurate bottom detail with less coverage, while a wide cone angle displays a larger area with perhaps more targets. But those targets are spread out over a larger area, and it's unclear exactly how close they are to your boat. When you've located a fish with a narrow-beam transducer, you know that it's near or under your boat. Measured at –3 dB, an 8-degree transducer covers an area whose diameter is about 1/6 of water depth (scans a 3-foot circle in 18 feet of water); a 20-degree transducer covers an area whose diameter is about 1/3 of water depth (6-foot circle); a 38-degree transducer, one whose diameter is about 2/3 of water depth (12-foot circle).

The disadvantages of low-frequency systems are that they usually don't work well in water less than 10 to 15 feet deep, and they don't penetrate deeper water as well as high-frequency systems. But a narrow-beam transducer (8 degrees) can concentrate sound energy and reach deep water, even several hundred feet down. For this reason, deep-water anglers on the Great Lakes often prefer low-frequency units. High-frequency systems, however, usually offer better target separation in shallower situations.

Because there are advantages to both frequency ranges, a few manufacturers offer sonar units able to operate at dual frequencies. A common dual frequency transducer operates at 50/200 kHz. A second design offers a dual-beam transducer whose frequency stays the same but whose cone width can be set for either 9 or 18 degrees. Yet another design is built around transducers containing multiple crystals of the same frequency; each scans in a different direction—right, left, or center—thus creating a wider beam of coverage.

TRANSDUCER POWER

Power determines how deep sonar penetrates; more powerful units can send a signal deeper into water and detect its return. For deepwater fishing, a 3,000-watt unit performs better than a 500-watt one. The latest units boast up to 8,000 watts peak-to-peak. But how much power do you need? Bottom hardness, salinity, plankton concentrations, interference from other electronic devices, and receiver sensitivity are factors affecting the depth a unit can penetrate.

Two aspects of sonar power should be factored into your decisions about how much sonar to buy: edge detection and target separation.

Edge detection—The strongest signal is generated by objects directly below the axis of the transducer. On the edges of that sound cone, energy decreases. Powerful locators— sonar units— help detect targets at the edges of the cone better than less powerful ones.

Target separation—Another aspect of sonar power is a unit's ability to detect and display objects like fish, rocks, and weeds. Greater power can drive sound waves to lake bottom in deeper water, making possible the separation of objects that lie close together. Most units with midrange frequency can separate targets about 3 inches apart in shallow water. That is, if a fish is 4 inches above bottom, a midrange unit can show the fish as a mark above bottom. But if a fish is just 2 inches off bottom, fish and bottom are likely to blend into a single image. Similarly, if three fish are below your boat and all the same distance from the transducer, only one fish will be displayed even though the fish are at different depths. Target separation widens in deeper water, so the more powerful a unit is, the greater likelihood that it can bounce off bottom and separate objects in close proximity to each other.

How much edge and target separation to buy depends on where you do most of your fishing. If you rarely fish deeper than 30 feet and bottom there is relatively firm, 300 watts may be adequate. If you fish soft-bottomed lakes or deeper water, you'll get more satisfaction from a 2,000- to 3,000-watt unit.

PIXELS

Another important feature of LCD units is the number of pixels, or "picture elements," it has—those tiny squares that produce the image on your graph's screen. The vertical pixel count (VPC) determines your screen's resolution, and the better the resolution, the more detailed the display. Vertical pixels break the column of water below you into segments. The more segments, and the smaller segments it gets broken into, the more information that's provided. Current VPC on most units is 200 to 500. In 30 feet of water, one pixel on a screen with a VPC of 100 represents about 3.5 inches. One pixel on a screen with a VPC of 350 at the same depth represents about 1.5 inches. Horizontal pixel counts also can be important, as the screen width, along with chart speed, determines how much of the history of the underwater world remains on the screen before scrolling away. Buy as high a pixel count as you can afford. Powerful units cost more, but they're worth the price.

Hard Bottom

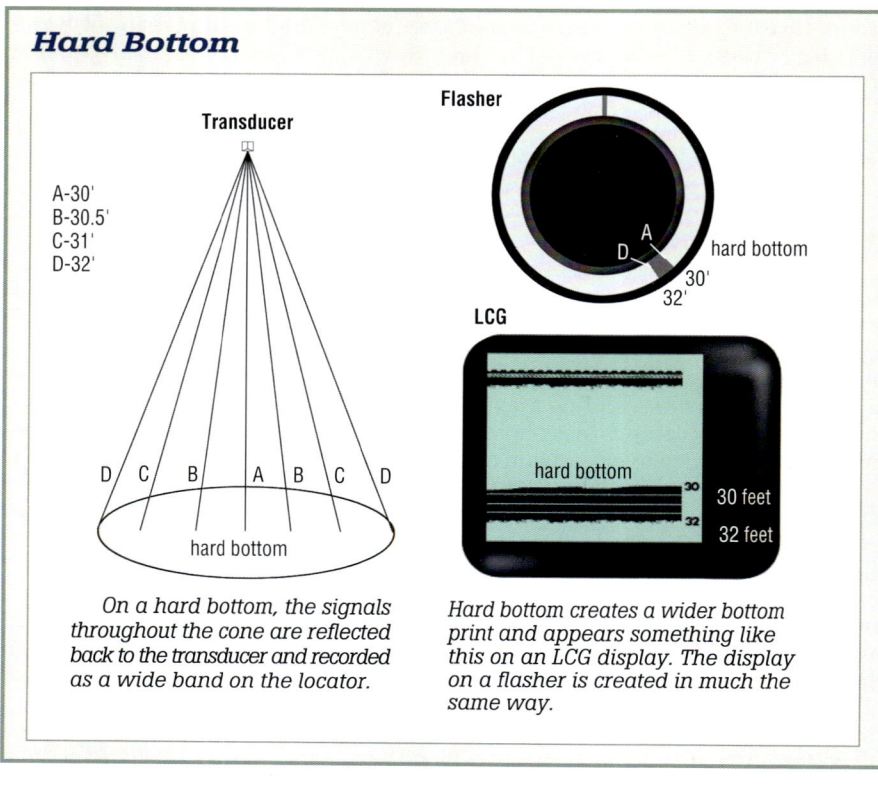

On a hard bottom, the signals throughout the cone are reflected back to the transducer and recorded as a wide band on the locator.

Hard bottom creates a wider bottom print and appears something like this on an LCG display. The display on a flasher is created in much the same way.

166 Critical Concepts . . . All About Finding Crappies

Soft Bottom

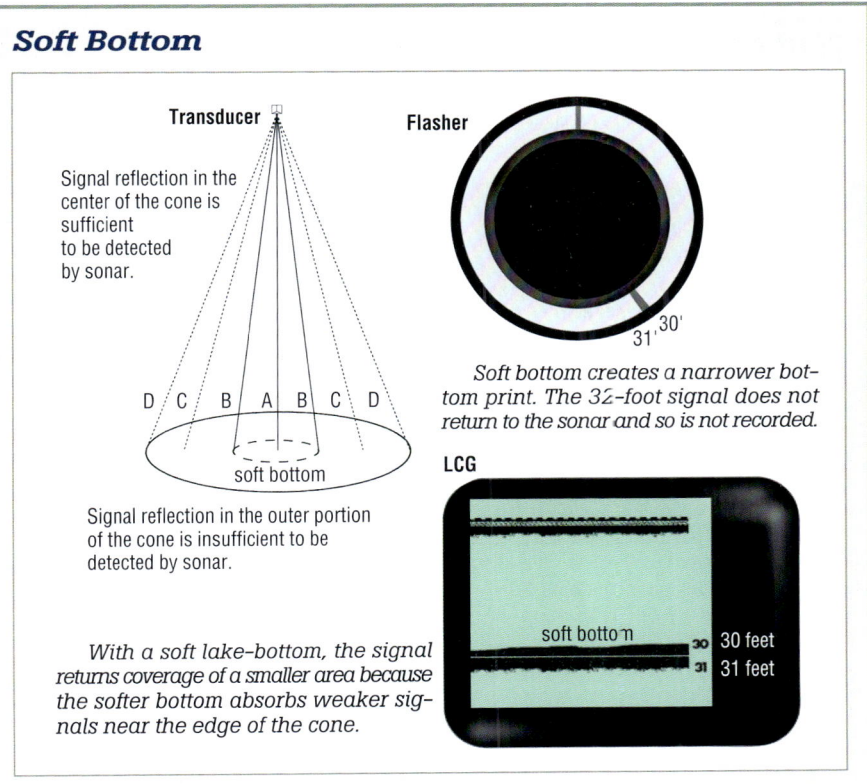

Transducer

Signal reflection in the center of the cone is sufficient to be detected by sonar.

Signal reflection in the outer portion of the cone is insufficient to be detected by sonar.

With a soft lake-bottom, the signal returns coverage of a smaller area because the softer bottom absorbs weaker signals near the edge of the cone.

Flasher

Soft bottom creates a narrower bottom print. The 32-foot signal does not return to the sonar and so is not recorded.

LCG

soft bottom — 30 feet
31 feet

INTERPRETING SONAR

Both deep water and soft bottoms tend to return a weak signal. In deep water, the signal travels a long way on its round-trip from surface to lake bottom and back to the surface again. As it travels, it weakens and becomes harder to detect, translate, and display. On soft bottoms like muck and silt, much of the signal is absorbed by the substrate. To improve readings over such substrates, turn up the unit's sensitivity in manual mode to a level higher than the default one the unit's auto mode selected. In water shallower than 5 feet, the return signal can be too strong because of the short distance it travels. In this case, auto mode may not reduce the sensitivity enough to produce a clear picture. Instead, the whole screen may "gray out." To adjust, turn down the sensitivity in shallow water or over a hard bottom, thereby providing a narrower cone angle. In deeper water or over softer bottom, increase sensitivity to provide a broader cone angle.

Vegetation provides another set of challenges for adjusting sensitivity. It's common for fish to hold along edges of weedlines or above the tops of weedbeds. Locators set in auto mode have difficulty handling such situations. If you increase sensitivity to penetrate to the bottom in a weedbed, the screen will be saturated and lack detail. Remember that increasing sensitivity raises the unit's listening ability, not the locator's power. When you power up in auto mode in dense vegetation, you get a strong return signal because vegetation is a good reflector,

Night

Watching sonar during long nights of crappie fishing tends to torch your night vision. You can simply dial down the backlighting on a Lowrance unit by hitting the "power/light" button, but there's a "night viewing" setting. It dims the readout with, for instance, a black background with a green bottom and fish marks to avoid being blinded by the light. Hit the "menu" button twice to get to the "screen menu," then arrow to the right. Scroll down to "display mode" and hit "enter"—then scroll down to go from "normal" or "high contrast" to "night viewing," and hit "enter." Your night vision will thank you.

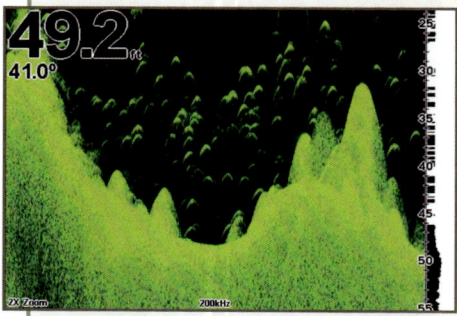

sending back a strong signal that lacks detail because of the multiple surfaces of the plants' leaves. Your unit is on overload. To reduce its sensitivity around vegetation, use the sonar in manual mode, experimenting with sensitivity settings to learn which works best.

The sensitivity control is the locator's most important function. Learn how it affects what you see on screen, so the unit works for and not against you. Launch on a favorite body of water and check familiar locations. Position your boat in shallow water, deep water, over hard bottoms, soft bottoms, rockpiles, and around vegetation. See how the unit interprets each of these areas. Adjust its sensitivity settings to see how doing so affects the information displayed. Decide which work best in situations you're familiar with. Doing so will give you more confidence in your sonar's capabilities.

FINE-TUNING

Today's sonars are highly sophisticated—some even include a computer-style hard drive. Faced with multiple buttons and arrows, which lead to layers of menu options, most anglers opt for the auto button. And given that this setting provides serviceable images on most good units, that's as far as many go. But to achieve the best possible depiction of bottom, bait, and fish, given the computer-like capabilities of modern marine technology, adjustments are needed.

SPLIT SCREENS

Before delving into sensitivity, colorline, and so forth, consider your fishing style. Are you structure-fishing or setting up a trolling spread for open water? For structure, try switching your unit to split-screen zoom mode. That way, the nuances of bottom are displayed on both sides of the screen. Moreover, the zoom window is powerful enough to pick out individual fish lying on bottom. Dropping a jig in the unit's cone angle shows your presentation in relationship to the fish, perhaps even their approach toward it. You can mark crappies in zoom mode and watch them rise off bottom or out of a school to inspect and strike bait.

On the other hand, full-screen mode is preferable for the wide-screen view of what lies below. It's possible to go into the "sonar setup" menu to create upper and lower depth limits to read specific bands—say, 20 to 40 feet—to zero in on bait and fish with greater accuracy. If you primarily troll, however, split-screen mode may not be for you—wide-screen view is better for this application.

COLORLINES

Next up: The crucial setting of sensitivity. While it was once important to crank the sensitivity almost to 100 percent with black-and-white units, color screens operating with higher power levels no longer require full-tilt sensitivity. Rather, the best way to set it is to turn it up until clutter and distortion fill the screen to the point of unreadability. Then back off until the screen clears itself of all but a little sprinkling that looks like a dusting of pepper. Then back off one or two more clicks for good measure. You'll need more sensitivity in deeper water, less in water shallower than 15 feet. Fish show in shades of red and orange, depending on their size and location in relation to the sonar's cone angle.

That brings us to colorline, the modern version of grayline, once the standard way black-white units provided separation of targets from bottom. On a color screen with colorline, you're better able to see fish on structure and even in weeds. For most applications, start with a colorline range of 75 to 90 percent, then adjust as needed.

To dial-in specific numbers, experiment with the colorline settings until the bottom shows a black, defining line with yellow underneath it. Then increase the colorline until the yellow has a hint of red in it; reduce the level from there until the red disappears, then increase by a click or two. At this setting, changes in the sonar return indicate both fish and differences in bottom content.

Turning the "Pages"

Want to adjust settings on one half of the screen but not the other, or zoom in on the sonar rather than the GPS when the unit's in split-screen mode? The answer is to hit the "pages" button twice. If you're clicking "zoom" and it's zeroing in on sonar magnification, but instead you want to zoom in on the GPS on the other side of the screen, punching "pages" twice allows you to zoom in on GPS. Likewise, hitting the menu button allows you to further adjust the GPS. It works in the other direction, too, to take you from GPS back to sonar.

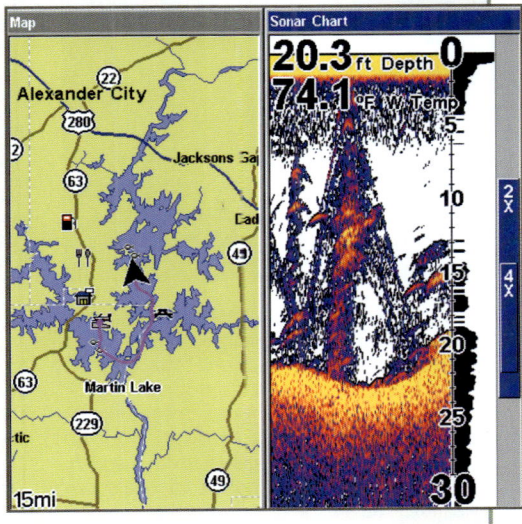

SELECTING SPEEDS

Although cranking settings to maximum is no longer needed in modern sonars, a couple of parameters are best taken to the limit—that is, to a 100-percent setting. Ping speed and chart speed both affect how fast impulses are dispatched and returned to the sonar unit. Ping has to do with the rate at which the sonar's signal is sent out, returned, and interpreted by the unit's processors. Furthermore, keeping ping at max rather than frequently adjusting it is going to yield a semblance of consistency in what you're seeing—all the better for your own interpretation.

Setting chart speed at max, which influences how fast the picture moves or scrolls across the screen, accomplishes something similar. At 100 percent, the read-out shows what's being displayed at the fastest rate possible for the best possible real-time viewing, with better fish arches in the shape of elongated, upside-down smiles rather than more compact, inverted V's.

SIDE-IMAGING SONAR

In 2005, Humminbird introduced a new type of sonar. Their high-end units have Side-Imaging (SI) sonar color imagery plus GPS map navigation features. At roughly $2,000, the Humminbird 987c SI is about the most expensive sonar and GPS unit available. But experienced anglers have found the SI to be a better searching tool than standard units.

Side-Imaging Snapshots

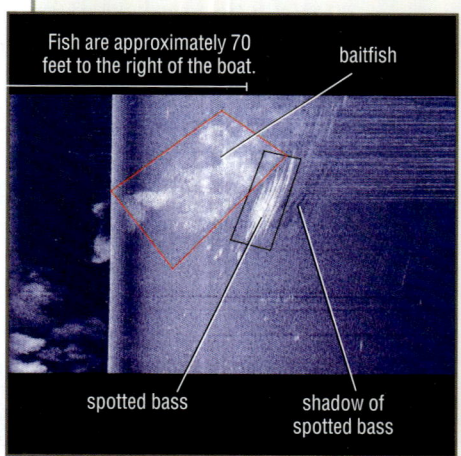

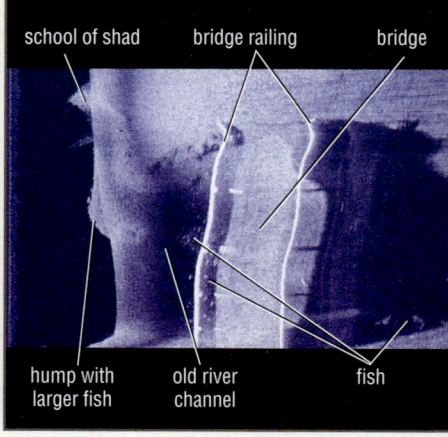

1) Mike Bucca, a guide (tritonmike.com) at Lake Allatoona, Georgia, located this school of baitfish surrounded by suspended spotted bass with his Humminbird 987c SI in SI mode. Bucca reported catching five of these large spots by vertically working a ballhead jig with plastic stickbait attached. The shadows of the bass indicate these are fish echoes.

2) One of several images of an underwater bridge and surrounding area that Ralph Manns screen-captured. Referring to several pictures of the same structure or cover objects from several angles greatly aids interpretation of what is shown in the imagery.

Buyers gain a new search capability that simplifies the process of finding cover and structure likely to hold fish. SI allows an angler to make passes down a shoreline or around important structures and mark spots as waypoints. The angler can then return to fish each waypoint to see if the spots are productive. Users more rapidly learn new waters and gain knowledge about underwater features they already fish.

One drawback is that fish returns are smaller and more difficult to identify in SI imagery compared to standard vertical sonars. Schools of small baitfish appear as murky clouds rather than dark blobs. Fish the size of crappies or yellow bass may appear as small white dots, and individual gamefish like bass aren't much different from the returns created by stumps on bottom; but this is a cover-location tool, and effective use always has a learning curve.

Although gamefish and baitfish show as separate returns in SI imagery close to the boat, fish echoes farther to the side are mixed in with returns from the bottom and are more difficult to see. The clue that an SI return is a fish rather than a bottom or cover echo is a matching fish shadow farther away. Side imaging can help an angler locate and relocate moving schools of predator fish in relatively open water, but this is a bonus feature, not a primary benefit.

Beds of underwater vegetation are visible as marbled or bumpy bottom, but the soft edges of many submerged weedbeds may be indefinite. The prime benefit of

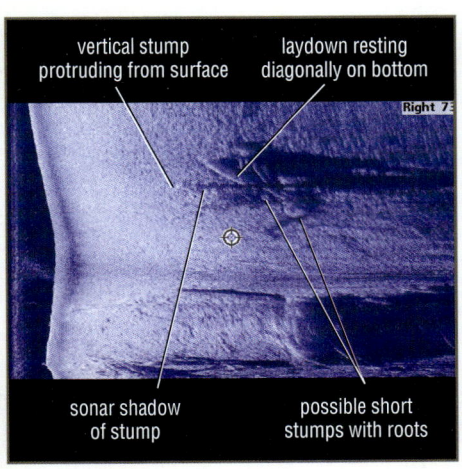

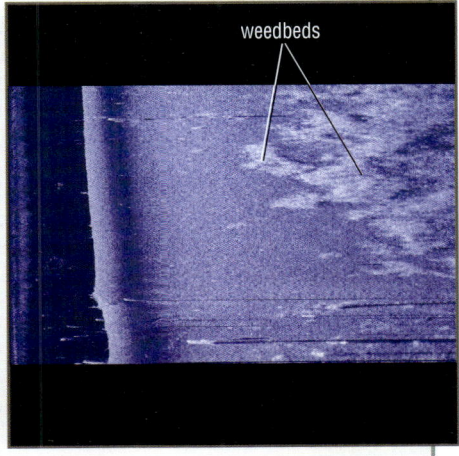

3) The ability of the SI to reveal details of underwater cover is shown here. This stump with a cluster of laydowns at its base produced two 6-pound largemouths at Lake Fork. The shadow reveals the large stump of the main trunk that protrudes from the surface. The SI revealed a second laydown resting diagonally on the bottom.

4) A bed of milfoil, coontail, and filamentous algae at Lake Fork. Not all weedbeds are this distinct or provide as sharp a return. Note that the SI sees right into clumps of vegetation, so the front edges of beds merge with the vegetation behind them. In some cases beds merely looked like bubbles or bumps on the bottom.

Tools for Fine-Tuning Crappie Location

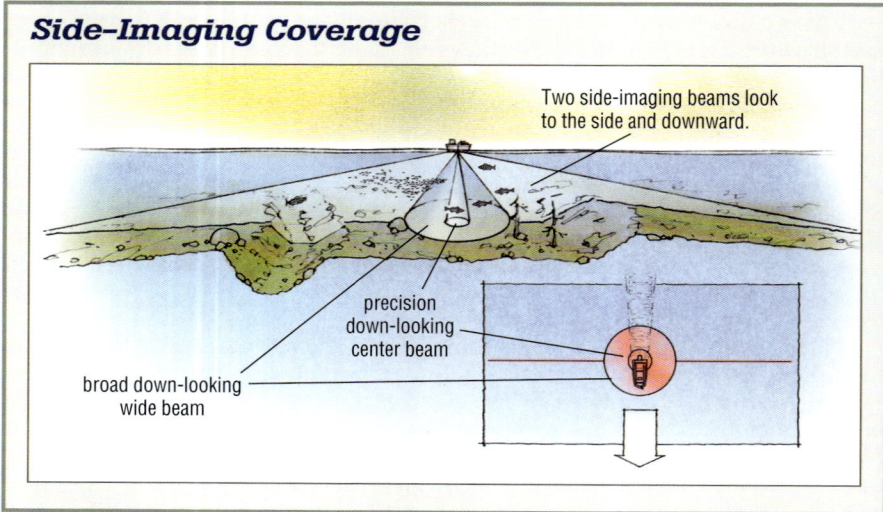

Side-Imaging Coverage

SI is in definition of hard elements. Rockpiles and the deep edges of riprap are clear. Bridge construction and cover near pilings are revealed. Laydowns and underwater brush seen as blobs on bottom with vertical sonars become distinct logs and trees with defined branches. The clarity of various images recorded with the SI can be seen on the Humminbird website (*humminbird.com*). The increased fishing capability created by such detail is much like having photographs of exposed cover in a reservoir or lake.

While the unit has many positive features, anglers should also be aware of its limitations. The SI unit's transducer must be located externally on the stern of a boat. The system works best at speeds under 10 mph and on straight-line courses, as turns distort the imagery.

How the stern is shaped and the outboard motor mounted influence whether the unit can "see" well to either side. Nothing may be placed in the line of sight to the sides of the transducer, and external mounting exposes the transducer to possible damage. Yet reasonably careful operation avoids damage, even in reservoirs with abundant standing timber and stumps.

Beginners with the SI system learn to better identify echoes and use other features on every outing. If you're a non-techie, you may find the complexity of menus and some options non-intuitive, but learning the details is rewarding. Users need to buy a map chip and may want another chip to record images for later review on a personal computer.

GLOBAL POSITIONING SATELLITE (GPS) SYSTEMS

The Global Positioning Satellite system is the most important locating technology to be introduced to fishing since the introduction of the depthfinder. Its forerunner, Loran-C, deciphered your location by triangulating a series of signals from radio towers, signals that often were weakened or lost due to variations in weather.

GPS was developed for the U.S. Department of Defense, and its first widespread use was during the Gulf War. Drawing on a network of satellites orbiting some 11,000 miles above the earth, a GPS unit can triangulate locations for latitude and longitude to within 5 to 20 feet.

Not surprisingly, the number of anglers who own GPS units has skyrocketed. Prices have fallen and new technologies have appeared for both boat-mounted and handheld units. Many new sonar units also have GPS capability, and split-screen mode allows an angler to view bottom features and position simultaneously.

Anglers use GPS for better positioning accuracy, marking spots, mapping, and charting routes within water bodies. GPS mapping systems offer electronic displays of lakes, rivers, and their shorelines. In the mid-'90s when GPS units first appeared on the scene, maps were cartridge-based and quite basic. They displayed freeway systems, state roads, midsized to large lakes and rivers, and medium to large towns. Background maps typically covered the entire U.S., as well as parts of Canada and Mexico. Greater topographic detail became available when manufacturers introduced cartridges or digital memory cards that enhanced designated areas on background maps. These provided additional useful navigational information— buoy markers, reefs, channels, and water depths. Extent and detail of coverage varies and certain computer applications are required, so check features before you buy electronic maps.

Mapping systems are available in chart-by-chart or seamless options. The chart-by-chart method is a digital version of the paper maps you've worked with for years, and it carries with it the same problem—differences of scale when you move from one map to another. The seamless method scrolls across a map with a uniform scale. The quality of mapping details is a function of two factors, the electronic file in the map cartridge and the acuity of your display monitor. In the case of a typical LCD screen, the total pixel count and the screen's ability to react to light are the factors determining detail. Coarse screens may not adequately display all of the information available on a cartridge, particularly small details.

Keep in mind that zooming down to a small scale may not increase detail. It may mean instead that what you saw at 2 miles is only bigger at 0.2 mile, not more detailed. Different levels of detail should appear at different zoom or scale levels. For example, contour lines, small reefs, and islands that may not appear on a 20-mile scale should become visible on a 3-mile scale. Check to make sure that the mapping system you buy offers this capability.

The appearance of CD-ROMs in the GPS lineup means that instead of buying a handful of cartridges to cover all the areas you travel for outdoor activities, you can now cover the entire country in great detail with one or two CDs. When you load a mapping CD—such as Lowrance's MapCreate or Garmin's Road and Recreation and MetroGuide U.S.—the program appears on the monitor. Select or outline the area you want transferred to your GPS unit. The

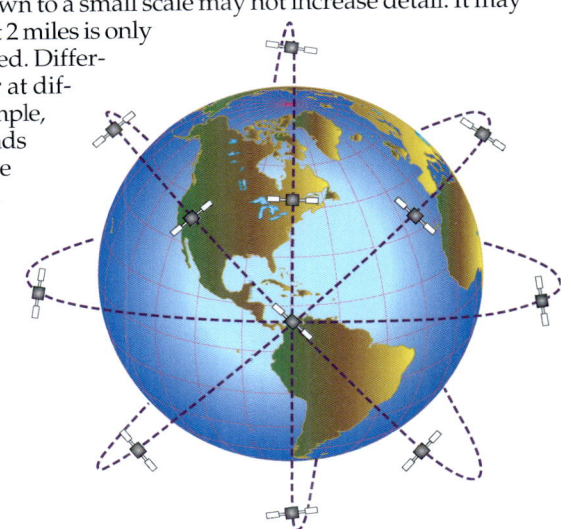

Global Positioning Satellite systems use a constellation of 24 satellites covering the earth in precise orbits about 11,000 miles out in space. As many as 12 satellites are available for signal transmission and receiver reception at any one time.

The latest GPS units allow you to manage waypoints and trails for more efficient navigation.

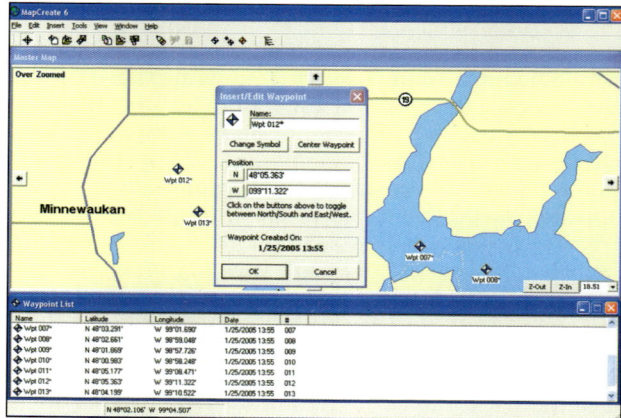

transfer is done through a data cable that attaches to the computer's data port. Mapping programs allow you to create or customize your own maps, so you can choose the details you want displayed—small streams, rural roads, restaurants, street names, navigational aids, state parks, and so on.

Once you've selected a map area for downloading, the information is transferred into a "flash memory" (typically, 2 to 8 MB of memory on a blank cartridge or MMC card that fits in your GPS unit). Depending on the level of detail you've chosen, a single file can include a state the size of Georgia.

Mapping giant DeLorme recently entered the GPS mapping scene, and their GPS PN-20 hand-held receiver can display both DeLorme maps and aerial imagery. Their Topo USA map software is included.

GPS APPLICATIONS

Marking waypoints is another strength of GPS systems. You can mark important points like home port, boat ramps, brushpiles, and reefs on your GPS maps so that you can avoid hazards or accurately return to fishing spots, even in bad weather or at night. Thanks to contour maps offered by such companies as Lakemaster, C-Map, Fishing Hot Spots, Lowrance, and Navionics in memory card, CD, and website formats, you can add waypoints to existing contour maps. When you're working on your computer with mapping systems, such as those produced by Fishing Hot Spots and Waypoint Technologies, you can move your mouse to spots and set them as waypoints. The system numbers your waypoints and you can name them for better identification. Marking underwater points, inside turns, and sunken islands is simple. This information can then be downloaded onto your GPS unit.

Most GPS units let you place markers or icons on the screen to mark fish or interesting structure for future reference. Most anglers don't bother to punch in names for locations of caught fish, as they expect them to change, but icons can help define a locational pattern. You can enter them on your computer later or log them into a notebook in case of GPS unit failure. GPS also is a safety feature, provided your batteries don't go dead. Even on familiar waters, anglers can become disoriented in fog, heavy rain, or other severe weather. Waypoints, icons, or saved trails can lead you to your destination or back to the ramp. GPS has turned many shoreline casters on big lakes into open-water anglers, thanks to the technology's ability to get them back home over featureless, expansive waters.

DEAR CRAPPIE DIARY

In-Fisherman Senior Editor Steve Quinn reports that on May 7, 1996, he and a companion landed 46 crappies ranging from a little one of a half pound to a couple of toads that pushed 15 inches. He doesn't have a photographic memory—instead, he's kept a record of his fishing excursions since 1978. Keeping detailed fishing records may not be for everyone, but Quinn and many other avid anglers enjoy doing it and gain interesting and valuable information on fishing trends that help define new patterns. Records serve as a check on the memory. "Often I recall a trip from memory," he says, "then look back at the data and find that I've exaggerated, or sometimes have underestimated the catch. Water temperatures and precise dates are readily lost, as well, by the frail human memory."

Quinn began his diary by using a commercial version (more on these shortly). He soon expanded data entries to include the length of the fishing day and precise location; times of catches, along with length and weight; lure or bait used, including size and color; air and water temperature, pH, and clarity; the moon phase; and weather observations.

"Keeping up with record-keeping isn't always easy," he admits. "The sooner you record data after the trip, the more accurate it will be. Precise time of day can be elusive, though the significance of this aspect may not seem critical to some anglers. But if you're interested in testing for effects of solunar periods on catch-rates or catches of big fish, times must be quite exact."

THE VALUE OF RECORDS

Quinn's stack of files stands some 30 inches high and weighs nearly 22 pounds. "I often refer to these records when returning to a body of water after not fishing it for a while," he says, "or to check on seasonal patterns that worked in the past. Records also help me as an editor and writer, as I can accurately call forth information on water temperatures, catch-rates, lure and bait preferences, and so on. They're also a great starting point when planning a trip."

An example of the type of data sheet used by Steve Quinn. Add or delete fields to capture the information you're interested in. Also consider a computer database program instead of a paper-based system.

ANGLING REPORT

Location		Hours Fished		Date	
Barometer		Moon Phase	ph	Water Clarity	
Weather		Water Level		Boat Used	
Air Temp		Water Temp		Companion	

Time	Species	Weight	Length	Bait Used	Color	Size	How Fished

"Records also can be a pleasant source of nostalgia," he adds. "As you review catch records, you relive the moment to an extent, recalling with satisfaction how you pieced together the eternal fishing puzzle and made a good catch, or how the fish flummoxed you once again. During the winter months, it's entertaining to go back and review the past year or years, looking for week-long or month-long hot bites, or other trends in the data."

Anglers interested in solunar effects or whether moon phase affected the catch can now perform analysis on a large set of data. Those with a more scientific bent and perhaps some training in statistics can apply tests to see whether apparent differences in catch-rates, say between full and dark moons, actually are significant.

Record-keeping software—In recent years, several fishing diary software packages have emerged, allowing easy recall and analysis of the information entered. You can then select for review by time of year, fish species, trolling applications, reservoir type, moon phases, and more. Obvious advantages to electronic records are quick analysis of data for time of year, fishing location, or species sought. With a keystroke, all pertinent records can be summoned, rather than thumbing through scores of loose hardcopy.

The most advanced record-keeping system we've seen so far is the Prologue Systems (*prologuesystems.com*), a fishing log that works in conjunction with today's fastest growing data management device, the hand-held Pocket PC PDA that uses Windows Mobile. With the unit in a waterproof pouch, you can record catches and information as you fish. The system costs $39.99 (not including your mobile hand-held computer).

When using GPS, it's wise to record locations of waypoints in a hardcopy logbook. Daily fishing records work fine for this too, as key information will include body of water, waypoint number, and date, as well as latitude and longitude. Handwritten records serve as back-up in case of unit loss or power failure, and also help organize a growing collection of GPS data.

Many anglers object to the time required to keep full and accurate records. Indeed, it can be tedious when work schedules or other activities become demanding. Some simply cannot sit down and do this, or don't care to.

It's also admittedly possible that going back and checking past patterns and catch locations might keep some anglers in a rut. Constantly referring to records could keep you doing what worked in the past, instead of breaking new trails and perhaps discovering a better fishing pattern, bait, or location. To avoid such a rut, try to balance following old paths with new experiments, based on changing water conditions, season, or other variables.

CHARTING WEATHER

Cold fronts seem a never-ending plague for springtime anglers, and they provide a time-honored excuse for poor fishing. The connection between barometric pressure—the actual weight of the atmosphere pressing upon us—and fish behavior has been a hotbed of discussion and puzzlement since the days of Izaak Walton in the 17th century.

In our rational minds, we tend to minimize such effects because changes in air pressure are impossible to see and difficult to envision. Air, after all, seems weightless. Biological researchers have not devoted much attention to the effects of barometric pressure on fish. When they have, results have been unclear and often conflicting.

As a result, the effects on fish remain mysterious, a source of endless curiosity, bringing frequent questions to *In-Fisherman* staff at fishing seminars, in letters to the editor, and on our Web forums. Some anglers suggest that biologists should do studies to better define how such slight changes in our atmosphere could affect creatures living below the water's surface. But with many more urgent projects, intense research into this topic isn't likely anytime soon.

It's reasonable to assume that any direct effects of air pressure, along with wind, cloud cover, solar radiation, and other atmospheric changes that coincide with barometric fluctuations, would be more pronounced in shallow water—generally the domain of crappies, especially early in the year. Moreover, crappies are common throughout the U.S. and southern Canada, a huge landlocked region boasting some of the most tumultuous weather changes on the planet.

BAROMETRIC BASICS

Earth's weather is affected by a never-ending series of high- and low-pressure fronts that generally move from west to east in that part of central North America sandwiched between the Rocky Mountains and the Appalachians. The term "front" applies to the leading edge of these air masses, which may be warmer and of lower pressure (warm fronts) or cooler with high pressure (cold fronts).

A barometer measures the pressure exerted on the local environment by the atmosphere. It reports pressure as inches of mercury called millibars—an inch of mercury, for instance, equals 33,864 millibars. This system dates to the late 19th century when Norwegian meteorologist Vilhelm Bjerknes defined a formula for measuring atmospheric pressure. Barometric pressure is greatest at sea level and decreases with elevation, thus the need to adjust instruments for local elevation.

As commonly reported on the nightly TV weather news, barometric readings are noted as inches of mercury, ranging from 28.5 (extremely low) to 31 (extremely high). Avid weather watcher and *In-Fisherman* reader Irvin Decker of Issaquah, Washington, notes that the midpoint of atmospheric pressure is 29.92 inches of mercury.

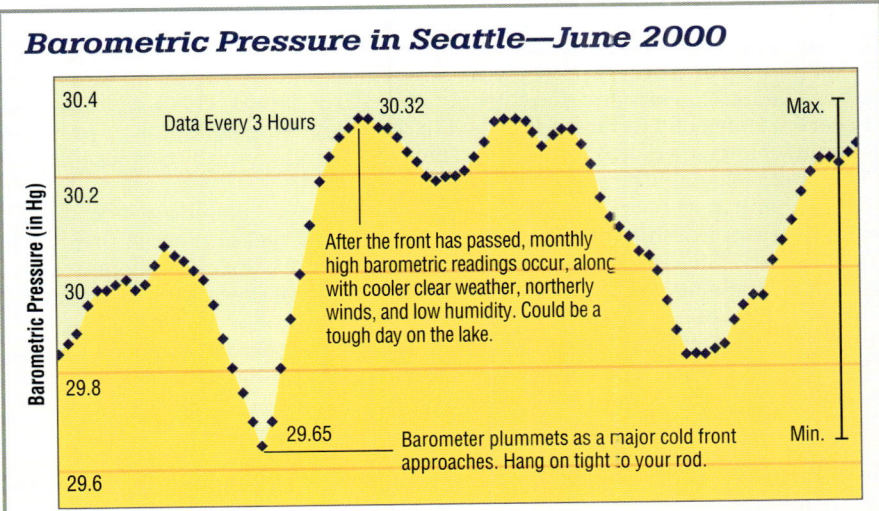

During June 2000, *In-Fisherman* reader and avid weather watcher Irvin Decker recorded barometric readings in Seattle made by the National Weather Service every three hours. "Barometric pressure varied between 29.65 and 30.32," he reports. "A major front passed near the middle of the month, resulting in a pressure drop of 0.67 inches of mercury."

During June 2000, Decker recorded barometric readings made by the National Weather Service in Seattle every three hours. "Barometric pressure varied between 29.65 and 30.32," he reports. "A major front passed near the middle of the month, resulting in a pressure drop of 0.67 inches of mercury. To put that in perspective, the highest barometric pressure ever recorded was 32.0 in Siberia in 1968. The lowest occurred in the eye of a typhoon in 1979 at 25.9."

Following several days of stable, mild weather with increasingly hazy skies, the approach of a cold front brings a falling barometer, along with increasing clouds and wind. According to the typical scenario, bass at this time feed actively, and good catches are common as a weather system approaches. After the front passes, the barometer rises rapidly, accompanied by clearing skies, northwesterly winds, and lower temperatures, particularly at night.

During these conditions, best termed "postfrontal," the bite is tougher. Good catches can still be made, but typically on smaller baits fished slowly in thick cover, where groups of bass have gathered. While trolling small crankbaits and mid-sized tubes may have worked as the front approached, miniature plastics and finesse hair jigs fished adjacent to weed clumps or in thick brushpiles may be the best way to tempt bites from crappies on the back side of the system. Anglers persisting with faster-moving horizontal baits likely catch smaller crappies, and not too many of those. Every experienced angler has experienced such changes.

WEATHER EFFECTS

In-Fisherman researcher Ralph Manns downplays the direct effect of barometric pressure on fish behavior. "A fish with a gas bladder needs only to swim up or down a foot or two to experience as great or greater a pressure change as that created by all but the largest natural pressure changes—say, a hurricane.

"A fish might notice itself floating or sinking a few inches in response to a change in air pressure, but it experiences larger pressure changes as it shifts depth several feet while hunting prey, escaping predators, or changing location.

"Black bass and other species with closed gas bladders use their bladders to achieve neutral density and thereby hold at constant depths. This weightlessness conserves energy by reducing the need to swim to hold position. If air pressure or depth changes, a fish with a gas bladder slowly and naturally adjusts bladder pressure to re-establish equilibrium."

Weather expert Irvin Decker adds, "Freshwater fish, including largemouth bass and crappies, shift depths from the surface to 15 feet or more in their feeding activities. This difference in depth represents a pressure change many times greater than the maximum barometric pressure change ever recorded on earth.

"I believe that barometric pressure changes associated with fronts bring with them secondary effects—wind, thunderstorms, cloud cover, changes in temperatures, and changes in light intensity—that do affect fishing success. Actual pressure changes alone do not have any direct effect on fishing, as is so often stated."

Manns concludes: "Biologists have never identified physical mechanisms or sensory systems that would specifically allow fish suspended at neutral density to sense relatively small changes in water pressure associated with barometric pressure shifts. Biologists have, however, long postulated that clouds, waves, and changes in lighting affect hunting success by predators, by favoring species with eyes sensitive to low light levels, such as crappies." Research into bioenergetics suggests that fish conserve energy by not foraging when their likelihood of success is reduced, then begin actively feeding when conditions are more promising. How they know this remains unstudied.

BE THE WEATHERMAN

If you've heard one joke about weather prognosticators, you've heard 100. But let's face it—the job's not easy. Try your hand by acquiring weather testing equipment: There's no arguing the benefits of consulting a barometer regularly and being prepared to adjust locations and presentations accordingly. Tackle-box barometers are available from Airguide, Cabela's, and Bass Pro Shops for under $20. Be sure to tune your barometer to local altitude by checking a nearby weather station, airport, or weather website. Set the marker arrow (usually red) to match the local current barometer level. The Anglers' EDGE PLUS from Speedtech (*speedtech.com*) is a pocket-sized weather guide that graphs 24-hour trends in barometric pressure, along with listing sunrise and sunset times, weather forecasts based on barometric pressure, and feeding activity charts. It's programmed with the next 96 years of solunar and sunrise data for future reference. Throughout the day, check for rising and falling barometric conditions and approaching solunar periods. Larger and more sophisticated weather stations can be set up indoors with equipment mounted on buildings to gauge wind speed and direction, humidity, UV index, and other factors. For a large selection of models from under $100 up to $1,000, check *weathershack.com*, *weatherconnect.com*, or *bestnest.com*.

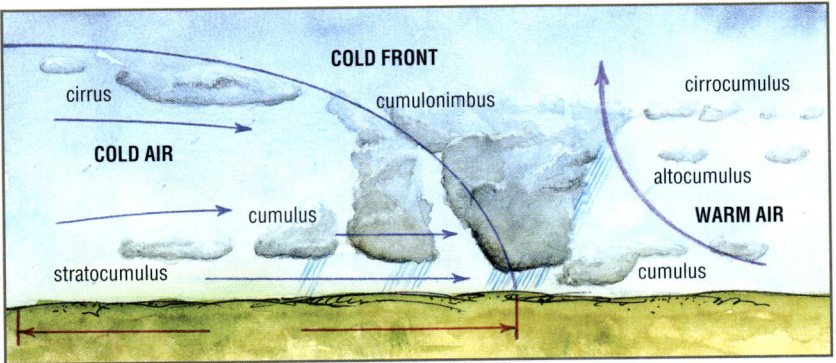

Cold Front

A cold front is defined as the transition area between a cold air mass moving into a warm air mass. At the front, cold air undercuts the warm air, lifting it upwards with a stronger thrust compared to the steady rise of air which is associated with a warm front. The cold front creates an unstable air mass and cumulonimbus clouds are formed which create thunderstorms along the cold air intrusion. All thunderstorms have two things in common—lightning and a rapid change in pressure.

Generally, pressure ahead of the cold front remains steady, then begins to fall. Once the cold front passes, pressure rises as a high-pressure system moves across the area. In a warm-front situation, pressure could remain steady after passage, or continue to fall.

DEALING WITH CHANGE

In most cases, the best time to go fishing is right now. If you wait for prime conditions, you'll likely find more pressing commitments spiking your trip.

Understanding the barometer's effects on bass can help you to select key depths and the most promising lure presentations. Though consensus is lacking on reasons for a tough bite following a cold front, there's little disagreement that fishing will be more challenging now than some days after the front has passed.

Cold fronts—Watching the barometer can help you tune your presentations to the mood of the fish. In general, best results after frontal passage come by fishing deeper. Another important modification is to use smaller baits and lighter line during postfrontal conditions. Livebait fished near the bottom continue to work, and for artificial lures, try vertical baits like minijigs that are effective when fished in cover and worked slowly.

Crappies typically aren't active or chasing prey under high-pressure conditions, but they will feed if an easy opportunity presents itself. Faster-moving horizontal baits like spinner jigs and mini-crankbaits usually don't produce well during high-pressure conditions.

Thin monofilaments or castable fluorocarbons hide the presentation better than heavier lines, and also allow small lures to move more naturally. Reduced line visibility also helps tempt bites from inactive fish. Naturally colored lures also are best. In short, fish deeper with smaller, slower-moving, natural-appearing lures.

Descending barometer—A falling barometer signals the approach of a front and often spurs a fast bite. Crappies often move shallower, following baitfish, and they feed toward the surface. It's a great time to fish small spinners or other fast-moving baits. Moreover, plankton rising in the water column in response to the falling barometer are concentrated on windblown banks, creating a great feeding opportunity for various species. In short, fish shallow with faster-moving baits.

Stable conditions—When the weather is stable and the barometer shows little fluctuation, fish tend to be scattered, as are preyfish. Fish hold at various depths, in different forms of cover, and show unpredictable activity levels. Various presentation patterns work, though none may produce outstanding catches.

If the barometer is falling from 30.1 or so, plan on covering water fast to find actively feeding fish, possibly near the surface. Once you find concentrations, expect a great catch. Focus on areas where crappies can corral baitfish, such as main-lake coves, bluff banks, tributary inflows, and necked-down areas. Carry crankbaits, rattlebaits, spinnerbaits, and buzzers.

If, on the other hand, the barometer is rising after a front has passed, pushing into the 30.4 range and beyond, switch presentation styles. Focus on smaller, natural-appearing baits that can be fished deeper and slower. Tune down your expectations, but fish hard, watching your sonar and your line carefully for soft bites.

Each new generation of fishing equipment and electronics brings more features and options into play. Whereas that first flasher technology lasted for decades, new and improved versions of electronics now seem to barrel through the fishing industry several times a year. As with computers—which most modern fishing electronics actually are—you hesitate to buy a particular unit because it's likely to be outmoded by the time you install it and first test it on the water. But get over your fears. You have to get your feet wet sometime, and now's as good a time as any to jump into the complex world of modern fishing technology. It will make you a better-equipped and more efficient angler.

Chapter 9
Ultimate Locational Factors

Finding Crappies Fast

SYSTEMS FOR NEW WATER

After elections, pollsters hang around the parking lot, taking what they call "exit polls." Basically, they ask who you voted for. In spring, some anglers perform their own version of such interviews. They fiddle with their boats, pulling out rods, taking off the tarp, and performing countless other chores that would be better done at home. But every angler returning to the ramp gets the third degree.

If you try to escape with a disclaimer like "Just caught a few," or "It was kinda slow," they buttonhole you, asking what kind, and how big, and what bait. And nothing gets them going as much as a glimpse of a few sizable crappies in the fish basket or livewell.

Finding Crappies Fast 181

Come spring, seems like everyone's catching crappies. Cast a minnow or small lure along any shallow, protected bay, and you'll likely get one or two. Little ones with big fins, big eyes, big mouth, and not much meat. Those big slabs are another breed altogether. Not literally, of course. They're just a couple years older. But in that time period, they adopt differing habits that separate them from the bankrunners.

Among America's most traveled anglers (excluding TV hosts, journalists, and the like) is Roger Bullock of Eugene, Oregon. In the past, he's graced *In-Fisherman* magazine with reports of hot spots for trout, bass, and crappies. Not only does the former postal worker travel a lot, but he keeps up with a network of fishing acquaintances around the country who help him choose his next angling destination.

PRE-TRIP PLANNING

From his home in Oregon, Bullock might foray to Alabama, stopping off in Kentucky and Illinois as the spring season advances north. He targets the hottest bites among the many species options across the country. He has to be able to find fish fast on unfamiliar water.

If you're after a big-fish bite, you've got to go where the big crappies live. Sounds obvious, but it's not always easy to determine. Certain waters across the continent maintain a reputation for outsize crappies—Lake Weiss in Alabama, Melvern in Kansas, Kentucky Lake on the Tennessee-Kentucky line, Lake of the Woods straddling Minnesota and Ontario, Buggs Island (Kerr Reservoir) in Virginia-North Carolina, Lake Roosevelt in Arizona, Georgia's Lake Seminole, and many more.

Some of those waters seem to routinely produce big fish, many over 2 pounds, which is the benchmark of a real slab anywhere. Lake of the Woods and Kentucky Lake particularly come to mind for offering steady production. Many other top waters, including most major crappie fisheries, undergo cycles of production—boom periods followed by busts when both average size and numbers of crappies decline.

Gearing Up for Crappies

Roger Bullock emphasizes pre-trip planning, including studying maps and weather patterns, contacting local anglers and marinas, and bringing tackle and equipment for all contingencies.

Bullock tries to keep a pulse on these cycles, to hit the highs and miss the lows on various bodies of water. In some, crappie cycles are based on region-wide water levels, droughts, and excessive hot spells, so waters in the region follow a similar pattern. But other lakes feature cycles based on their own biological food webs that end at their shores.

"Maintain contact with top anglers around the lakes," he advises. "Some will be able to predict upcoming cycles and help you pick a good time to visit. I usually don't hire guides, but often they give me some excellent background information even without booking a trip. Of course, they may hope that you will end up hiring them or recommending their services.

"Most state fishery agencies run Master Angler programs like *In-Fisherman's*, giving awards for trophy-size fish. These lists are a great source of information on top trophy waters for all species of fish, but particularly valuable for panfish that vary so much in size potential from one lake to another."

TIMING

"Pretrip planning always pays off, "Bullock says. "I call several marinas around the lake and talk to bait-shop operators. They like to talk about hot lures and recommend various guides, but what I'm really trying to find out is when the spawn typically occurs. To catch the biggest crappies in a lake, I recommend fishing during the early phases of the actual spawn, when a few fish have started nesting. Like bass, the biggest crappies often nest first.

"At this time, the biggest crappies are shallow and typically easier to locate, usually holding in thick cover such as brushpiles, stumpfields, and thick beds of emergent grasses. You can trust that your well-honed crappie instincts will lead you to the fish.

"Of course, the timing of the spawn can vary from year to year, based on weather and water levels. I strongly advise planning a trip on the early side of the spawn because the prespawn also is an excellent time to find and catch big crappies. Better to be too early than late."

According to biological studies, extended water temperatures of at least 60°F draw crappies into spawning areas. Peak spawning activity for both black and white crappies occurs around 70°F. Crappie spawning in Florida may begin as early as February, while in the northern edge of their range, early June is typical.

The farther south the location, the longer the duration of the spawn—up to ten weeks in central Florida. In Minnesota, beds may be built and abandoned in less than 10 days. Keep that in mind when planning a trip to target spawn-time slabs.

MAP READING

Before Bullock travels, he also buys the best available map of the lake or reservoir. "Spawning invariably occurs in shallow areas," he says, "so scan the map for coves with large flats, positioned to provide protection from prevailing winds. National Weather Service maps generally show prevailing wind direction by season, or else talking with guides and local anglers will give you a good idea. And remember that, in general, coves in northwest corners warm first.

"The next key ingredient is cover. Mark coves that offer flooded brush at spring water levels, standing timber along the creek channel of a reservoir, or downed trees along the bank. The best coves also feature a rather deep channel leading from the main body of the reservoir, 20 to 35 feet in many cases.

"The channel provides the roadway for crappies to move into and out of protected areas. And the closer the deep channel approaches thick cover, the better. One last feature to look for is a steep rocky point within 1/4 to 1/2 mile of your chosen cove. I'm not sure why the rock is important, but over the years, I've found it to be associated with spring crappie hot spots."

Now that you've zeroed in on a top crappie spawning area, it's time to hunt for the big guys. "Masses of average-size crappies will spawn on the large sheltered flats in the backs of coves," Bullock says. "To find trophy-size crappies, follow the shoreline from the back of coves out toward a prominent main-lake point. Note any large shoreline irregularity or structure on the topo map—points, divots, and the like. The big ones favor smaller, better-defined spots for nesting.

"Then try to define any underwater ridges or breaklines that lead toward these shorelines from the deep water of the creek channel, or the deepest part of the cove in a natural lake. Larger fish favor isolated shoreline cover, with a drop-off to at least 12 feet within about 30 yards. Carefully note these spots and check them first when you get to the lake. These are lunker havens."

Most major crappie fisheries are large reservoirs, but Bullock notes that well-managed farm ponds, particularly in the West and Midwest, can produce giant crappies. Finding these waters takes research, but often you'll find sleepers close to home.

ON THE LAKE

Once you get to your destination, match actual shoreline and bottom features to what was depicted on your marked map. Some new topo maps like those from Fishing Hot Spots include grids for latitude and longitude, which allow you to mark waypoints on your GPS before you get to the lake. Track a route to the icon and you're there.

Note, though, that many maps aren't quite accurate, and some seem based on flights of fancy. Some older ones were crudely fashioned, based on a limited sampling. In other cases, bottom features change following floods or just gradual erosion and siltation. Some spots that looked great on the map may not be worth much. Use sonar to verify the map's indications of structure and cover.

"I've also encountered drastic changes in water level," Bullock says. "Unusually low water can leave prime spots high and dry. In less severe cases, the proper conditions are lost when the water becomes too shallow, either in the creek channel or along spawning banks. But as long as you have 20 feet in the channel, crappies will continue to use the general area, if abundant cover is present."

BACKTRACKING

Bullock recommends the first phase of the spawn for the hottest lunker bite. But, again, the vagaries of timing this event make it easy to miss. "If the spawn is still two to four weeks or so away, you can still salvage a great trip," he says. "Find primary areas you've identified on the map, then backtrack toward deeper water.

"As you move out toward the main lake, look for small ridges with rock or stump cover. Try to visualize the path that fish might take as they move from the deeper main lake back toward spawning areas. In southeastern reservoirs, crappies move gradually toward the extreme shallows, and they may slide back and forth along these mid-depth areas for several weeks if the weather is unstable.

"Even with the spawn weeks away, a warm, calm afternoon will propel crappies shallower. Check isolated shoreline cover late in the day—rock slides, fallen trees, or deep boat docks. Of course, a prolonged hot spell can send legions of fish into the shallows, yielding super-fast fishing."

Spring Hot Spots

Broad feeder creeks warm fast, attracting crappies in spring.

Search for submerged structure with sonar.

Bridges can lure concentrations of postspawn crappies.

Prespawn crappies hold along steep banks with thick woodcover.

levee

Crappies migrate into shallow bays once water temperatures stabilize above 60°F, then spawn in thick cover.

Look for big prespawn crappies at the junction of creek channels.

Channel bends with stumps can yield big crappies.

READING COVER

Across the country, most top crappie reservoirs offer lots of woodcover, stumps, standing timber, brushpiles, and cribs. Bullock notes that the placement of the wood is critical in determining its use by crappies. "Some lakes and reservoirs feature many steep bluff banks. Look for those with trees growing right to the waterline. Usually trees, or at least stumps, will be present below the waterline as well.

"These spots provide great cover for big prespawn crappies. Once you get on the lake, ease along and watch sonar for timber, as well as little rises in the bottom, rockpiles, and brushpiles planted by fishermen. Use your electric motor to more closely examine these areas. An outboard just doesn't allow enough lateral movement.

"If you spot good cover, don't fish it right away. The crappies will be spooked. Rest it for a half hour or more, then come back and anchor off the area and fish it thoroughly.

Crappie Spawning Location in Reservoirs

"Warm tributaries entering a reservoir are another major draw in spring," Bullock adds. "Big, wide tributaries tend to be slow-moving, allowing them to heat up before entering the lake. The key area is where the tributary's current stops and flat water begins.

"Now you need to find major brushpiles, sunken timber, or big stumps lying along the old creek bank in minimal current. The final ingredient is that the area receive lots of sunlight to warm it. These types of spots have produced trophy crappies for me over the years, in many different waters."

PRESENTATION POINTERS

Sometimes when you arrive at a lake early in the Prespawn Period, you'll locate spots and fish some of these high-potential areas but catch lots of small fish. In some situations, crappies of all sizes seem to mix at this time of year. Bullock advises, "If you're catching small ones, that doesn't mean the big ones aren't there, too. But the little ones often are more aggressive and quickly will take standard jigs and minnows.

"When you're catching small fish on big-fish spots, switch to gradually heavier and larger jigs and baits until you're no longer catching the little ones. At times, I've gone up to 3½-inch bass-style tubebaits rigged on 1/16- or even 1/8-ounce heads to catch 2-pounders, where only little ones had been biting standard baits. Crappie spinners select for big fish, too. By the way, larger baits are particularly selective for big crappies in darker water."

While Bullock says the Prespawn and Spawn periods deliver the best odds for trophy-sized crappies, he also recommends considering the period when spring shifts into summer and crappies disperse. "They tend to follow the same path out to the main lake that they used when moving into spawning areas," he notes. "Look for them initially outside the first distinct drop-off outside the spawning cove.

"You still can catch a big one now, but chances are lower than during the spawn. One tactic I use to find bigger fish at this time is slowly trolling small crankbaits that will run from 6 to 14 feet deep or so. Adding lead shot to the line will get them deep enough, because most little cranks run too shallow. I also use sinking crankbaits. I always troll with my electric, to ensure a slow pace; and I closely follow structure contours and make sure my lures pass through stumps, brushpiles, and other cover.

"If you mark big schools of crappies, try slow-rolling small-bladed 1/4-ounce spinnerbaits through the aggregations. Usually only the larger crappies will take a spinnerbait."

Slab Bait Selection

When searching for trophy crappies, Roger Bullock chooses larger baits that small fish won't tangle with. Try slow-rolling downsized spinnerbaits, casting spinners and bass-size tubebaits, or trolling small crankbaits with an electric motor.

NIGHT-FISHING

Fishing pressure can make crappies spooky, and activity seems to preferentially turn off the bigger fish. In response, Bullock's always prepared to fish after dark. "Night-fishing often produces more trophy-size bass and walleyes, and the same's true with crappies," he says. "Particularly during the Postspawn Period and in summer, night-fishing is a great way to increase both the number and size of the crappies you're catching.

"Most night anglers fish near bridges or other lighted structures close to a boat ramp. This works, but again, too much activity can make the big ones tough to tempt. I use floating and submersible lights to set up my own feeding zone. I choose an area with lots of baitfish present, often at the channel turn in tributary creeks, junctions of two creek channels, and other key areas. If a channel swings close to a bank with stumps or fallen trees, it can be a gold mine.

"Let the lights attract zooplankton and baitfish, and the crappies will come. Fish your floats just on the edge of the lighted areas, where the biggest crappies lurk. Or else cast baits toward the bank, away from the light. Big crappies seem to roam shallow at night, similar to bass. In my experience, moonlit nights have produced the most trophy-size crappies.

"Night-fishing also is an antidote to cold fronts that seem to haunt any springtime traveler. If a series of storms or fronts has put the crappies down, particularly the bigger ones, look for sets of large docks in the vicinity of spawning areas. At night, the big ones will hold under and around these structures, particularly if they're lighted. If they don't have lights, bring your own and set them out. Big crappies can't resist a big minnow on a float."

SELECTIVE HARVEST

Trophy-size panfish are the latest frontier for anglers who like big fish. As we've said in In-Fisherman, a 1-pound bluegill in most regions is rarer than a 6-pound bass and likely older. Same is true of a 2- or 2½-pound crappie, depending on the region you're fishing. In some especially productive waters, it takes a crappie close to 3 pounds to reach true trophy status, but consider that's half the size of the all-tackle record.

Once you catch such a fish, use catch-and-release or selective harvest as your guide to conservation of fish populations. For eating, keep only a reasonable number of smaller fish, releasing large or trophy-size fish to boost the quality of crappie fishing in the future.

Big crappies don't seem as critical to successful reproduction as big male bluegills, but releasing them certainly helps maintain trophy fisheries longer and may blunt the cyclical fall of many great waters. Keeping a special fish for a once-in-a-lifetime wallmount is fine, though top taxidermists now offer excellent replica mounts of crappies.

CRAPPIE WINDOWS TO THE NEW WORLD

Southern teams have a solid advantage in college baseball. The first crack of the bat echoes through the ivy by the first of February in Georgia and Florida. A month to six weeks after Gators and Bulldogs take the field, Wolverines and Buckeyes continue to practice indoors, waiting for glaciers to recede from the diamonds.

By the same solar coincidence, crack-of-the-bat crappies take to the shallows first in the South each year.

North or South, crappie fishing is a year-round activity. Well, OK—there's a week or two up North when the ice is too rotten to walk on. But shallow lakes open early, and deep lakes have safe ice longer; so most years, we see little or no pause in the activity. But, North or South, a window opens each spring when crappies are drawn up—a point in time when activity levels increase, and crappies coalesce into tighter groups in shallower habitat, or at least, closer to the surface.

What if you won the lottery and decided to follow that magic window north? The journey would last six months. The window pops open first in January, way down in southern Florida. It moves ponderously north in a band that looks something like the jet stream—extending east to west, bending north over here and back south over there, undulating slowly as it progresses to places like Santee-Cooper and Sam Rayburn in February, John Kerr Reservoir in early March, Kentucky Lake in early April, finally reaching Canada and the northernmost borders of the crappie world by June. Along the way, you'll see contrasts in methods, how anglers approach crappies, and how key depths and structures change, from lake to lake, while fishing the same, basic In-Fisherman calendar window throughout the natural range of the crappie.

IT OPENS

Early prespawn crappie bites are awesome for trophies but so-so for numbers, in many places. The movement is from deep winter haunts toward shallower water, closer to spawning habitat. Big clusters of fish become easier to find as they mill in traditional spots, staging at the mouths of creeks or shallow bays. Females are heavy with eggs, the bite becomes more aggressive, and fish are concentrated. Shallow crappie activity occurs first each year down in Florida, usually sometime between mid-January and early February, and progresses quickly up the coast with the Gulf Stream.

Santee-Cooper, South Carolina, benefits from the Gulf Stream. Situated about 50 miles or so from the Atlantic, the climate warms almost—but not quite—as fast as Florida's. It's a shallow flatland reservoir, with indistinct creek channels in the back ends of creek arms. Most of the lake is less than 25 feet deep. Pete Pritchard, a former fireman and a guide on Santee-Cooper for over 30 years, says crack-of-the-bat crappies appear in early March. "I don't book any crappie trips before March," Pritchard says. "In February, crappies are laying low in the main lake, holding right on bottom in 25 feet of water in the dead forests. It's hard to locate them in February, and few people try.

"When the water temperature hits about 58°F, crappies start moving and congregating. The time to be here is when they start staging around the mouths of creeks in 15 to 20 feet of water. That first bite in spring is all about trophies. You won't catch big numbers early on, but you catch good-sized fish. It's not uncommon to see a 3-pounder in March. When the water warms into the high 50°F range, I start looking for suspended fish on 20-foot flats leading into mouths of creeks. Unless you see crappies suspended, the bite's slow. The best bites occur when fish are suspended 10 to 15 feet down over those 20- to 24-foot flats.

"I put out 15 rods during that early bite, tightlining with no floats, putting lines at different depths with the rods in holders, trying to find out which depths the fish are biting at." Pritchard baits with live minnows on #1 Aberdeen hooks, placing split shot 6 to 8 inches above the bait and presenting it with short ultralight rods, 5 to 6 feet long. "I like that length because we're fishing vertically. We catch 25 apiece on an average day, ranging from 3/4 pound to 2½ pounds or bigger. They don't bite too well until they rise off the bottom."

The true shallow exodus comes a little later. "When the bite heats up on the brushpiles, the water will be 64°F or so," he says. "We've got brushpiles positioned strategically to intercept crappies as they move from the main body of the lake into the creek arms. They begin to spawn at 68°F, about the second week of April. Black crappies use cypress trees and root structures in 3 to 5 feet of water. White crappies look for bushes, old pad stems—something to stick their eggs on. I believe some of these white crappies, however, spawn unbelievably deep. In late March and early April, you'll catch fish with milt and eggs running out of them in 20 to 24 feet of water.

"About 47°F is as cold as the water ever gets here. The bite really heats up for numbers of fish in Postspawn, in May and June. In Prespawn, black crappies don't stay in those cypress trees, so timing is key. They move in for only an hour or so. They've usually finished spawning when whites start spawning."

Some 250 miles north of Santee-Cooper and 150 miles from the sea, the window on *John Kerr Reservoir* opens two weeks later—some time in mid- to late March most years. Kerr is a crappie factory. In contrast to Santee-Cooper, it's a classic hill-land reservoir, highly dendritic (lots of creek arms or "tribs") with a river channel that averages about 50 feet in depth. Covering 48,900 acres at normal pool level, it's the largest body of fresh water in Virginia, yet about 10 percent of it lies in North Carolina. Kerr regularly produces the largest crappies each year in both states.

In early March, crappies are staging, suspended over 20- to 25-foot channels in the major tribs like Buffalo Creek. By mid-March, as water temperatures reach the high 50°F range, crappies begin moving into 2 to 4 feet of water in submerged terrestrial bushes. (This is so typical, we could use the same account to describe the early window in every hill-land reservoir in America, though some key factors that trigger movement do vary slightly, North to South.) Locals use traditional methods, fishing crappie minnows under slipbobbers, using a split shot to take the rig down a foot to three feet and securing the bait with a long-shank Aberdeen hook. Experienced anglers pitch jigs in the 1/32- to 1/16-ounce range tipped with minnows or plastic tails, swimming the package over the top and down the outside edge of the brush. Another method that's catching on is to target crappies with small spinnerbaits, like the 1/8-ounce Terminator, during extended periods of stable weather, covering water quickly when crappies are most active.

When Crappie Windows Open

This map refers to the start of the prespawn crappie bite, one of the hottest of the year. Crappies begin to move shallow as the window opens and spawn most years as it closes. Windows open in spring south to north, in a band that crosses the country from east to west. As late winter gives way to spring, this band moves north at a rate of approximately 150 miles per week during an average year. As the earth slowly tilts on its axis and the sun approaches the Tropic of Cancer, shining more directly on North America, spring moves ever northward. Crappies respond similarly to similar conditions throughout their range, doing the same things at 45°F in Texas as in Minnesota. But 45°F water often can't be found in Minnesota before late April, two months after the Sam Rayburn crappie bite catches fire.

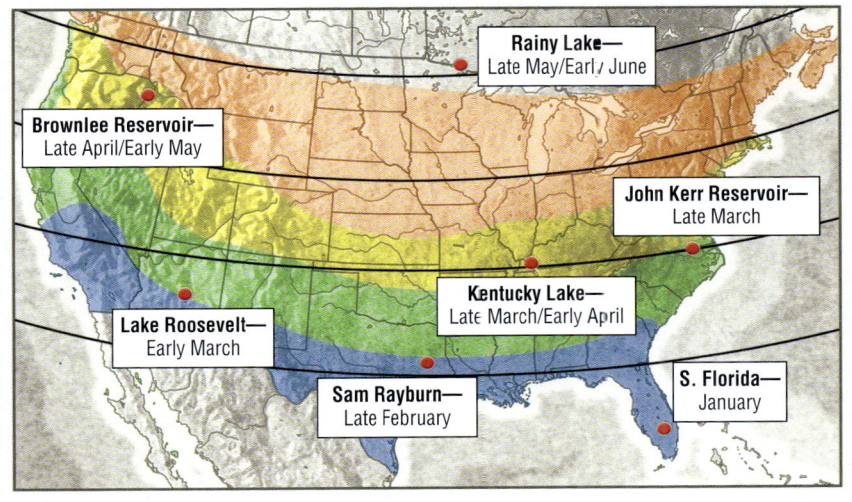

A recent creel census on Kerr revealed that crappies average close to 13 inches—well over a pound. It's one of a few lakes in North America that consistently produces 3-pound crappies, year after year. Late March represents the crack of the bat for trophy seekers. That's when the big egg-laden females glide into the shallows for the first time, becoming more vulnerable, more concentrated, and easier to find. One key thing to remember about crappies in any environment at this time of year is the fact that they return to the same shallow spots to forage year after year. Many call this first shallow movement a "prespawn movement," but that isn't quite accurate. They first come to the shallows to feed heavily during stable weather, and they often vacate the shallows after cold fronts. Actual spawning usually follows several weeks to a month later.

Kentucky Lake provides an interesting case in contrasts. Like John Kerr, Kentucky Lake is a hill-land reservoir, and it's located at precisely the same latitude as Kerr. Yet, being situated 650 miles to the west, the window opens a little later without the influence of warming oceanic currents passing nearby.

Malcolm Lane, owner of the Hook Line & Sinker Guide Service (270/388-0525), says the first really shallow movements take place in early April most years. "If I were going to plan a trip here, I'd pencil in the first two weeks of April," Lane says. "At the beginning of March, with the water temperature still in the low 50°F range, crappies are just beginning to stage at the mouths of the bigger creek arms, suspending off creek channels over 25-foot depths. The first shallow movements take place as the water broaches 60°F, when crappies approach the banks in the creek arms and settle into woodcover in 3- to 6-foot depths."

Crappies in Kentucky Lake average over a pound, and many of the first to show up shallow weigh in at over 2 pounds. "They gradually move toward spawning habitat, which used to be in the 2-foot depths on bottom. Now they spawn on wood in 6 feet of water, because the water's clearer," Lane says. "The water hits 60°F sometime around the first of April, triggering crappies to move in and forage heavily on shad in that 5-foot zone."

"If I were going to plan a trip here, I'd pencil in the first two weeks of April when crappies are just beginning to stage at the mouths of the bigger creek arms."

In the clearing water, Kentucky Lake crappie gurus are turning to in-line spinners, like the #1 and #0 Mepps single-hook Aglia and Aglia Spin flies. "Or we throw a 2-inch Twister Tail on a 1/16-ounce jig. Everything is set up for 6-pound line on fairly long rods, so we can wrestle big fish quickly out of heavy cover. If it's flat calm and sunny or the bite's timid for some other reason, I go down to a #0 Mepps on 4-pound line. More and more people are throwing spinners here, because black crappies are taking over in this clearing water, and they suspend more than whites. When the water was cloudy, it was a white-crappie lake, but that's no longer the case.

"If I can get the depth figured out, I can count a spinner down and retrieve it so it stays in the strike zone, just over their heads. We cast jigs and spinners right into woodcover, too. Brush encourages algae, which draws minnows, which draws crappies into that 3- to 6-foot zone. I like to retrieve spinners close to the bottom and touch that wood as much as possible. Most people retrieve them too fast."

WINDOW'S SUNSET

In southern Minnesota, the ice goes off the lakes sometime in late March or early April. As everywhere else, the first shallow movement of crappies is largely determined by weather, and the "window" is expanded to a period that spans almost a month to accommodate the wild vagaries in weather at this time of year. At any point after the ice leaves, hot fishing can occur in depths of 2 to 5 feet in northern natural lakes. Sometimes we catch fair numbers of them in 5-foot depths through the ice in March, back in those black-bottom bays they invade every spring. But if the weather stays blustery and cold, fishing will be poor. The first "shirtsleeve days" after the ice recedes are the prime indicator. Stable weather during a warming trend—that's the key to early-season crappie success everywhere.

The day after the ice recedes from a lake, the temperature out in the main lake typically registers right around 40°F, unless the weather really turns sour, in which case crappies turn off and suspend beyond the first major drop-offs. Stable, warming weather is a different story. A shallow, dark-bottom bay on the north side of a lake, where the sun hits the water for the longest period during the day, can warm quickly into the high 40°F range. If so, the crappies will arrive before you do. When a cold front hits, crappies back out of these bays and revert to staging practices. It's typical to find them suspended 10 to 20 feet down over depths of 20 to 30 feet, just off points, bars, or channels leading into the bay.

Another pattern involves canals and marinas, where shallow water leads into protected areas. Canals can be natural or artificial, where paths have been dredged into a condo complex or group of homes to create boat slips. If the construction has only one way in and one way out, wind and convection currents can't blow the warm water out. These spots can produce some of the most sustained and consistent bites right after ice-out in the North Country, which also serves to prove a point: Crappies seldom spawn in marinas and boat-slip canals, suggesting that the first movement to shallow water is a foraging movement, not a true prespawn activity.

The earliest bite can be slow, so it requires slow, subtle presentations. Light 7-foot rods, 2- to 4-pound line, tiny jigs, and tiny minnows or maggots tend to produce best. Things can warm up quickly, in which case the window opens in early April. If cold weather persists, the window may not really open wide until early May. The time to be there is when the water hits 50°F, which can be hard to plan for. At that point, crappies reach their highest saturation point in those early foraging zones, and the hot ticket becomes a 1/32-ounce jig with a plastic tail on 4-pound line. Casting and slowly retrieving a jig with a 2-inch action tail can put 50 or 60 crappies in the boat in short order in Mississippi River backwaters between Red Wing, Minnesota, and La Crosse, Wisconsin.

Farther north, the window opens even later. Perhaps the hottest crappie bite in the North in recent times has taken place on **Red Lake** in Minnesota. Big black crappies roam this vast northern lake in huge schools these days. It's a shallow lake, with gradually tapering shorelines. Once crappies commit to the shallows, they have a long way to go to retreat back to deep water, and usually only back off into the 10- to 12-foot zone.

"If you had to pick one week to spend here," suggests Don Hudek, owner of Hudek's resort on Red Lake, "it should be about the first week of May. The fishing is consistently good at that time of year. During a cold spring, May 1st represents the first really hot shallow bite. In warm years, it will be the middle of the spawning run. Either way, the weather's usually getting nice by then."

From ice-out through the spawn, slipbobbers, light jigs, and minnows are most popular on Red Lake, but Hudek fishes on bottom. "I like a floating jig and a minnow on a Lindy Rig." This is basically a sliding sinker ahead of a 1- to 3-foot leader. "It's more versatile," Hudek says. "You can cast or drift to cover more water, and the fish are shallow (generally 4 to 8 feet), so they won't be too far from bottom most days. Most of the areas the crappies use are pretty featureless, and weeds are rarely a problem early. A sudden 1- to 2-foot drop in the bottom is significant and can collect hundreds of crappies." A minnow can be tail-hooked on a small floating jighead. When the rig is left to rest on bottom, the floating head holds the minnow up, struggling against the jig to reach bottom—a powerful trigger early on.

Just across the Canadian border, the window finally closes once and for all, but not until mid-June. People from down South are always shocked to find 2-pound crappies this far north, and **Rainy Lake** has a ton that size. Rainy Lake sprawls across the international border between Minnesota and Ontario. "It's a pretty big window up here," according to Barry Woods of Woody's Fairly Reliable Guide Service. "It can happen in the first week of May or the first week of June. It all has to do with water temperature and weather. Water temperature is pretty warm when the crappies move in really shallow, right around 50°F. On Rainy, the first hot shallow bite can take place in pencil reeds or on shallow rockpiles. I look for them first along the north shore of shallow, weedy bays. If you can find steep, marshy banks with overhanging brush along those northern shorelines, that's good. If you've got a proven rockpile, sit right on it. You might not see anything for several hours and suddenly, there they are. They seem to move in and move off several times over the course of the day.

"You have to have several warm days in a row to trigger them," Woody says. "Another method for locating them is to work along reed lines and dap with 20-foot poles and 6-pound line, because sometimes they move right into areas 1 foot deep that you can't cast to. I prefer to use 2- to 4-pound line out on the rockpiles. Makes it sporty. You don't need a slipbobber. They're not that sensitive. When they're ready, they start eating, and they'll pull a beach ball under. A tail-hooked minnow on a light jig is the standby, but a tube or puddle jumper works really well, too. Sometimes isolated reedbeds, out in the middle of nowhere, produce the hottest bites. Where reeds are sparse, a Beetle Spin or Mepps spinner works really well, too.

"Crappies run a pound to 1½ pounds, and it's common to catch a few 2-pounders. Occasionally we catch one over 17 inches. They start to spawn in water temperatures in the low 60°F range, here. The water doesn't even reach 70°F until July most years. In the river sloughs and backwaters leading into Rainy, the timing is the same. Be here early May to early June, find a beaverhouse in black, marshy water, and fish the groove that beavers create in the bottom leading into the house. The water is cloudy and crappies feel rather safe. Occasionally you can really pound them in there. On Rainy Lake, you have to find the right bay. You'll know when you find it," he says, "because crappies literally take over the shallows once the weather stabilizes."

Somewhere north of Rainy, the natural range of the crappie comes to an end. Dotted throughout this near-wilderness are little lakes and rivers that represent the final frontier. Long lifespans allow crappies to grow huge up there, many living out their lives without ever seeing a hook. Most of the locals could care less about crappies up there, what with giant walleyes, pike, muskies, and smallmouths surrounding them in every direction. Pinpointing the time when crappie fishing first heats up early in the far North requires a little more research before you go.

Final Factors _____ **Chapter 10**

Where the Slabs Are

**ULTIMATE CRAPPIE
LOCATIONAL
FACTORS**

In-Fisherman editors sat down to talk crappies several times during the formulation of this second crappie book in our Critical Concepts series. The roundtable discussion centered on a series of questions: Where are the biggest crappies, why are they there, and how long will they persist?

"First you have to determine what constitutes a big crappie," says Editor In Chief, Doug Stange. "Two pounds is big wherever you go. In Texas, Minnesota, Florida, or Canada, a 2-pounder is not only considered big, but quite possible to catch. Do we have another species like that?"

A 10-pound largemouth might be considered big in Florida but impossible in Minnesota, where the state record is currently 8 pounds and some change. Walleyes, which range much farther north than either crappies or largemouths, become progressively smaller as you approach the far northern edge of their range. In Minnesota, an 8-pound walleye is just big, not special, because numbers of 10-pounders are caught every year. In northern Manitoba or Saskatchewan, an 8-pound walleye is huge beyond belief, and a 12-pounder would have to be flown in from someplace way down south like, well, central Saskatchewan (Tobin), where 15-pounders are registered most years.

Most species have easily identifiable zones where giants can be targeted. For smallmouth bass, *In-Fisherman* recently mapped out a trophy rectangle, which basically covers Tennessee and parts of surrounding states—where all of the specimens weighing 10 pounds or more have been caught. The biggest largemouths persist in Florida, California, and specific lakes in Texas and Arizona. The Giant Muskie Belt extends from the St. Lawrence River to Minnesota along the border between the U.S. and Canada, yet the range of the biggest pike includes parts of that belt and extends north to the tundra. The Slab Crappie Rectangle (if it exists) is a much more difficult place to identify.

> *Most species have easily identifiable zones where giants can be targeted. . . . The Slab Crappie Rectangle, if it exists, is a much more difficult place to identify.*

The state record black crappie in Minnesota (5 pounds even) is not that much different from the state records in Mississippi (4 pounds, 4 ounces), Georgia (4 pounds, 4 ounces), or Alabama (4 pounds, 5 ounces). In fact, Minnesota's record fish is bigger, as is Michigan's (4 pounds, 12 ounces), which is odd considering that crappies do not range much farther north than largemouth bass. That would seem to make the crappie a "southern fish." (The South does tend to grow bigger white crappies, which do not typically fare as well in clear water, and northern waters tend to be clearer.) So why are the biggest specimens of black crappies occurring in the North?

"In Georgia, a 5-year-old specimen is ancient, and probably weighs almost 3 pounds," *In-Fisherman* Senior Editor Steve Quinn points out. "In Minnesota, a 5-year-old is just reaching 1 pound, yet a crappie reaching 7 years of age is pretty common up here. Northern fish live a bit longer." If not taken out by anglers, a pretty tough assignment for a crappie these days.

"Fishing pressure has intensified and it certainly complicates the hunt for big fish," Quinn says. "In fact, the chances of catching a 2-pound crappie in many of the places where we used to find them 20 years ago are slim to none. The catch-and-release ethic—so popular among trout, bass, and muskie fishermen these days—never caught on for crappies and, possibly, never will."

"Right here, in the general area of the In-Fisherman offices," Stange adds, "we used to fill stringers with 2-pound crappies in Lake Edward, Leech Lake, Upper Portage Lake, and several others. Chances of catching crappies that size in those lakes now are poor at best." We all bit our tongues, wanting to ask if those "stringers" might be the reason. But we were all guilty, before the ethics and logic of conservation convinced us to stop taking home more than we absolutely needed to kill.

We discussed regulations and the need for conservation, but catch-and-release lakes for crappies seem a long way off. "Length limits are pretty much out of the question here in Minnesota," Quinn says. "Biologists say they just won't make a kid measure a bluegill." Which seems fair enough. But how do we guarantee your kids will be able to take their kids to a lake where they might find a few 2-pound crappies—especially in the North, where it might require 10 years to replace them? Most panfish anglers continue to keep the larger crappies they catch, those specimens weighing over a pound. Some anglers continue to cull out smaller crappies, replacing them with bigger ones while releasing fish they know won't survive. Not only do anglers largely resist returning big crappies to the water, but many are willing to fight tooth-and-nail against all proposed quality regulations for panfish.

Gord Pyzer, one of two Field Editors for *In-Fisherman* and former Ontario fishery biologist, says, "The problem isn't managing fish, it's managing people. That's the dilemma. Managing angler expectation is difficult, and many anglers care only about numbers and never will care if they catch a 2-pound crappie.

"Certainly those bigger fish are old fish," he says. "Pressure has a huge bearing. For instance, if we didn't have such intense interest in bass up here these days, every smallmouth you'd catch on Rainy Lake would be 4 to 5 pounds. The same thing goes with crappies. A 14-inch crappie up here is 14 to 15 years old, averaging a little better than an inch a year. With climate change, you're going to see massive changes in this fishery. We know that a 1°C (1.8°F) change in average daily temperature has a phenomenal effect on smallmouths. We're now seeing an average increase of 3°C in this region. Ice-out occurs two weeks earlier, resulting in a 15-fold increase in smallmouth numbers, because recruitment is so much higher. Crappies will respond to this change in precisely the same way. Not only will recruitment increase, but crappies will grow faster. I'm certain this is happening, from what I'm seeing.

"It's a positive thing up here for crappies, but not for trout and salmon. In British Columbia's Fraser River, which receives the world's largest run of pink salmon, temperatures have been lethal for adults when they return to the river during their traditional spawning windows, for the past 4 or 5 years in a row. And that's happening with just a 1°C rise in average daily temperatures.

"Crappies will benefit from global warming, up here on the northern end of their range," says Pyzer. "We're seeing huge schools of young-of-the year crappies where I've never seen them exist before. They're moving and colonizing—actually spreading their range and taking over more parts of these larger, deeper lakes, in areas that were too cold or too deep in the past. Back bays in those areas used to be too cool, and that factor is changing." Which complicates the identification of a Slab Crappie Zone even further.

THE QUEST FOR TRUE SLABS

"The key elements surrounding the quest for big fish don't change," Stange says. "You pick the seasons of greatest vulnerability, find the right seasonal habitat, and try to hit a window of optimal weather conditions. But step one is targeting water where it's not only possible but likely to run across fish in the 2-pound range. Spring is the primary time to find crappies shallow, but you have to hit one of two narrow windows in spring on many lakes. Last-ice is prime time Up North, and the early Prespawn Period is critical everywhere. Both periods are short, volatile, and given to extreme weather fluctuations that make timing the bite difficult."

"A number of lakes in South Dakota have crappies over 2 pounds," says *In-Fisherman* Editor Jeff Simpson. "But to go there and expect to catch them that big? Unless it's timed perfectly, you probably won't find them. They seem vulnerable only on a seasonal basis, only in those key windows, and those might last several days or several weeks, depending on weather."

"That's what makes Red Lake in Minnesota so remarkable," Quinn responds. "Some legitimate 3-pound crappies have been weighed there in the past few years and fish in the 2-pound range can be found almost year 'round."

The phenomenal Red Lake crappie fishery is unique for a variety of reasons. It was created by the overharvest of walleyes. Crappies moved in to fill that niche, became abundant, and grew quickly in the void left by walleyes. But what remains remarkable about Red Lake's trophy crappies is that they continue to persist, even though walleye numbers are back to normal, despite the fact that biologists predicted the crappie population would crash.

Last-ice is prime time Up North, and the early Prespawn Period is critical everywhere. Both periods are short and volatile.

"Given everything we've said, is it possible to map a zone where anglers can target a 3-pound crappie and expect a reasonable chance for success?" Stange asks. "As always, private ponds provide the best shot. But where could the average angler, taking a one-week vacation, expect any real chance at a 3-pound crappie? Is there a region we can point him to?"

"Might as well point a shotgun at a map of North America," offers Senior Editor Matt Straw. "In recent months we've received numerous reports of 3-pound crappies being caught in Arizona, California, Mississippi, and Oklahoma. I don't have to hear from anyone on Kerr Lake along the North Carolina-Virginia border to know somebody probably caught one there recently. But if there's a Trophy Crappie Zone right now, it's contained within a relatively small arc in northern Mississippi."

In-Fisherman's many Top-10 lists of trophy crappie lakes over the years typically include one of these four lakes: Arkabutla, Sardis, Enid, and Grenada. For some anglers and guides we know, 3-pound crappies are relatively common in these Mississippi waters. Legends of giant slabs swirl around Arkabutla like a swarm of gnats. According to retired fishery biologist Jim Robbins of Mississippi, "Several commercial fishermen netting catfish and buffalo have taken crappies that exceeded the world record over the past several years. Very few homes are situated on it, and it's about 20 minutes south of Memphis, Tennessee. A lot of 3-pound crappies are weighed in here every year. Sometimes a lucky angler catches several over 3 in a day."

Not far east of the "Arc of Slabs" is a little-known reservoir called Miller's Ferry, a favorite of longtime *In-Fisherman* contributor, Roger Bullock. "Crappies consistently average over a pound at Miller's Ferry," Bullock says. "And quite a few 3-pound giants are weighed in at the Minnow Bucket [a local bait shop] every year."

"Don't forget Florida," Stange adds. "Florida might be the last overlooked bastion

The Arc of Slabs

of big crappies on the planet. The Stick Marsh and Farm 13 in eastcentral Florida have produced numbers of 3-pound crappies in the past few years."

One of our favorites has always been Lake Roosevelt in Arizona (when it has water, of course), where the growth rate for crappies might be the fastest anywhere (over 15 inches in 4 years). Crappies take off quickly during the wet years on Roosevelt, where they can find extensive habitat for both spawning and foraging in the miles of flooded brush that cover the shorelines in spring. It's a pitching game with jigs and plastics, and landing a 3-pounder can be a real challenge.

A list of the most consistent and prolific big-crappie waters in America over the past 3 or 4 decades has to include Toledo Bend in Texas and Santee-Cooper in South Carolina. But for most waters, trophy potential changes with conditions, predator counts, water levels, variability in recruitment, and other factors. So, the list changes as the trophy potential of most lakes around the continent tends to wax and wane year by year. Lakes identified on our map not only provide the best shot at a bevy of 2-pounders (possibly a 3), but have also been the most consistently productive over time.

THE FINAL WORD ON CRAPPIE LOCATION

To know the latitude of a lake, the lake type, a little about the forage base, the cover options, and prevailing water conditions is to know something about crappie behavior there, without ever having to visit. Knowing all those things and a lot more, however, won't deliver you to crappie nirvana every day on the water.

Select Age-to-Size Analysis

WATER BODY	SIZE AT 4 YEARS
Roosevelt Lake, Arizona	15.12"
Norris Lake, Tennessee	12.92"
Moultrie Lake, South Carolina	12.6"
Rainy Lake, Ontario	10.2"
East Osceola Lake, Iowa	9.64"
Fort Gibson, Oklahoma	9.44"
Ouachita Lake, Arkansas	9.2"
Lake Oahe, South Dakota	7.12"
Average of 25 different lakes in Oregon	8.44"
Kimball Lake, New Brunswick	6.28"
Three Forks Lake, Montana	4.88"

(From various aging studies conducted across the continent, involving scale analysis of at least 75 black crappies from the 4-year age group in each fishery listed. Measurements are averages of total lengths of specimens examined.)

Weather, changes in the forage base, a sudden abundance of insects, water temperature, a gradual change in water clarity, and a variety of other factors can impact location on a daily or even an hourly basis. At the end of a long list of factors that can be measured come those that cannot. Like hunches: At the end of a long day of searching, a hunch often plays a bigger role than any of us might like to admit, but there it is. Very few if any among us can say we've never been stumped by those specs, those calicos, those papermouth slabs.

We've all been amazed to find crappies in 5 feet of water when they were supposed to be deep, and vice-versa. And we've all been stumped by crappies suspending over deep water when conventional wisdom demands the use of dense cover. When hunches begin to deliver results more often than not in these situations, we start calling them informed guesses. Arriving at the lake with confidence only to be handed a day-long puzzle is a challenge we all face from time to time. And few things in angling are more satisfying than following a hunch that finally solves the puzzle. A foundation of knowledge can transform your hunches into something more, and that's what this book is all about.

Research leads to waters that produce the best numbers, the biggest fish, or sometimes both. Look at the lake on a map: An instant understanding of the lake type and how crappies commonly relate to features found in such lakes pops up on your mental monitor. The process has begun. What follows is a pretty fun ride, because it means involving ourselves directly in the web of life surrounding the crappie. To understand crappies to the fullest possible extent requires knowledge of shad and shiners, muskies and bass, insects and plankton, watershed dynamics, weather, dissolved oxygen counts, and a lot more. Everything is connected.

Living things are never simple. A crappie has a brain the size of a pea, yes. But that brain is infinitely more complex than our most advanced computer. When your laptop can wander off, somehow avoid being stolen or run over by a truck, identify an outlet, plug itself in for recharge then travel miles to find its own way back home, we might accept arguments to the contrary. Until then, being outwitted by a crappie is no reason to hang your head. The more we know, the more we realize we don't know. Life continues to adapt and evolve. Crappies too, so the ride can't end here. The next Critical Concepts book on crappies revolves around presentation, which can also be used to locate fish. Lures and presentation options that cover water fast, triggering crappies with speed or appeals to curiosity, are the next steps in the fine-tuning process.

And so it goes. In other words, the final word on crappie location will never be printed, until crappies (or humans) cease to exist. As Albert Einstein noted, "The only really valuable thing is intuition."

State Crappie Records

STATE	SPECIES	LBS	OZ.	WATER BODY
■ Alabama	Black crappie	4 lbs.	5 oz.	private pond
	White crappie	4 lbs	9 oz.	Lake Martin
■ Arizona	Black crappie	4 lbs	10 oz.	San Carlos Lake
	White crappie	3 lbs.	6 oz.	Lake Pleasant
■ Arkansas	Black crappie	4 lbs.	9 oz.	Oladale Lake
	White crappie	4 lbs.	7 oz.	Mingo Creek
■ California	Black crappie	4 lbs.	1 oz.	New Hogan Lake
	White crappie	4 lbs.	8 oz.	Clear Lake
■ Colorado	Black crappie	3 lbs.	4 oz.	private pond
	White crappie	4 lbs.	7 oz.	Northglen Lake
■ Louisiana	Black crappie	3 lbs.	8 oz.	Toledo Bend
	White crappie	3 lbs.	9 oz.	private pond
■ Michigan	Black crappie	4 lbs.	12 oz.	Lincoln Lake
	White crappie	3 lbs.	4 oz.	Stoney Cr. Lake
■ Minnesota	Black crappie	5 lbs.		Vermilion River
	White crappie	3 lbs.	15 oz.	Lake Constance
■ Mississippi	White crappie	5 lbs.	3 oz.	Enid Reservoir
■ N. Carolina	Black crappie	4 lbs.	15 oz.	Asheboro Lake
■ Ohio	Black crappie	4 lbs.	8 oz.	private pond
■ Oklahoma	Black crappie	4 lbs.	10 oz.	Ottawa Pond
	White crappie	4 lbs.	15 oz.	Kingfisher Pond
■ Oregon	Black crappie	4 lbs.	6 oz.	Pond Corvallis
■ Virginia	Black crappie	4 lbs.	10 oz.	private pond
■ Washington	Black crappie	4 lbs.	5 oz.	Lake Washington
■ Wisconsin	Black crappie	4 lbs.	8 oz.	Gile Flowage

Catch More Crappies
GUARANTEED!

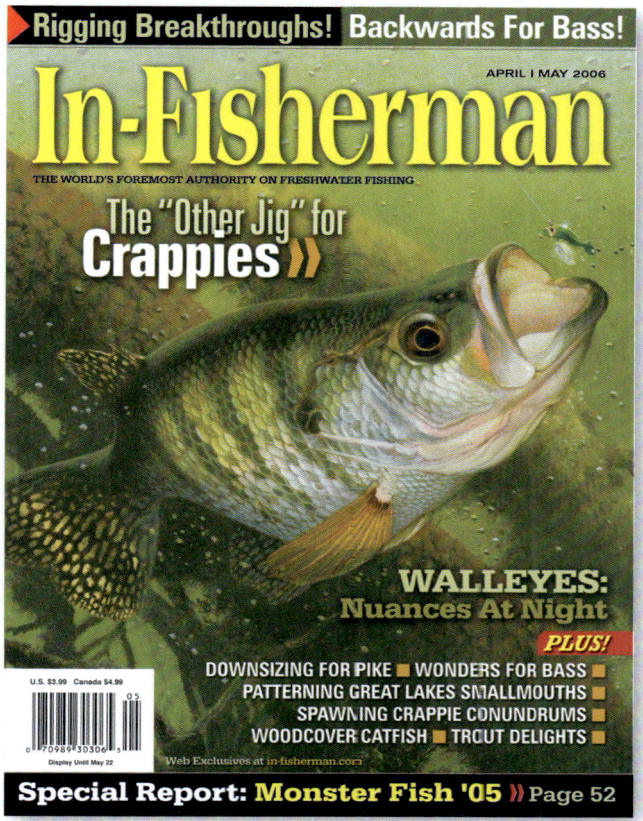

Every issue of In-Fisherman magazine features articles loaded with exclusive panfish-catching information from the In-Fisherman staff. No wonder it's subscribed to by the top anglers in the country.

START CATCHING MORE BASS. *SUBSCRIBE NOW!*

Call 1-800-441-1740 or subscribe online at www.in-fisherman.com

Visit The Top Fishing Destination In The World

TIPS FROM THE EXPERTS

In-Fisherman pros provide tips and advice to help you catch more fish.

IN-FISHERMAN MERCHANDISE

Great deals on Award-Winning books, videos, and more.

RECIPES

Fish are nutritious and delicious—especially when prepared from an In-Fisherman recipe.

BIG FISH GALLERY

Show off your catch and see what our readers are catching.

FISH ID

Not sure what you just caught? Look it up here.

ASK THE EDITORS
Our experts answer your freshwater fishing questions.

in-fisherman.com

BEST FISHING TIMES
Plan to be on the water when the bite is hot.

PROFESSIONAL WALLEYE TRAIL

Watch tourney results as they happen or sign up with a pro!

IN-FISHERMAN TV & RADIO

See what's on tap this week for IF TV and locate the IF Radio station in your area.

In-Fisherman
TEACHING THE WORLD HOW TO FISH!
ON THE INTERNET
7819 Highland Scenic Rd, Baxter, MN 56425